100 CLASSIC HIKES IN

COLORADO

100 CLASSIC HIKES IN

COLORADO

Great Plains / Front Range / Rocky Mountains / Colorado Plateau

Scott S. Warren

THIRD EDITION

THE MOUNTAINEERS BOOKS

THE MOUNTAINEERS BOOKS

is the nonprofit publishing arm of The Mountaineers Club, an organization founded in 1906 and dedicated to the exploration, preservation, and enjoyment of outdoor and wilderness areas.

1001 SW Klickitat Way, Suite 201, Seattle, WA 98134

© 2008 by Scott S. Warren

Third edition, 2008

Manufactured in China

Copy Editor: Brenda Pittsley
Cover and Book Design: The Mountaineers Books
Layout: Jennifer Shontz, Red Shoe Design
All maps and photographs: Scott S. Warren

Cover image: *Treasure Falls in the South San Juan Mountains*
Frontispiece: *Emerald Lake in Rocky Mountain National Park*

Library of Congress Cataloging-in-Publication Data

Warren, Scott S.
 100 classic hikes in Colorado / Scott S. Warren.—3rd ed.
  p.   cm.
 Includes index.
 ISBN 978-1-59485-024-0
1. Hiking—Colorado—Guidebooks. 2. Backpacking—Colorado—Guidebooks.
3. Trails—Colorado—Guidebooks. 4. Colorado—Guidebooks. I. Title.
II. Title: One hundred classic hikes in Colorado.
 GV199.42.C6W37 2007
 796.51'09788—dc22

                                        2007036469

CONTENTS

PLATEAULANDS

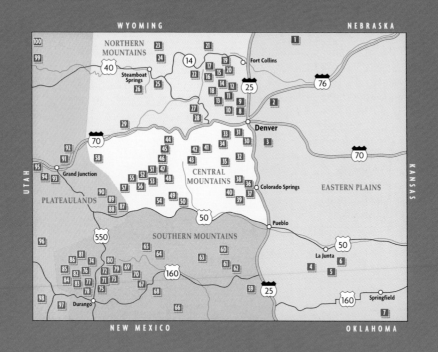

WYOMING
NEBRASKA

NORTHERN
MOUNTAINS

100
99

40

Steamboat
Springs

Fort Collins

14

25

76

Denver

70

92
95
94 93
Grand Junction

91
58

90
89
88 87

PLATEAULANDS

CENTRAL
MOUNTAINS

70

3

Colorado Springs

EASTERN PLAINS

KANSAS

UTAH

550

96

SOUTHERN MOUNTAINS

Pueblo

50

160

La Junta

50

4
5

6

98
97
Durango

160

25

Springfield
7

NEW MEXICO
OKLAHOMA

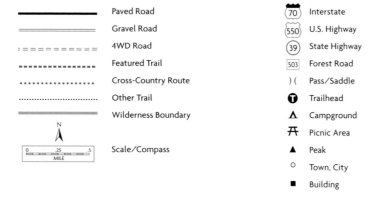

LEGEND

———————	Paved Road
═══════════	Gravel Road
= = = = = = = = =	4WD Road
▬ ▬ ▬ ▬ ▬ ▬	Featured Trail
• • • • • • • • • •	Cross-Country Route
....	Other Trail
▒▒▒▒▒▒▒▒▒	Wilderness Boundary

N

| 0   .25   .5 | Scale/Compass |
| MILE | |

70	Interstate
550	U.S. Highway
39	State Highway
503	Forest Road
) (	Pass/Saddle
T	Trailhead
Λ	Campground
⊼	Picnic Area
▲	Peak
○	Town, City
■	Building

HIKE NUMBER AND NAME	DIFFICULTY	SEASON	HIGHLIGHTS
Half–Day Hikes			
1. Pawnee Buttes	easy	All year	prairie, scenic buttes
4. Santa Fe Trail	easy	All year	prairie, history
6. Vogel Canyon	easy	All year	prairie, prehistory
10. Forgotten Valley	easy	May–Nov	forest, meadows, history
11. Lake Isabelle	easy	Jul–Sep	forest, alpine lake, mountain scenery
14. Emerald Lake	moderate	Jul–Oct	forests, lakes, mountain scenery
18. Calypso Cascades	easy	Jun–Oct	forest, cascades
19. Mount McConnel	moderate	Mar–Nov	forest scenery
29. Hanging Lake	strenuous	All year	canyon scenery, hidden lake, waterfall
30. Roxborough State Park	easy	All year	red-rock formations, history
31. Mount Falcon	easy	May–Nov	forests, foothills scenery, history
32. Devils Head	moderate	Jun–Oct	forests, mountain scenery, fire lookout
34. Mount Goliath Research Natural Area	easy	Jul–Sep	alpine scenery, bristlecone pines
36. Red Rock Canyon	easy	All year	red-rock formations, history
40. Boulder Creek	easy	All year	forests and meadows, geology
56. Beckwith Pass	easy	Jun–Oct	nice mountain scenery
61. Great Sand Dunes	moderate	All year	sand dunes, scenery
63. Penitente Canyon	easy	All year	interesting canyon, geology, history
75. Spud Lake	easy	Jun–Oct	forests, lake
83. Sharkstooth Pass	moderate	Jul–Sep	mountain scenery, high pass
84. Geyser Spring	easy	Jun–Oct	forests, interesting geology, geyser
87. Dillon Pinnacles	easy	All year	interesting geology
88. Oak Flat Loop	moderate	All year	stunning canyon vistas, geology
89. Exclamation Point	easy	May–Oct	incredible canyon scenery, geology
91. Mount Garfield	strenuous	All year	far-reaching desert vistas, geology
95. Rabbits Ear Mesa	easy	All year	desert scenery, river corridor
97. Petroglyph Point	moderate	Apr–Nov	canyon scenery, prehistoric rock art and cliff dwellings
99. Harpers Corner	easy	All year	incredible canyon scenery
Short Day Hikes			
2. Barr Lake	easy	All year	lake, waterfowl, prairie
3. Castlewood Canyon	easy	All year	prairie, canyons
7. Picture Canyon	easy	All year	prairie, canyons, prehistory
8. Bear Peak	strenuous	May–Oct	mountains, scenery
9. Green Mountain Loop	strenuous	Apr–Nov	mountains, forest
12. Mount Audubon	strenuous	Jul–Sep	great alpine scenery

13.	Arapaho Glacier	moderate	Jul–Sep	alpine scenery, view of glacier
16.	Little Yellowstone	moderate	May–Oct	forest, geological oddity, history
37.	North Cheyenne Cañon	moderate	Apr–Nov	riparian plant life, stream, canyon scenery
38.	Waldo Canyon	moderate	Apr–Nov	forest scenery
39.	The Crags	easy	Jun–Oct	forests, geological formations
41.	French Pass	moderate	Jun–Oct	alpine scenery, Continental Divide
46.	Hagerman Tunnel	easy	Jun–Sep	mountain scenery, fascinating history
49.	Browns Cabin	strenuous	Jul–Sep	mountain scenery, history
50.	Waterdog Lakes	strenuous	Jun–Sep	lakes, forest, scenery
54.	Lamphier Lake	moderate	Jul–Sep	forests, lake, mountain scenery
59.	West Spanish Peak	strenuous	Jul–Sep	tremendous summit, far-reaching vistas
62.	Mosca Pass	moderate	Jun–Oct	forests, mountain scenery
65.	Powderhorn Lakes	moderate	Jul–Sep	forests, mountain scenery, lakes
67.	Fourmile Falls	moderate	Jun–Oct	forests, waterfalls
73.	Highland Mary Lakes	strenuous	Jul–Sep	great alpine scenery, lakes
74.	Ice Lake Basin	strenuous	Jul–Sep	wonderful mountain scenery, lakes
77.	Goulding Creek	strenuous	Jun–Oct	forests, meadows, history
78.	Animas City Mountain	moderate	Mar–Nov	forests, scenery, easily accessible
80.	Bear Creek	strenuous	Jun–Oct	rugged canyon scenery, history
81.	Blue Lakes	strenuous	Jul–Sep	high mountain scenery, lakes
90.	Gunnison Gorge	moderate	All year	canyon scenery, river corridor
92.	Main Canyon	easy	All year	canyon scenery, wild horses
93.	Monument Canyon	moderate	All year	canyon scenery, high desert
96.	Dolores River Canyon	easy	All year	red-rock canyons, river corridor, rock art
98.	Sand Canyon	easy	All year	canyon scenery, cliff dwellings
100.	Chokecherry Draw	easy	All year	remote, drainage, history
Long Day Hikes				
5.	Picket Wire Canyonlands	moderate	All year	prairie, canyons, history, paleontology
15.	Flattop Mountain	strenuous	Jun–Oct	alpine scenery, forests, Continental Divide
17.	Mirror Lake	moderate	Jul–Sep	forest, alpine lake
20.	Emmaline Lake	moderate	Jul–Oct	forests, lakes, mountain scenery
22.	Baker Pass	strenuous	Jul–Sep	great mountain scenery
25.	Sarvis Creek	moderate	Jun–Oct	forest scenery, streams
27.	Upper Cataract Lake	moderate	Jul–Oct	forests, lake, mountain scenery
28.	Eccles Pass	moderate	Jul–Oct	alpine scenery
33.	Resthouse Meadows	moderate	Jun–Oct	forests, mountain scenery
35.	Wigwam Park	moderate	Jun–Oct	forests and meadows, nice stream

42. Mounts Democrat, Lincoln, and Bross	strenuous	Jul–Sep	14,000-foot summits, alpine scenery, history
43. Buffalo Peaks Loop	moderate	Jul–Sep	nice mountain scenery, forests
44. Notch Mountain	strenuous	Jul–Sep	great mountain scenery, historic landmark
45. Fancy Pass	strenuous	Jul–Sep	mountain scenery, lakes
47. Mount Massive	strenuous	Jul–Sep	14,000-foot summit, alpine scenery
48. Elkhead Pass	strenuous	Jul–Sep	high pass, mountain scenery, 14,000-foot peaks
51. Lost Man Lake	strenuous	Jul–Sep	alpine scenery, lakes
53. Electric Pass	strenuous	Jul–Sep	high mountain pass, lake, scenery
58. Crag Crest	moderate	Jul–Sep	interesting mountain scenery, geology, lakes
60. North Crestone Lake	strenuous	Jul–Sep	mountain scenery, lake, forests
66. No Name Lake	strenuous	Jun–Sep	mountain scenery, alpine lake
68. Quartz Lake	strenuous	Jul–Sep	mountain scenery, lake
69. Redcloud and Sunshine Peaks	strenuous	Jul–Sep	two 14,000-foot summits, great scenery
72. Crater Lake	moderate	Jul–Sep	forests, mountain scenery, lake
79. Wetterhorn Basin	moderate	Jul–Sep	mountain scenery, alpine meadows
82. Sneffels High Line	strenuous	Jun–Sep	mountain scenery, forests, accessible
85. Navajo Lake	strenuous	Jul–Sep	alpine scenery, lake, forests
86. Lizard Head	strenuous	Jul–Sep	mountain scenery, stunning geological formation
94. Rattlesnake Arches	strenuous	All year	great canyon scenery, natural arches
Short Backpacks			
23. Red Dirt Pass	moderate	Jul–Sep	lake, mountain scenery
52. Snowmass Lake	strenuous	Jul–Sep	great mountain scenery, lakes
55. Silver Basin	moderate	Jul–Sep	great mountain scenery
57. Tater Heap Loop	strenuous	Jun–Oct	mountain scenery, forests, nice streambeds
64. Wheeler Geologic Area	moderate	Jul–Sep	mountain scenery, geologic formations
71. Chicago Basin	strenuous	Jul–Sep	mountain scenery, high pass, history
Extended Backpacks			
21. Rawah Lakes	strenuous	Jul–Sep	forests, great alpine scenery, lakes
24. Wyoming Trail	moderate	Jul–Sep	great mountain scenery, lakes
26. Lost Lakes–Devils Causeway	moderate	Jul–Sep	lots of alpine scenery, lakes
70. Continental Divide	strenuous	Jul–Sep	incredible alpine scenery, lakes, forests
76. Colorado Trail	strenuous	Jul–Sep	incredible alpine scenery, forests

INTRODUCTION

When most people think of Colorado, they think of mountains. And why not? With its array of mountain ranges, fifty-three 14,000-foot peaks, and thousands of slightly lesser summits, Colorado is the most mountainous of the lower forty-eight states. In fact, Colorado's average elevation of 6800 feet makes it the highest state in the union. Surprisingly, despite these lofty statistics, only a third of Colorado's area is covered with mountains. Spanning much of the eastern half of this rectangular state are the Great Plains—expansive shortgrass prairies broken up by the occasional shallow canyon and a lone butte or two—while the slickrock canyons and mesas of the Colorado Plateau encompass the western quarter. It is from these three provinces—the Rocky Mountains, the Great Plains, and the Colorado Plateau—that Colorado draws its geographic diversity, allowing it to provide some of the best opportunities for hiking and backpacking in the nation.

TOPOGRAPHY

Few states can match Colorado's widely varying topography. Moving from east to west, you first encounter the flat and seemingly featureless grasslands of the state's eastern plains. As part of the Great Plains, this land is naturally treeless, save for a few cottonwoods that sidle up to rivers and creeks. A variety of grasses and some beautiful species of wildflowers grow here instead. Looking out across this land, you might think at first glance that there are no places worth exploring. Longer contemplation would reveal canyons that dissect portions of this terrain, and a few buttes and mesas that interrupt the horizon on occasion.

As the plains roll westward, they suddenly run up against the dramatic rise of the Rocky Mountains. Defined in the northern half of the state by a chain of summits known as the Front Range, and by the Pikes Peak massif, the Wet

Mountains, and the Sangre de Cristo Range to the south, Colorado's first battalion of summits stands in sharp contrast to the horizontal stretch of the plains to the east. Within the space of only a few miles, these peaks rise to elevations of 13,000 and even 14,000 feet. Beyond them the mountains continue in such ranges as the Sawatch, Gore, Park, Elk, West Elk, and San Juan mountains. In all, Colorado encompasses some fifty different mountain ranges.

In contrast to the singular grasslands environment that characterizes the eastern plains, the sudden changes in elevation that Colorado's Mountains provide are responsible for a variety of ecosystems, courtesy of the widely varying climates. Forming a natural boundary that separates the eastern slope and the western slope of the mountains, the Continental Divide also plays an important role in determining local weather patterns. Because the Divide winds for more than 600 miles through the state, Colorado gives rise to a number of important rivers, including the North Platte, Arkansas, Rio Grande, San Juan, and Colorado, to name five.

In the western portion of the state, the high mountains give way to the deeply dissected canyon country of the Colorado Plateau. Although this transition is not as abrupt as the one between mountains and plains, the contrasts are definitive. A land of relatively little rain, much of the Colorado Plateau can be considered upland desert, especially when compared to the snowy mountains to the east. Deep red-rock canyons, high mesa tops, and an assortment of other features add considerable variety to the topography. Extending well into Utah, Arizona, and New Mexico, the Colorado Plateau encompasses about a fifth of Colorado.

CLIMATE

Colorado is a land of many climates. Among its high mountains, deep snows and below-zero nighttime temperatures grip the land for much of the year. With the arrival of spring, however, the snow begins to melt, and by June or July these mountain lands are experiencing more comfortable conditions—though severe local thunderstorms can wrack the mountains on most afternoons during July and August. These storms typically feature brief but heavy periods of rainfall or hail, and plenty of lightning. They become less frequent come September, and by the end of the month or early October the first snows begin to fall. Although these initial wisps of winter usually melt off, heavier snowfalls soon follow to again blanket the high country.

While the mountains are experiencing heavy snows and cold temperatures in the winter, however, Colorado's western canyons may feature relatively mild conditions with plenty of sunshine and afternoon temperatures that hover near the 50-degree mark. During the summer months, these canyons can see temperatures around the century mark. As for the plains region, winds and cold temperatures regularly buffet its open expanses in the winter, but the land remains mostly snow free. By contrast, sweltering temperatures are commonplace in the summer across the plains.

PLANT LIFE

Eastern Plains

In the areas where croplands have not replaced the natural prairie, the eastern plains of Colorado feature a comparatively homogeneous mix of grasses and forbs. Grasses include such species as blue grama, buffalo grass, Kentucky bluegrass, big bluestem, Indian grass, and cheatgrass; forbs include evening primrose, goldenrod, milk vetch, Russian thistle, prickly pear cactus, and yucca, among others.

Mountains

The broadly varying elevations within Colorado's mountain lands translate into very different plant communities. Dependent mostly on elevation and, to some extent, on local topography, these ecosystems can be broken up into five distinct life zones.

The Upper Sonoran zone, which features stunted forests of pinyon pines and junipers, is typical of the lower foothills. It ranges from less than 5000 feet to 6000 feet.

At the next level, taller ponderosa pines, as well as some Douglas-firs and Gambel oaks, characterize the Transition zone. The Transition zone begins around the 6000-foot level and extends up to about 8000 feet.

A bit cooler in overall temperature and blessed with more precipitation is the Canadian zone. The Canadian zone harbors some Douglas-firs throughout, but also subalpine firs and Engelmann spruce. This Engelmann spruce and subalpine fir mix is widespread throughout Colorado's mountains above 9000 feet. Aspen groves are also common in the Canadian zone; aspens commonly pioneer disturbed ecosystems such as burn areas. Lodgepole pine is also found in this zone in the central and northern reaches of the state. Left to their own, lodgepole pine stands can grow quite thick.

Creating a buffer between the Canadian zone and the topmost Arctic-Alpine zone, the Hudsonian zone is home to hardy tree species such as bristlecone and limber pines, as well as Engelmann spruce and subalpine fir. Because of the harsh climate that prevails at these elevations, spruce trees often grow in stunted and twisted thickets known as krummholz forests. Blasted by near-constant cold and wind, such trees have little chance of growing tall and straight.

Finally, above timberline is the Arctic-Alpine zone, a treeless terrain dominated by flowering annuals and perennials, grasses, and occasional thickets of willow. Timberline in Colorado ranges from about 11,000 feet in the north to 11,500 feet across the southern portion. The Arctic-Alpine zone features some of the same species of plants that are found above the Arctic Circle, such as phlox.

Plateau

West of the mountains, across the canyons and mesas of the plateau region, elevations are low enough to ensure that the Upper Sonoran zone is most prevalent. Here, pinyon pine and juniper are the most common species of trees. Mountain mahogany, Utah serviceberry, Mormon tea, yucca, and a variety of small cacti are also plentiful.

Bristlecone pine cone at Dream Lake, Rocky Mountain National Park

Riparian

The diverse plant communities in the riparian ecosystem are of great importance in Colorado, especially in the arid plateau region and the eastern plains. Blessed with a reliable source of water, such as a perennial or frequently flowing stream, riparian areas support cottonwood, box elder, ash, and willow trees, as well as a variety of undergrowth such as wax currant, hawthorn, bulrush, cattail, and poison ivy.

WILDLIFE

Colorado's different provinces are home to an incredible variety of wildlife. Among the species that favor the mountains are mule deer, elk, bighorn sheep, mountain goats, black bears, mountain lions, coyotes, bobcats, an increasing number of Canada lynxes, pine martens, perhaps some wolverines, snowshoe hares, cottontail rabbits, and a variety of squirrels, chipmunks, and other rodents. Pronghorn antelope, white-tailed deer, badgers, and prairie dogs inhabit the eastern plains, while desert bighorn sheep are found in some parts of the plateau region.

Among the hundreds of species of birds that call Colorado home are golden and bald eagles, peregrine falcons, prairie falcons, American kestrels, prairie chickens, western meadowlarks, Steller's jays, Clark's nutcrackers, and magpies.

USING THIS BOOK

This book serves to introduce hikers and backpackers to one hundred of Colorado's best hikes. To lessen the impact on the environment, all of these hikes follow established trails. If you leave these routes to hike cross-country, do so at your own risk. While most of the hikes access a particular destination, such as a lake or a mountain pass, some follow loop routes to take in a variety of locations. Hikes from all regions of the state are included, but, unsurprisingly, most hikes fall within the mountainous areas. No special effort was made to focus on lesser-known hikes (which would have led to the omission of some truly incredible excursions), so some of the trails covered are very popular. If crowds are not your cup of tea, try to plan your trip for the off-season or during a weekday.

Information Blocks

Each hike begins with an information block that presents essential facts at a glance. These facts will help you decide whether or not a hike is right for you.

- The **Distance** listing gives the hike's total mileage. This figure reflects the entire distance, whether for a loop hike, a hike along an out-and-back trail, or a one-way hike that begins and ends at different trailheads. For example, if an out-and-back hike follows a route that is 6.4 miles long, the distance in the information block would be 12.8 miles round-trip. If the trail instead makes a loop, the distance would be listed as a 12.8-mile loop. In the few cases where a point-to-point hike is discussed, the distance is stipulated as one-way; a shuttle is necessary for these hikes.

- While determining the **Difficulty** of a hike is subjective at best, the ratings presented here reflect the hike's total elevation change, its overall grade, and, to some extent, its distance. The three levels of difficulty are easy, moderate, and strenuous. Most short hikes are rated as easy, but a short hike that climbs steeply might be rated as moderate

Elk in Rocky Mountain National Park

or even strenuous. Similarly, some longer hikes are rated as moderate or strenuous simply because they are longer.

- As with the difficulty rating, trying to determine the **Hiking time** for a route is an uncertain science. Hikers walk at different speeds and some take more breaks than others. This book tries to balance each route's length with its overall elevation change to come up with a consistent determination of the total time that each hike should take. These times tend to be conservative to better prepare hikers with beginning abilities. Remember, the hiking times are only estimates.

- **Elevation** figures indicate the range in elevation covered by the hike. The first figure is the trailhead elevation and the second figure is the hike's high or low point, depending on whether the route gains or loses elevation.

- The **Management** listing identifies the government agencies that manage the trail. Entities include the Bureau of Land Management, national forests, national parks, national monuments, national grasslands, state parks, and municipally owned parks and open spaces. The organizations listed are also a source for maps.

- **Wilderness status** indicates whether the hike crosses an established wilderness area or wilderness study area. These areas are covered by specific regulations (see the Wilderness Etiquette section later in this chapter).

- The **Season** entry indicates when a particular route will probably be free of snow. These listings are conservative; some routes can open a month earlier or close a month later, depending on how severe the winter has been or will be. Check with the managing agency with questions concerning the condition of a trail or access to a trailhead.

- The **Maps** listing indicates which United States Geological Survey (USGS) 7.5-minute topographic maps apply to the hike. Keep in mind that some USGS maps are out-of-date, however, and

might not indicate recent changes in a route or omit a new trail completely. USGS topographic maps should be used in conjunction with other maps, such as those produced by the U.S. Forest Service, the Bureau of Land Management (BLM), the management agency, or commercial publishers.

- Following the information blocks, a **Getting there** section provides driving directions to the trailhead, or trailheads in the case of one-way routes, and parking.

Maps and Profiles

A topographic map illustrates each hike in this book, but you should bring along the actual topo maps that show more of the surrounding area.

Each chapter also includes a trail profile. Round-trip hikes show the elevation profile for the first half of the hike only, since the route returns to the starting point along the same trails. Loop hikes and a few one-way hikes are depicted from start to finish.

Hike Descriptions

Each hike description begins with an introductory paragraph, and then presents a descriptive guide to the route, including distances, grade changes, trail difficulty, trail conditions, intersecting trails, and natural features such as forest types or geological formations. Historical anecdotes are occasionally included and some information on side routes is also provided to give readers ideas about other hiking possibilities in the area. The final paragraph in the descriptions provides information on the availability of water, potential hazards, specific regulations, and other special considerations.

WILDERNESS ETIQUETTE

Many of the hikes in this book enter established wilderness areas where specific regulations apply. Some hikes explore the backcountry reaches of national and state parks, which have their own rules. Other hikes cross parcels of public domain that are open to multiple uses. No matter what hike you choose, however, you should follow a set of commonsense, environmentally

Gnarled bristlecone pine at The Crags

friendly rules. Many of these edicts of wilderness etiquette are stipulated in the Wilderness Act of 1964.

As dictated by the Wilderness Act, all forms of mechanized travel are prohibited in wilderness areas. This includes hang gliders, motorcycles, and mountain bicycles. Because some off-road bicyclists believe that this regulation does not or should not apply to them, mountain bikes present a particularly pressing problem in some locales. Keep in mind that all trails within wilderness areas, and most in national parks and monuments, are off-limits to bicycles. Where mountain bikes are allowed, be sure to watch for the occasional out-of-control rider. Bicyclists are learning that irresponsible riding leads to additional trail closures, but a few still ride as though their fun takes precedence over other trail users.

The Wilderness Act also prohibits the use of chainsaws, generators, and other mechanized equipment in wilderness areas. Commercial enterprises such as livestock grazing, pack outfitting, and guide services are allowed only by permit. Keep in mind that individual wilderness areas can carry added regulations. Because dogs can disturb wildlife and other hikers, they are usually prohibited in the backcountry of national parks and monuments, as well as in most state parks and specific areas within national forest and BLM lands. The best plan is to leave your dog at home, but if you do take your pet along, it is important to keep it under control (preferably on a leash) at all times.

To lessen their impact on Colorado's backcountry, hikers should follow the regulations in the Wilderness Act of 1964—as well as leave-no-trace guidelines—in the backcountry and when camping at the trailhead.

- Do not build campfires; use a stove instead.
- Avoid camping on sensitive areas, such as mountain meadows and fragile desert soils.
- Camp at least 100 feet from all trails, streams, and lakes, and use existing sites whenever possible. Some heavily used areas might have additional regulations concerning where you can camp.
- Never cut down standing trees—dead or alive.

- Do not leave behind any structures or nails.
- Do not dig holes or trenches, and do not level or trench around tent areas.
- Use biodegradable soap, bury all human waste at least 200 feet from water, and pack out toilet paper and hygiene products.
- Travel in small groups.
- Never cut across switchbacks or walk over sensitive areas such as cryptogamic soil (i.e., soil encrusted with lichen).
- Pack out all litter.

All plants, animals, rocks, and historical relics should be enjoyed only within their natural setting. These rules are often the law within national parks and monuments, and in state parks. Although they do not always apply to areas administered by the Forest Service and BLM, they should be followed just the same. Where historical and archaeological artifacts are concerned, all antiquities of historic and prehistoric origin are fully protected on all federal lands. The looting of Indian artifacts has become an alarming problem, especially in the southwest corner of Colorado. The best rule where ancient artifacts, cliff dwellings, and rock art are concerned is look but do not touch.

BACKCOUNTRY SAFETY

Hiking Colorado's backcountry can be a pleasurable experience, but there also can be hazards—especially for those who are unprepared. Before setting out into the plains, mountains, or canyons of the state, you should be aware of potential hazards and how best to avoid them. The most common potential problems are described briefly here. A list in the appendix suggests books with more detailed information concerning safety in the backcountry.

Hypothermia

The weather in Colorado's high country can change suddenly without notice and hikers need to be prepared for all possibilities. Even during the summer, the sun can be shining one moment and a storm brewing the next. Because winds, cold rain, hail, and even snow can accompany such changes in weather, hikers should be aware that hypothermia can be a life-threatening situation. Hypothermia occurs when the body's core temperature drops to dangerous levels. Symptoms include uncontrollable shivering, deteriorating speech, impaired judgment, drowsiness, and weakness. Often, the victim is unaware that he or she is sick.

While hypothermia can kill in only a few hours, it is readily treatable, even in the field. Replace wet clothing with dry as soon as possible, and place the victim in a warm sleeping bag. It also might be necessary to huddle with the victim to share body warmth. Give warm liquids and high-energy food, and then seek medical help at once. Of course, the best plan of action is to avoid hypothermia altogether by staying dry and warm in the first place, carrying spare clothing and raingear, and eating plenty of high-energy foods.

Lightning

Perhaps the most omnipresent threat to visitors in Colorado's backcountry is lightning. Lightning can strike anywhere and anytime there are clouds in the area. Thunderstorms build in Colorado's high country nearly every afternoon during the months of July and August. Often violent in nature, such storms hit the upper elevations with incredible ferocity—you don't want to be in any exposed location such as above timberline, on a mountain or ridge top, on canyon rims, or in other prominent places where lightning would naturally strike.

As with hypothermia, an ounce of prevention can go a long way. Plan your trip so that you are off the mountain by noon or shortly after. If you do get caught in a storm, experts suggest that you huddle in a flat area or depression, get rid of any metal objects, and stay away from trees. Deeper caves can provide a safe hideout, but avoid tents, shallow alcoves, the base of rocks, and gully bottoms. The safest place to be, by far, is in your vehicle.

Flash Floods

Although flash floods are not particularly common in Colorado's high country, they can occur. They are somewhat more common in the canyons of the plateau region and even in some

Wildflowers in the San Juan Mountains

drainages in the eastern plains. The tricky thing about flash floods is that you may be experiencing sunny weather while it rains torrents upstream. In these cases, a wall of water can crash down upon an unsuspecting hiker with little or no warning. If you are caught off guard, get to higher ground immediately. Do not try to cross flooded areas until the water subsides.

Wildlife

Attacks on humans by mountain lions and black bears have been on the rise across the country in recent years, largely due to an increase in the number of people living near wild areas. Where bears are of concern, store food, including toiletries, in a bear-resistant container. If you do not have access to one, hang your food bag at least 12 feet up in a tree and away from your tent. It is also a good idea to cook at least 300 feet downwind from camp. The smell of food is the surest way to invite a bear into your camp. Go to *www.bearsmart.com* for additional information on avoiding bear problems, as well as for updated information.

Mountain lions still have a healthy fear of man in Colorado's unpopulated areas and are not considered a menace. If you come face-to-face to one, do not run. Try to appear as large as possible and fight back with sticks and rocks if attacked.

Rattlesnakes are common in the lower elevations, but they will try to shy away from people when they can. Encountering a rattler is most likely if you leave the trail to explore rocky areas. If you have a close encounter, step away carefully and seek immediate medical attention if bitten.

Giardia

Within the last few decades, *Giardia lamblia* has become so widespread that you should assume that no surface water—streams, creeks, lakes, and so on—is safe to drink without being treated or purified first. A microscopic organism, giardia causes severe diarrhea one to two weeks after it gets into your digestive system. Fortunately, giardia is easy to avoid. While most chemical treatments do not safeguard against giardia, boiling water for ten minutes or longer does. Some effective filter systems are also available

Mule deer in Rocky Mountain National Park

today; read the label to make sure your system can screen out giardia. If you are out just for the day, the simplest means of prevention is to pack enough water for the entire hike.

Getting Lost and Found

Like many outdoor skills, the ability to find your way through the backcountry is enhanced with experience. Most of the hikes in this book are straightforward enough to introduce novice hikers to Colorado's backcountry, but the possibility of getting lost still exists. First-time hikers should not travel alone and veteran hikers should think twice about soloing on harder routes. If you plan to leave established trails, be prepared with a compass, topographic maps, and the orienteering skills to use both. In any case, you should always let someone know where you are going and when you will return. If you do get lost, remain calm; with luck, another hiker will happen along shortly. If not, a search party will eventually be sent once whomever you told realizes you are overdue.

BEFORE YOU GO

A little preparation can make all the difference between having a fun and successful excursion and enduring a miserable or unsafe experience. The best place to begin is in selecting your equipment. You will need sturdy yet comfortable hiking shoes. Good soles and plenty of ankle support are especially important when tackling steep and rocky terrain. While shorts and a tee shirt might seem like enough clothing when you set out, be sure to pack long pants and a long-sleeved shirt as well. A warm jacket is a must, as is raingear—a poncho or rain parka and pants. Exposure to the sun is intense in alpine areas and in the canyons and plains, so you also will want to bring sunblock lotion and a wide-brimmed hat. Mosquito repellent is also useful.

Whether you are setting out for the morning or overnight, you will need a comfortable pack. The market is filled with high-tech packs that make carrying weight as painless as possible. A lightweight tent, a warm sleeping bag, and a sleeping pad will help ensure a comfortable night's rest. Given the fact that campfires are environmentally unfriendly, a lightweight stove for cooking is essential on overnight trips, and a backpack cook kit will simplify meal preparation.

In addition to basic clothing and equipment, you also should always carry the "Ten Essentials," even if you plan to be out only for the day. The ten essentials that follow detail a systems approach to preparedness; your pack should include:

1. Navigation (map and compass)
2. Sun protection (sunglasses and sunscreen)
3. Insulation (extra clothing)
4. Illumination (headlamp or flashlight)
5. First-aid supplies
6. Fire (firestarter and matches/lighter)
7. Repair kit and tools (including knife)
8. Nutrition (extra food)
9. Hydration (extra water)
10. Emergency shelter

A NOTE ABOUT SAFETY

Safety is an important concern in all outdoor activities. No guidebook can alert you to every hazard or anticipate the limitations of every reader. Therefore, the descriptions of roads, trails, routes, and natural features in this book are not representations that a particular place or excursion will be safe for your party. When you follow any of the routes described in this book, you assume responsibility for your own safety. Under normal conditions, such excursions require the usual attention to traffic, road and trail conditions, weather, terrain, the capabilities of your party, and other factors. Keeping informed on current conditions and exercising common sense are the keys to a safe, enjoyable outing.

—The Mountaineers Books

Opposite: One of the two impressive Pawnee Buttes

EASTERN PLAINS

A land of shortgrass prairies, farms, and ranches, Colorado's eastern plains might seem to have little if anything to offer hikers. Indeed, the number of hiking destinations in this eastern third of the state is limited, but the ones that do exist are real gems. Most come in the form of shallow but interesting canyons, three of which hold unusual and fascinating treasures of the past. Another hike follows the historic Santa Fe Trail for a short distance. The hike around Barr Lake reveals the rich wildlife of the region, and the walk to Pawnee Buttes revels in the quiet beauty of the high plains. Standing in sharp contrast to the near vertical topography of the state's mountainous region, these walks each offer something memorable.

1 PAWNEE BUTTES

Distance: 3 miles round-trip
Difficulty: Easy
Hiking time: 2 hours
Elevation: 5420 to 5200 feet
Management: Pawnee National Grassland
Wilderness status: None
Season: Year-round
Maps: USGS Pawnee Buttes, Grover SE

Getting there: From Fort Collins, drive 45 miles east on Colorado Highway 14. After passing through Briggsdale, continue for another 13 miles and turn left toward the nearly abandoned town of Keota on County Road 103. Drive 4.5 miles north to Keota, then continue 3 miles north on County Road 105. Turn right onto County Road 104 and drive 3 miles to County Road 111. Turn left and drive 4.5 miles to where a secondary road turns north. Follow this route less than a mile to the signed trailhead. From the highway, each turn is signed for Pawnee Buttes access.

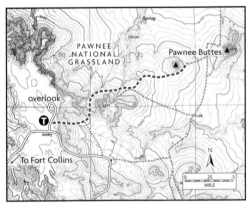

Rising a few hundred feet above the surrounding shortgrass prairie, the Pawnee Buttes are both the crowning jewel of the 193,060-acre Pawnee National Grassland and the destination of a short but rewarding hike. The trail passes some interesting plant communities and badlands formations, and offers the opportunity for hikers to enjoy a surprising variety of wildlife.

The hike begins by dropping easily from the trailhead into a broad drainage. A popular route, this trail is well established and easy to follow. Near the drainage bottom, the route passes through a gate in a fence to reach the next drainage north. On either side of the trail are low sandstone bluffs that look like they might be fun to explore. These areas are off-limits from March 1 to June 30, however, to protect nesting birds of prey, so be sure to stay on the trail. In addition to falcons, these grasslands are also home to golden eagles and hawks. Songbirds are plentiful, and you might glimpse some deer or pronghorn antelope.

As the trail winds its way into another shallow drainage, notice the scattered juniper and squawbush, plus prickly pear cactus and yucca. Also growing in the vicinity of the buttes are the easternmost stands of limber pines. Wildflowers grow in prodigious numbers along this trail during the late spring and summer months. After climbing easily out of the drainage bottom, the trail then continues on toward the imposing buttes, which are less than 0.5 mile to the northeast. The actual hiking route ends at a private property line marked by a sign. Formed from sedimentary rock deposited during the Oligocene and Miocene epochs, the Pawnee Buttes are actually remnants of a once-higher plain. The surrounding terrain was subsequently eroded away by runoff during the last glacial age. After enjoying the buttes up close, return to your car by the same route.

Obey all signs concerning the disturbance of nesting birds of prey. Disturbing any archaeological or paleontological artifacts is strictly prohibited. If you plan on camping, regulations stipulate that you must be at least 200 feet from the Buttes, the trail, stock tanks, windmills, and parking lots, and at least 0.25 mile from any trees. Mountain bikes are prohibited and dogs must be on a leash. Watch for flash floods in the wash bottoms and be wary of rattlesnakes, especially off trail. Water is not available along this hike, so bring plenty. Be sure to respect the rights of private property owners in the area.

Cactus blossoms near Pawnee Buttes

2 BARR LAKE

Distance: 9-mile loop
Difficulty: Easy
Hiking time: 6 hours
Elevation: 5100 feet
Management: Barr Lake State Park
Wilderness status: None
Season: Year-round
Maps: USGS Brighton, Mile High Lakes

Getting there: From Denver, drive northeast on Interstate 76 to the Bromley Lane exit (exit 22). Follow Bromley Lane east to Picadilly Road and turn south. The park entrance is a little more than a mile down this road. The trail begins at the nature center and picnic area, which are at the end of the road within the park.

Situated in the plains northeast of Denver, Barr Lake offers an interesting oasis for people and wildlife alike. With a 1900-acre surface area when full, the lake serves as a stopover for a variety of migratory birds. As of 2007, the lake has also hosted a bald eagle nesting site for 20 years—the oldest such nesting site of the few that exist along the Front Range region. This hike follows a 9-mile trail that circles the entire lake.

From the trailhead, at the nature center, begin by turning left immediately after crossing the Denver and Hudson Canal. This canal parallels the trail along the lake's southeast shoreline. Because the trail actually follows the service road for the canal, the going is extremely easy.

Immediately after crossing the canal, the Niedrach Nature Trail branches off to the right. Take

Gazebo boardwalk at Barr Lake

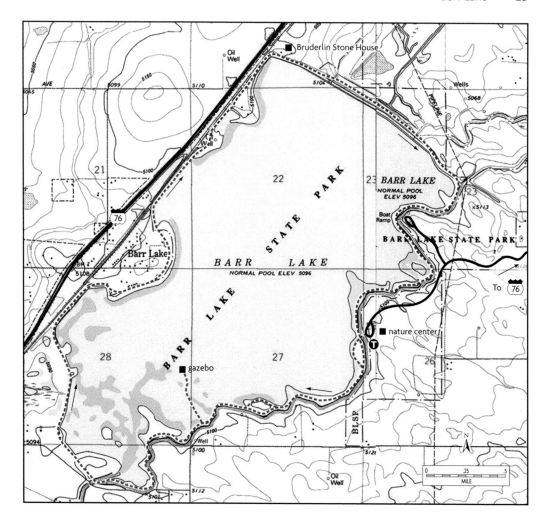

this short side route to access a boardwalk that leads to the lake's shoreline and penetrates the forest of cottonwoods that lines the lake. Besides breaking up the horizontal axis of the plains, these trees add variety to the natural environment. The nature trail soon returns to the main trail, where the hike continues clockwise around the lake.

In addition to cottonwood stands, you also pass some small meadows where foxes and mule deer might be spotted, especially at dawn and dusk, and a few short side trails lead to observation stations on the lakeshore. These small structures provide screens for bird-watching. Possible sightings at Barr Lake include Canada

geese, and a variety of ducks, grebes, great blue herons, egrets, and more.

At 1.3 miles, the trail reaches the turnoff for a covered observation gazebo located at the end of a long boardwalk that extends out over the lake. From this pleasant spot, you can observe waterfowl up close—that is, when the water level is high. Because Barr Lake is used to store water for irrigation purposes, it can drop considerably during the late summer and fall, leaving the gazebo high and dry. It is still a nice place to visit, nevertheless. A telescope there allows observation of distant birds, as well as a glimpse of a bald eagle nest that sits in a large cottonwood to the west. You might even see one or both parent birds perched in the branches nearby and eaglets in the nest.

Although many visitors turn back after visiting the gazebo, the trail continues on around the southwest end of the lake, where it crosses the lake's inlet. Some interesting cattail marshes are encountered along the western portion of the shoreline. As the route reaches the lake's northwest side, the quiet solitude is washed away by noise from the nearby interstate highway and by an occasional passing train. An old homestead, the Bruderlin Stone House, which dates back to the 1880s, is located along this section of the trail. It has been renovated and now serves as headquarters for the Rocky Mountain Bird Observatory. The trail then reaches the dam, which spans more than a mile across the lake's

northeast side. You can cross the dam on either the Upper Crest or Lower Crest Trail. The upper offers a view of the lake while the lower passes a prairie dog town. From the dam, the trail continues along the eastern portion of the lake, passing a boat ramp and another observation boardwalk. It is possible to see owl and hawk nests in this area, as well as nests of other species. At 9 miles, the trail returns to the trailhead. Be sure to pay a visit to the nature center either before or after your hike.

Because the southern end of Barr Lake is included in a wildlife refuge, dogs are not permitted along this section of the hike. Fishing and boating are prohibited as well. Stay on established trails at all times. Bring plenty of water to drink and binoculars for bird-watching.

3 CASTLEWOOD CANYON

Distance: 6.1-mile loop
Difficulty: Easy
Hiking time: 4 hours
Elevation: 6600 to 6200 feet
Management: Castlewood Canyon State Park
Wilderness status: None
Season: Year-round
Maps: USGS Castle Rock South, Russellville Gulch

Getting there: From Castle Rock, drive 7 miles east on Colorado Highway 86 to Franktown. Turn south on Colorado Highway 83 and drive 5 miles to the park entrance. Stop at the visitor center to pick up a brochure with a detailed map of the park trail system, then drive to the trailhead at the picnic area at Canyon Point.

Castlewood Canyon is located in the plains region southeast of Denver. Etched by Cherry Creek, this canyon includes several ecological communities that blend together in a relatively small area. They include surprisingly tall stands of timber, verdant riparian areas, fragile prairie grasses, and more. Add to these natural features a poignant lesson in man's attempt to control nature and you have a special place indeed.

The hike begins by following the Lake Gulch Trail northwest along a mesa top for a short distance before descending through scattered ponderosa pines and thick patches of Gambel oak to the canyon bottom. The 0.8-mile Lake Gulch Trail drops 200 feet to reach the Inner Canyon Trail at a creek crossing. Turn left at this intersection to follow the Inner Canyon Trail for a short distance north to the site of an old dam. Built in 1890 to harness Cherry Creek for irrigation purposes, this cut-rock dam had problems almost from the beginning. After springing leaks within its first years, the 65-foot-high, 630-foot-long dam finally burst following heavy rains in

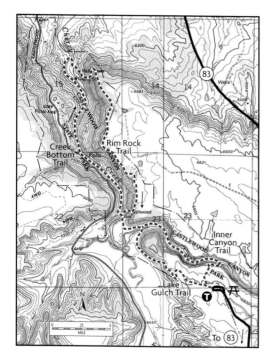

View from the Lake Gulch Trail

August of 1933. The wall of water created by the 200-acre reservoir killed two people and caused $1 million in damage. Today, only a small portion of the dam still stands, but the lessons are vivid just the same.

At the dam site, the trail crosses the main wash bottom to reach a trailhead on the northwest side of Cherry Creek. Here, it picks up the Creek Bottom Trail to trace the canyon floor downstream for a little more than 1.5 miles. This section of the hike visits the riparian community supported by Cherry Creek's perennial flow of water. Occasional flash flooding helped shape this riparian area, precluding the growth of some plant species while fostering others. Poison ivy figures among the plants found along this corridor—watch out!

At the north end of the Creek Bottom Trail, the hike turns right at a trail intersection to take up the approximately 2.1-mile Rim Rock Trail; the left-hand route leads less than 0.5 mile along the Homestead Trail to the park's west entrance. From this trail intersection, the Rim Rock Trail climbs steeply—about 300 feet in less than 0.25 mile—to gain the east rim of the canyon. Perhaps the most interesting portion of the entire hike, the rim provides the best views of the canyon below and reveals an interesting mix of prairie grass-lands and ponderosa pine forests. These forested areas are part of a much larger ecosystem known as the Black Forest. Stretching across a 40-mile-by-75-mile area of the eastern plains, the Black Forest features stands of ponderosa pine that take advantage of suitable growing conditions found along slightly higher reaches of the plains. As you follow the Rim Rock Trail, you can also enjoy the interesting cliff faces that drop into the canyon. Known as Castle Rock Conglomer-ate, this rock is composed of sands and coarse pebbles that were cemented together some 34 million years ago.

At its south end, the Rim Rock Trail drops back into the canyon to meet with the nearly 1.2-mile Inner Canyon Trail at the dam site. This hike then returns to the trailhead by way of the Inner Canyon route through a side canyon up-stream before climbing about 100 feet back up to Canyon Point. Along this last leg of the hike, you will encounter more riparian growth, and see how stands of Douglas-firs take advantage of the north-facing canyon wall, which provides pro-tection from the elements and suitable ground moisture for the evergreens.

Although water is found along this hike, it is best to bring your own for drinking. Camping is prohibited within the state park, and dogs must be kept on a leash. Watch for flash floods during rainy periods, and avoid wandering off trail, as the surrounding vegetation is fragile. Also be mindful of rattlesnakes, especially along the Rim Rock Trail.

4 SANTA FE TRAIL

Distance: 6 miles round-trip
Difficulty: Easy
Hiking time: 3 hours
Elevation: 4410 to 4400 feet
Management: Comanche National Grassland
Wilderness status: None
Season: Year-round
Maps: USGS Timpas, La Junta SW

Getting there: This hike begins at the Timpas Picnic Area, which is 16 miles south of La Junta on US Highway 350. Upon reaching the nearly deserted town of Timpas, turn right onto County Road 16.5 and drive across the railroad tracks to a picnic facility. The other end of this hike is reached by driving 3 miles northeast of Timpas on US 350 to Colorado Highway 71. Follow this road north for 0.5 mile to the Sierra Vista Overlook, located on the only high point for many miles around.

For some, the thought of hiking across a nearly featureless prairie within sight of a highway does not sound appealing. For the committed history buff, however, such an excursion can be irresistible, especially if the hike follows the actual route of the Santa Fe Trail. Thanks to the route's recognition as a National Historic Trail by Congress in 1987, it is possible to visit and enjoy many different portions of the trail. Here, you can walk a stretch of the famed trail delin-eated by stone markers.

Beginning along a short nature trail that heads west from the Timpas Picnic Area, the 3-mile stretch of the Santa Fe Trail running northeast to the Sierra Vista Overlook offers what may be

A stone marker along the old Santa Fe Trail

the easiest hiking route you will ever find. This is because it traverses the shortgrass prairie, a completely level land of ankle-high grass. As for the route itself, instead of being an actual tread, the way is marked every 0.25 mile or so by a waist-high stone marker easily visible from a distance. These trail markers lead you in a virtually straight line from the Timpas Picnic

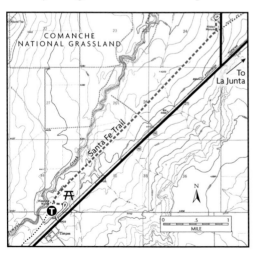

Area to the Sierra Vista Overlook. You can also see the overlook on the horizon, as well as US Highway 350, which is visible less than 0.5 mile to the right.

While the hike itself holds little challenge or intrigue, the fact that you are following the Santa Fe Trail is indeed of interest. A trade route rather than one of emigration, the Santa Fe Trail runs for 900 miles, from Independence, Missouri, to the city of Santa Fe in what is now New Mexico. Because the Spanish government trade had prohibited trade with America, the Santa Fe Trail did not become a reality until Mexico gained its independence in 1821. Within just six weeks, the first trader, William Becknell, set out from Franklin, Missouri, to sell his wares in Santa Fe. Encouraged by the Mexican government, commerce quickly boomed as traders from both nations were eager to tap into a new market. The Santa Fe Trail included two branches almost from the beginning: the more direct Cimarron Route, which followed the normally dry Cimarron River from Dodge City through Oklahoma to Watrous, New Mexico, and the Mountain Route, which followed the Arkansas River west into Colorado and then south over Raton Pass. The longer Mountain Route, initially desirable because of the availability of water, became even more popular with the establishment of Bents Fort near the present-day town of La Junta in 1833. Commerce on the Santa Fe Trail continued after 1848, when the United States seized control of the territory from Mexico, and did not end until the first train reached Santa Fe in 1880.

Visions of the Santa Fe Trail along this hikeable stretch must be conjured up more by your imagination than by physical evidence. Look out across the prairie and get a feel for what it must have been like for those early traders headed to Santa Fe, with the seemingly ever-present winds buffeting your face and the numbing expanse of flat terrain stretching westward to the barely visible snowy summits of the Rockies (the Spanish Peaks, Sangre de Cristo Range, Greenhorn Mountain, and Pikes Peak are all visible on a clear day).

Be sure to pack water as there is no potable water available on this hike. Also, watch for rattlesnakes, tarantulas, and scorpions while walking the prairie. Keep in mind that federal law protects all historic relics.

5 PICKET WIRE CANYONLANDS

Distance: 17.4 miles round-trip
Difficulty: Moderate
Hiking time: 12 hours
Elevation: 4660 to 4320 feet
Management: Comanche National Grassland
Wilderness status: None
Season: Year-round
Maps: USGS Riley Canyon, Beaty Canyon, O V Mesa

Getting there: To reach the trailhead, drive 13 miles south from La Junta on Colorado Highway 109 to County Road 802. Turn southwest, and drive 8 miles to the intersection with County Road 25. Turn south on County Road 25 and drive about 6 miles to the bulletin board for the Picket Wire Canyonlands. The trailhead is 3.3 miles to the east along Road 500, a high-clearance, two-wheel-drive (2WD) route that might be impassable when wet. A parking area marks the trail's start. Remember that all vehicles must stay on the roadway.

The relatively deep and expansive canyon system carved by the Purgatoire River might come as a shock for the first-time visitor to the plains region of eastern Colorado. Some 350 feet deep and rimmed by substantial cliff faces of sandstone, these canyons offer truly wonderful hiking opportunities where access is permitted. One such place is the Picket Wire Canyonlands area south of La Junta. This area offers some surprising canyon scenery along with a treasure chest of paleontological, prehistoric, and historic delights. The name Picket Wire originated with the way in which French trappers pronounced the Spanish-inspired name, Purgatoire. Locals have held on to the misnomer ever since.

From the parking area, this hike follows an old pasture road that is closed to motorized vehicles (managing agency trucks and other specially permitted vehicles are excepted) by a pipe gate. Beyond the gate, the road drops steeply into Withers Canyon, a side drainage of Picket Wire Canyon. The route descends 350 feet in the first 0.3 mile to reach the mostly level

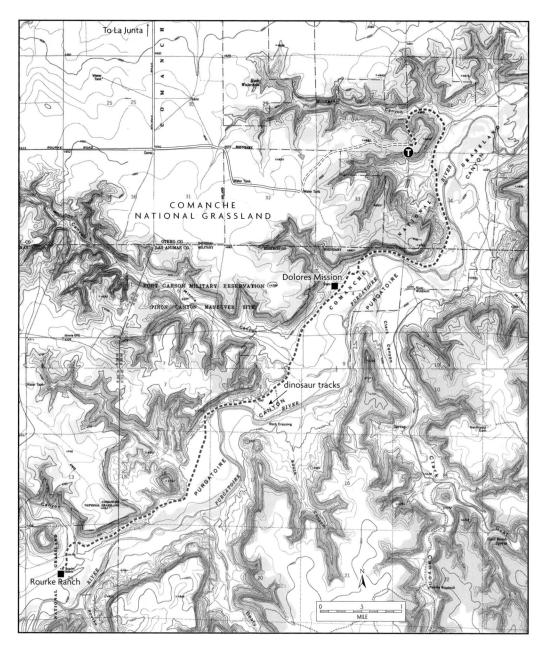

canyon bottom. From here, it continues following the old road south to the open main canyon of the Purgatoire River, about 1 mile from the trailhead. After turning right here, the trail follows a mostly level four-wheel-drive (4WD) road for the rest of the way.

In the few places where the trail runs directly adjacent to the Purgatoire River, you can see that the waterway is not very large. It is, nevertheless, one of the more substantial streams that flow across the arid plains region of southeastern Colorado. In places where the river is out

The trail into Picket Wire Canyon

of sight, its meandering course is often marked by tall cottonwoods growing along its banks. Willows, tamarisks, and a variety of other water-loving plants are also common in the Picket Wire Canyonlands. Wildlife includes mule and white-tailed deer, badgers, coyotes, antelope, bighorn sheep, and mountain lions.

A short distance beyond the trail register are the crumbling remains of an adobe homestead. One of a handful of old structures in the area, it serves as a reminder that the late 1800s saw some settlement activity in the Picket Wire Canyonlands. A second reminder comes 3.7 miles from the trailhead in the form of the Dolores Mission, which was established in the late 1800s. Remnants of the building, along with a nearby cemetery, are visible today. In other stretches of the hike, you also might happen upon prehistoric rock art that dates back between 300 and 4500 years. Although little is known about the prehistoric inhabitants of the area, it is thought that they were nomadic hunters who occasionally passed through these canyons in search of game.

Farther on—a little more than 5 miles from the trailhead—the hike takes you even further back in time with the longest mapped and recorded dinosaur track site in North America, continuing for 0.25 mile and containing more than 1300 individual footprints. These tracks were set 150 million years ago by enormous brontosaurs and smaller, meat-eating allosaurs as they walked across a muddy shoreline. Preserved in the Morrison Formation, these tracks are evidence of social behavior among younger brontosaurs—namely that they traveled as a pack in a single direction. Today, the tracks are visible in a shelf of bedrock that runs adjacent to the river.

Beyond the dinosaur track site, the route continues for another 3.4 miles to reach the Rourke Ranch, which, like the Dolores Mission, dates back to 1871. Before being sold in 1971, this ranch grew from 40 acres to more than 52,000 acres in size, making it one of the largest cattle operations in this part of the state. From the Rourke Ranch, it is 8.7 miles back to the trailhead. If your time is limited, you might want to turn back sooner, perhaps at the dinosaur track site or the Dolores Mission. In any case, you will have experienced the wonderful scenery and the interesting natural history of the Picket Wire Canyonlands.

The Picket Wire Canyonlands are open to mountain bikes but closed to all motorized vehicles. Because camping is prohibited in the canyonlands, you will have to complete your hike within a day. Bring plenty of water, as water from the Purgatoire River is not drinkable. Watch for rattlesnakes and scorpions. Keep in mind that flash floods have been known to occur within these stream bottoms. Also note that federal law protects all cultural resources within the Picket Wire Canyonlands. Collecting artifacts is strictly prohibited.

6 VOGEL CANYON

Distance: 2.25-mile loop
Difficulty: Easy
Hiking time: 2 hours
Elevation: 4400 to 4300 feet
Management: Comanche National Grassland
Wilderness status: None
Season: Year-round
Map: USGS La Junta SE

Getting there: The hike begins at the Vogel Canyon Picnic Area, reached by driving 13 miles south from La Junta on Colorado Highway 109. Turn right at the sign for Vogel Canyon and drive southwest for 1 mile on County Road 802. Turn left at an intersection and continue south for about 1.5 miles to the picnic area.

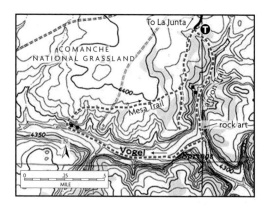

While the nearby Picket Wire Canyonlands (Hike 5) offer a stunning contrast to the expansive plains that stretch south of La Junta, considerably smaller Vogel Canyon provides a more intimate break. Graced by both natural beauty and relics of the past, this small canyon system is a real joy to visit. Four hiking trails have been established in Vogel Canyon; this hike follows the Canyon and Mesa Trails to complete a 2.25-mile loop.

From the trailhead, follow the Canyon Trail through a V-shaped cattle guard (to the left of the gated fence crossing) and then south among scattered juniper trees. Stone cairns mark the way along this stretch. Within 0.25 mile, this trail begins dropping into the head of a shallow side canyon. The well-defined Canyon Trail is easy to follow as it continues down the wash bottom for another 0.25 mile or so. Along this first segment of the hike, some old stone foundations near the canyon rim to the west are the remains of the Westbrook homestead, which dates to the Depression era. Farther on, at the base of the canyon's east wall, are petroglyphs (images carved into the rock) left behind by prehistoric inhabitants of the area.

A little more than 0.5 mile from the trailhead, the Canyon Trail reaches one of two springs found in Vogel Canyon. Crowded by a few cottonwoods, some cattails, and a tamarisk or two, this reliable source of water not only made it possible for ranchers to homestead in the canyon, but it also attracts wildlife such as deer and antelope. At the spring, the Canyon Trail intersects with the Mesa Trail, which heads west up the main fork of Vogel Canyon. Turn right at this junction to continue along the Mesa Trail as it follows Vogel Canyon upstream. The trail begins to fade away, but because the route continues along the flat canyon bottom, and thanks to a few stone cairns, it is not difficult to follow.

About 0.75 mile from the intersection with the Canyon Trail, the route climbs the canyon rim to the north to return to the trailhead. To find this short ascent out of Vogel Canyon, watch

Trailside wildflowers in Vogel Canyon

for stone foundations to the right on the canyon floor. These are the remains of a stagecoach stop along the Barlow and Sanderson Mail and Stage Line, which was active between 1872 and 1876. Less than 100 yards beyond these ruins, look for two stone cairns that mark a turn in the trail leading north through some rocks. Climb less than 100 feet to reach the top of the canyon rim, and continue north across the mesa top for a short distance until you find another cairn. From here, look eastward for additional markers that can be followed back to the trailhead. This section of the route passes among scattered junipers and encounters more stone ruins. In sections where no stone markers exist, just keep heading east. As you near the trailhead, look for a wooden crossover that provides access over a fence running north to south. Soon after the crossover, you reach the Overlook Trail, which is graveled for wheelchair access. Turn left onto this trail to return to the trailhead.

Watch for rattlesnakes, tarantulas, and scorpions along this hike, especially when away from established trails. Bring drinking water, as the water in Vogel Canyon is not potable. Do not disturb rock art and other historic sites along the way.

7 PICTURE CANYON

Distance: 4-mile loop
Difficulty: Easy
Hiking time: 2 hours
Elevation: 4300 to 4450 feet
Management: Comanche National Grassland
Wilderness status: None
Season: Year-round
Map: USGS Tubs Spring

Getting there: From Springfield, drive 20 miles south on US Highway 287 to the small town of Campo. Turn right onto County Road J and continue west for 10 miles to County Road 18. Turn left and drive 5 miles south to the signed right turn for Picture Canyon. Drive less than 2 miles south to the Picture Canyon Picnic Area at the road's end.

As the name suggests, Picture Canyon is home to some interesting examples of Native American rock art, but this unexpectedly memorable place in southeastern Colorado also offers hikers

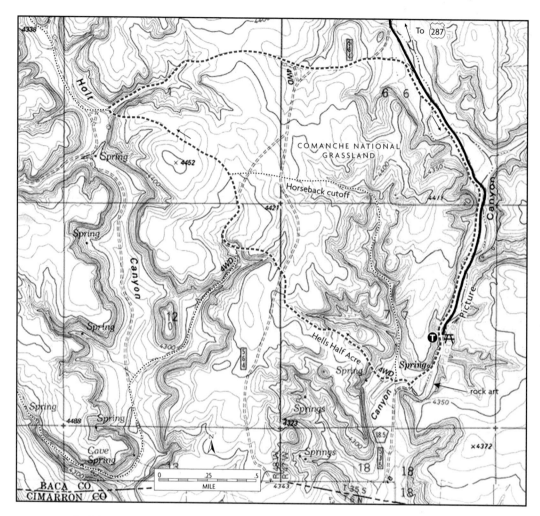

some wonderful canyon scenery, unusual geologic formations, and an interesting collection of
flora and fauna. Hikers can explore Picture Canyon on a 4-mile loop that visits its unique natural
and cultural features.

From the picnic area, the route follows Picture Canyon downstream for about 0.3 mile
along an old road that is closed to most vehicles.
Upon reaching an area where the canyon begins
to widen, you might want to pay a visit to the
rock art scattered along the canyon's east wall.
Although these pictographs (painted on the
rock) and petroglyphs (carved into the rock)
have been badly vandalized over the years, they
still present a fascinating collection of ancient
images. Some drawings, such as one of a horse,
cannot date before the time that these beasts
of burden were introduced to the West by the
Spanish—sometime after AD 1600. Other images
are far older, however, as archaeologists have
unearthed camps in the area that date to AD 500
and earlier. One of the more unusual rock art images in Picture Canyon is a series of vertical lines
crossed by a longer horizontal line. Found in several locations across southeastern Colorado and
neighboring Oklahoma, these strange designs
so closely resemble a form of Old World writing
known as Ogham that some scholars believe the
region might have been visited by the early Celtic
people of Ireland as long ago as 200 BC Most

Petroglyph in Picture Canyon

around the corner. Cedar signposts mark the rest of the route from this point. These markings are especially helpful since the actual trail may be overgrown along many stretches. Within 0.25 mile of entering this side canyon, the trail turns west at a check dam that spans the wash bottom. From this point, follow the side canyon for another 0.3 mile to an area of interesting rock formations known as Hells Half Acre. Here, look for a post that points the way up through a rocky area to the north. No tread exists along this stretch, but the trail markers eventually lead to the canyon's rim and the flat mesa top above. Blue grama grass, buffalo grass, cholla cactus, prickly pear cactus, yucca, and other plant species in this prairie ecosystem contrast with the trees, cattails, and thick shrubs found along portions of the canyon bottom below.

From the canyon's rim, head northwest for 0.75 mile to a side canyon that drops into the next drainage to the west. Follow rock cairns down this side drainage. Upon reaching the main canyon in less than 0.25 mile west, turn right and follow the drainage upstream to a beautiful little natural arch and a rock formation known as the Wisdom Tooth. Beyond the arch, the route follows an old road a little way before turning due east. It then takes up a faded road and follows it eastward along the head of a side canyon. This portion of the route offers a great view of the surrounding prairie. You can also see Oklahoma to the south. The hiking route soon reaches a graveled county road, which in turn drops back to the Picture Canyon Picnic Area, which is about 1.5 miles from the arch.

Watch for prairie rattlesnakes and other venomous creatures, especially when venturing beyond the established trails. Bring drinking water, as any water found along this hike should be treated before drinking. Be sure not to touch or deface in any way the fragile rock found within the canyon. Keep in mind that federal law protects all historic and prehistoric artifacts.

archaeologists doubt such a scenario, though these carvings do pose a mystifying question about prehistoric America. When visiting these or any rock art panels, be sure not to touch, trace, or disturb the images in any way.

After enjoying Picture Canyon's rock art, return to the trail and follow it north up a side canyon that feeds into Picture Canyon just

Opposite: North St. Vrain Creek in Wild Basin

NORTHERN MOUNTAINS

This exploration of Colorado's northern mountains—those highlands north of Interstate 70—covers various reaches of Rocky Mountain National Park, but it begins with a pair of hikes in the foothills of the Front Range near Boulder. It also reveals some wonderful hikes in national forest lands adjacent to the park before moving on to the Park Range near Steamboat Springs. To the south rise the interesting Flat Tops Wilderness and the impressive Gore Range, which possess a handful of small jewels and some of the largest parcels of wilderness in the state.

8 BEAR PEAK

Distance: 7 miles round-trip
Difficulty: Strenuous
Hiking time: 5 hours
Elevation: 5600 to 8461 feet
Management: City of Boulder Open Space and Mountain Parks
Wilderness status: None
Season: May to October
Map: USGS Eldorado Springs

Getting there: From Boulder, drive south on Colorado Highway 93 to Colorado Highway 170 and the turnoff for Eldorado Springs. Turn right and drive 1.6 miles to the South Mesa trailhead on the right. The Doudy Draw trailhead on the south side of the road accesses more open-space land to the south.

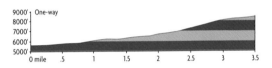

The city of Boulder has set the pace for open-space preservation among Colorado's Front Range communities. Some 43,000 acres of prime foothills acreage have been set aside and many miles of hiking trails and numerous trailhead facilities have been established. One of the more interesting, and most challenging, of these hiking routes climbs through the South Boulder foothills to the top of Bear Peak. At 8461 feet, Bear Peak misses out at being the tallest in the area by a few feet. It does, however, provide one of the most comprehensive views of the Boulder area below and the plains beyond.

To begin the hike up Bear Peak, follow the Mesa Trail from the trailhead across South Boulder Creek and then immediately turn left at the first trail junction onto the Homestead Trail. A few feet beyond, turn right onto the Towhee Trail. These intersections, as well as all other trail junctions in the area, are well marked by small

metal signs. Nearby stands a beautiful stone structure known as the Doudy-Debacker-Dunn House. First homesteaded in 1858 by Sylvester Doudy, the surrounding area was sold to John Debacker in 1869 for $500. The portion of the home that is still standing dates back to 1874.

Heading northwest from the homestead site, the Towhee Trail climbs easily for about a mile along the bottom of Shadow Canyon—be sure to note the different riparian species of plants that grow along the small stream flowing through the drainage. Included in this plant community are cottonwood trees, willows, wild plums, chokecherries, hawthorns, and a fair amount of poison ivy. Attracted by the wild fruit, black bears might be seen along the Towhee Trail and dogs must be leashed along this portion of the hike. The Towhee Trail ends at a junction with a short connecting trail that leads to the Shadow Canyon Trail.

Upon reaching the Shadow Canyon Trail, about 1.5 miles from the trailhead, bear left and

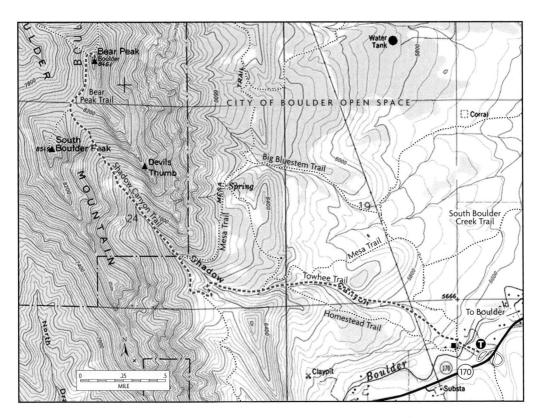

The rocky summit of Bear Peak

continue up the trail, which follows an old road. After circling south for a short distance, the route re-enters the Shadow Canyon drainage bottom where a left turn continues northwest, directly up Shadow Canyon. Continuing to the right, the Mesa Trail cuts north along the eastern front of Bear Peak.

Upon turning up Shadow Canyon proper, the route becomes considerably steeper, tackling an impressive 1600 vertical feet over the next mile. At the top of this drainage, the Shadow Canyon Trail reaches a saddle and an intersection with the Bear Peak Trail, which continues right to climb another 0.4 mile to the summit. A left turn at this intersection leads a short distance to the top of 8549-foot South Boulder Peak.

Shortly before reaching the Bear Peak summit, the route intersects two trails—the Bear Peak West Ridge and Fern Canyon Trails—that drop north into the Bear Canyon drainage. To reach Bear Peak itself, hikers will have to negotiate a final pitch of hand and toeholds. Although this final terrain is not technically challenging, caution should be used. From the top, you will enjoy tremendous views of Boulder directly northeast and the city of Denver to the southeast. Toward the west, you can also take in vistas of the considerably higher Indian Peaks region.

Be sure to bring plenty of drinking water on this hike, as none is available. Dogs are permitted in some places and restricted in others. Check current regulations established by the City of Boulder Open Space and Mountain Parks before setting out. Also check current regulations posted at the trailhead. Horses are commonly encountered along this trail system; be sure to allow plenty of room for their passage. And watch for lightning during thunderstorm activity.

9 GREEN MOUNTAIN LOOP

Distance: 3-mile loop
Difficulty: Strenuous
Hiking time: 3 hours
Elevation: 5800 to 7200 feet
Management: City of Boulder Open Space and Mountain Parks
Wilderness status: None
Season: April to November
Map: USGS Eldorado Springs

Getting there: To reach the Gregory Canyon trailhead, where this hike begins and ends, drive 1.5 miles west on Baseline Road off Colorado Highway 93. A small fee is charged for trailhead parking. If this trailhead lot is full, park at nearby Chautauqua Park and follow the Baseline Trail less than 0.5 mile to the Gregory Canyon trailhead.

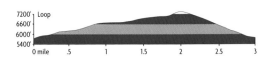

Rising impressively along the Front Range, the Flatirons provide a dramatic backdrop for the city of Boulder. They also form the centerpiece for the beautiful and surprisingly wild Boulder Mountain Park. With many miles of backcountry trails, this park is a worthwhile destination for hikers.

A challenging route explores Gregory Canyon along three different trails. Collectively, the entire hike constitutes the Green Mountain Loop.

Begin by following the Gregory Canyon Trail west up the bottom of its namesake. Watch for poison ivy along most of this stretch, especially in the canyon bottom. A short distance from the trailhead you will encounter the lower end of the Saddle Rock Trail, the return route for this loop. Keep right on the Gregory Canyon Trail. This verdant lower section of the canyon is a favorite haunt for bird-watchers. A variety of birds frequent the area, including a number of colorful songbirds. As for flora in the area, beyond the leafy canyon bottom evergreen species include ponderosa pine and Douglas-fir. A variety of wildflowers can be spotted as well.

Shortly, the Gregory Canyon Trail begins a 900-foot climb to the head of the drainage. Although most grades are moderate in difficulty, some stretches are strenuous. Some portions are rocky, as well, but the route is well defined the entire way. As you climb, you begin to gain views of Boulder and the plains beyond, framed by the canyon walls.

At the ridgeline, continue southwest for a short distance to where the route meets a narrow dirt road. Turn left here and follow the road (now part of the Ranger Trail) to the Green Mountain Lodge, a rustic log structure that can be rented for group events. From the lodge, continue up a

single-track trail that climbs steadily southeast through a heavily forested area. Within a half mile, the Ranger Trail reaches the west end of the E. M. Greenman Trail. Turn left on the E. M. Greenman Trail and begin the return leg of this hike. A right here would continue up the Ranger Trail to the summit of Green Mountain (8144 feet). This climb is arduous and would add an additional 2.5 miles to the hike.

After turning left at the Ranger and E. M. Greenman intersection, the route climbs steeply through more forest before reaching a junction with the Saddle Rock Trail. Turn left here to complete the last 1.3 miles to the trailhead. The Saddle Rock Trail is incredibly steep in places, so take care when descending. Also be thankful that you did not have to climb up this trail. Along the upper portion of the Saddle Rock Trail are commanding views of the Indian Peaks to the northwest and Longs Peak to the north. Boulder and the eastern plains also come into better view.

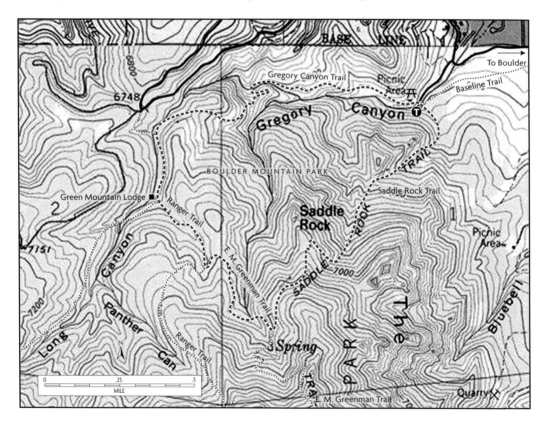

A trail sign in Gregory Canyon

Since you are actually behind the northernmost Flatiron, you might be able to watch rock climbers in action. Formed as horizontal layers of the Fountain Formation, the Flatirons were tilted upward during the time the Rockies were uplifted, 65 million years ago. Once in the bottom of Gregory Canyon, the Saddle Rock Trail ends at the junction with the Gregory Canyon Trail. Turn right and continue a short distance to the trailhead.

Boulder Mountain Park is popular and attracts a lot of other trail users, including trail runners. Dogs are permitted along many trails (though not all) and specific rules apply. Check the regulations first before setting out with your dog. Fires and camping are not permitted. Use caution when descending steep sections of trail. Bring plenty of water, as none is found along the hike.

10 FORGOTTEN VALLEY

Distance: 2.4 miles round-trip
Difficulty: Easy
Hiking time: 2 hours
Elevation: 7800 to 8200 feet
Management: Golden Gate Canyon State Park
Wilderness status: None
Season: May to November
Map: USGS Black Hawk

Getting there: From Golden, drive north on Colorado Highway 93, then turn left onto the Golden Gate Canyon Road (Colorado Highway 46). Follow this road 14 miles, turn right at the park visitor center, and drive 2.4 miles to the Bridge Creek trailhead.

The map shows Golden Gate Canyon State Park with Buffalo Trail, Forgotten Valley, City Lights Ridge, Mountain Lion Trail, Burro Trail, Picnic Areas, and the route to the visitor center. Elevation markers include 8931, 8449, and grid references 25, 30. A scale bar shows 0, .25, and .5 MILE.

secrets as well. One easy-to-reach destination within the park that offers hikers scenery and a palpable taste of the past is Forgotten Valley.

This hike begins by following the Burro Trail north to cross Ralston Creek within the first 0.25 mile. It then climbs steeply before leveling off to continue up a more moderate grade that contours the hillsides. As it ascends, the route encounters scattered stands of ponderosa pine, small meadows, and sporadic clumps of aspen. Later on, you might notice spruce and fir growing on the shaded north-facing slopes. Nearly 0.5 mile from the trailhead, the Burro Trail intersects with the Mountain Lion Trail. Turn left onto the Mountain Lion Trail, which the hike will follow for the rest of the way to Forgotten Valley. Turn left again at a second junction shortly after this intersection. A short distance farther still, a 0.5-mile side trail turns left to access City Lights Ridge, a high point with some nice vistas. All of these trail junctions are signed. From the City Lights Ridge Trail junction, it is 0.7 mile of mostly level hiking along the Nott Creek drainage to Forgotten Valley.

Forgotten Valley features a stock pond plus a handful of antiquated buildings. First homesteaded in 1876 by a Swedish immigrant named

Covering some 14,000 acres of the Front Range west of Denver, Golden Gate Canyon State Park harbors not only a number of beautiful natural areas but also some rather alluring historical

Old homestead in Forgotten Valley

Anders Tallman, this out-of-the-way meadow was occupied by his descendants until 1955. During their stay here, the Tallmans kept milk cows, raised cattle and chickens, and grew vegetables. The main structure was once a school. Anders Tallman purchased the building and moved it here in the 1870s. The state acquired the land in the 1970s. From Forgotten Valley, the Mountain

Lion Trail branches up a side drainage, while the Buffalo Trail continues along Nott Creek. Turn-around here to return to the trailhead.

Bring water on this hike, as it is not available along most of the trail. Be aware that mountain bikes and horses are permitted on this trail. It is possible to camp at Forgotten Valley by registering for one of several backcountry sites.

11 LAKE ISABELLE

Distance: 4.2 miles round-trip
Difficulty: Easy
Hiking time: 3 hours
Elevation: 10,500 to 10,868 feet
Management: Roosevelt National Forest
Wilderness status: Indian Peaks Wilderness Area
Season: July to September
Map: USGS Ward

Getting there: This hike begins near Brainard Lake, which is 5 miles west of the village of Ward, at the end of Brainard Lake Road (County Road 102). Ward is located along Colorado Highway 72, which runs from Estes Park to the Denver metropolitan area. Upon reaching Brainard Lake, follow the signs to the Long Lake trailhead. If this parking lot is full, you can park at the Niwot Mountain Picnic Area and follow the Niwot Cutoff Trail to where it connects with the main route at Longs Lake. A fee is charged to enter the Brainard Lake Recreation Area.

The easy, pleasurable hike to Lake Isabelle offers one of the best and most readily accessible introductions to the high country just west of the Denver area. It is also one of the most popular hikes along Colorado's Front Range.

From the Long Lake trailhead, this hike begins on the Pawnee Pass Trail. A mere 0.2 mile in, the route reaches scenic Long Lake and an intersection with the Jean Lunning Trail. The Pawnee Pass Trail skirts the lake to the north, while the 1.2-mile Jean Lunning Trail branches left. Crossing the Long Lake outlet before continu-

ing around the south side of the lake, the Jean Lunning Trail then connects back up with the Pawnee Pass Trail west of the lake to offer casual hikers a circumnavigation of the lake itself. The Jean Lunning Trail also connects with the Niwot Cutoff Trail, which runs east to the Niwot Mountain Picnic Area. Because the Long Lake area is popular and parking at the Long Lake trailhead is limited, there is a good chance you will have to park at the Niwot overflow area. If so, add a little less than a mile to the hike's total mileage.

Beyond Long Lake, the Pawnee Pass Trail continues west to wind among beautiful forests of spruce and fir. At 2.1 miles from the trailhead, a short climb reaches the east end of Lake Isabelle. Continuing along the north shore of Lake Isabelle, the Pawnee Pass Trail begins climbing in earnest to eventually reach its namesake an additional 2.5 miles beyond. At 12,541 feet, Pawnee Pass is the objective of a much more ambitious hike than this one to Lake Isabelle. A second extension of this hike follows the considerably

The Indian Peaks rise above Lake Isabelle.

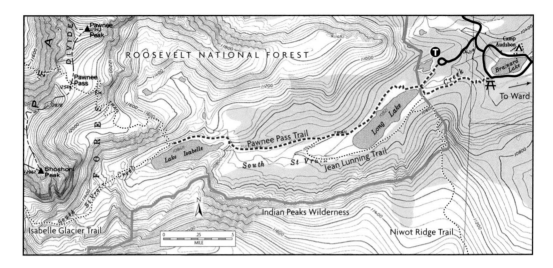

more rugged Isabelle Glacier Trail west from Lake Isabelle to a cirque high above.

Offering many memorable vistas, Lake Isabelle is best viewed from its east end where its still water reflects the rugged spine of the Indian Peaks beyond. This view may seem familiar, as it has graced highway maps, brochures, and the pages of many coffee table books.

Water is available along this hike, but it should be treated before drinking. Watch for lightning during frequent summertime thunderstorms. Camping is prohibited in this part of the Indian Peaks Wilderness from May 1 to November 30. Dogs must be on a leash. Expect to encounter many other hikers along the way.

12   MOUNT AUDUBON

Distance: 7 miles round-trip
Difficulty: Strenuous
Hiking time: 4 hours
Elevation: 10,400 to 13,233 feet
Management: Roosevelt National Forest
Wilderness status: Indian Peaks Wilderness Area
Season: July to September
Map: USGS Ward

Getting there: As with the hike to Lake Isabelle (Hike 11), This hike begins near Brainard Lake, 5 miles west of the village of Ward at the end of Brainard Lake Road (County Road 102). Ward is located along Colorado Highway 72, which runs from Estes Park to the Denver metropolitan area. Upon reaching Brainard Lake, follow the signs to the

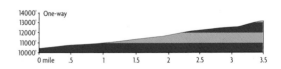

Mitchell Lake trailhead. A fee is charged to enter the Brainard Lake Recreation Area.

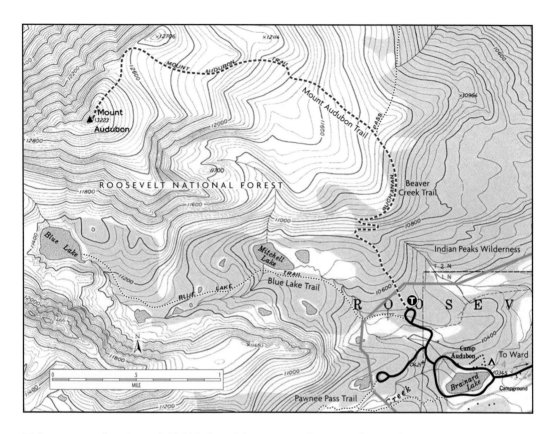

Rising to an elevation of 13,233 feet, Mount Audubon is one of the more prominent summits within the Indian Peaks Wilderness. Despite its lofty stature, however, this gentle mountain seems tame when compared to its immediate neighbors. Indeed, topped by a well-established trail, Audubon poses little challenge to the discerning climber. For the hiker who is simply out to enjoy some incredible views, on the other hand, this peak cannot be beat for the up-close views of the surrounding mountains and incredibly far-reaching vistas in all directions.

From the Mitchell Lake trailhead north of Brainard Lake, this hike follows the Beaver Creek Trail for 1.5 miles before turning left onto the Mount Audubon Trail. In this first 1.5-mile segment, the route climbs about 1000 feet along easy-to-moderate grades through forests of mostly Engelmann spruce and subalpine fir.

After bearing left on the Mount Audubon Trail, the route climbs steadily westward to gain another 2000 feet to the summit. This last segment of the hike ascends the east face of Mount Audubon to reach a small saddle just north of the peak. It then climbs strenuously up the last pitch to the summit. Some scrambling among boulders and rocks can be expected in this section. From the summit, you can look north past nearby Sawtooth Mountain into the southern end of Rocky Mountain National Park. The eastern horizon falls off among the foothills of the Rocky Mountains and the Great Plains beyond. To the west is a chain of mostly 12,000-foot peaks named after Indian tribes of the west—Paiute, Pawnee, Shoshoni, and Navajo. These especially rugged peaks carry the Continental Divide through the 76,586-acre Indian Peaks Wilderness. As part of the Front Range, the Indian Peaks were uplifted during the Laramide Orogeny, beginning 65 million years ago as a large block of Precambrian rock. The east faces of the Indian Peaks are characteristically more rugged than their back sides,

Rugged view from Mount Audubon

in part because this mountain block was tilted along its length during its uplifting. Within the last 2 million years, glaciers subsequently etched away at these peaks, adding to their ruggedness in the process. Looking south from Mount Audubon, the view takes in the southern portion of the Front Range, which includes Mount Evans and Pikes Peak.

Thanks to its proximity to the Denver-Boulder area, and because of the relatively easy access to the high country that the Brainard Lake area provides, the hike to Mount Audubon is very popular. Because of this, the Forest Service prohibits backcountry camping in the Brainard Lake area from May through November. Water is not available along this hike, so be sure to bring your own. Lightning is an almost daily threat during the summer, especially in the afternoon. General weather conditions can deteriorate rapidly as well.

13 ARAPAHO GLACIER

Distance: 7 miles round-trip
Difficulty: Moderate
Hiking time: 5 hours
Elevation: 10,121 to 12,700 feet
Management: Roosevelt National Forest, City of Boulder
Wilderness status: Indian Peaks Wilderness Area
Season: July to September
Maps: USGS Monarch Lake, East Portal

Getting there: The hike to the Arapaho Glacier overlook begins at the Fourth of July trailhead northwest of Nederland. From Nederland, drive 0.6 mile south on Colorado Highway 119/72 to the signed turnoff for the Eldora Ski Area. Turn right onto County Road 130 and drive 8.6 miles to the Fourth of July trailhead at road's end. The last 6 miles of this drive are rough and narrow but passable to most vehicles.

Nestled in a high alpine cirque in the south end of the Indian Peaks Wilderness, Arapaho Glacier is one of only a few glaciers remaining in Colorado. Although geologists are not sure whether these ice fields are left over from the last ice age or formed within the last few thousand years, they do show signs of movement characteristic of glaciers. The Arapaho Glacier falls within land set aside by the City of Boulder for its water supply and is off-limits to hikers. It is possible, however, to hike to the south ridge of South Arapaho Peak for a good look at the geologic anomaly.

Setting out from the Fourth of July trailhead, the hike begins by climbing easily among the spruce and fir forests typical of the area. The first mile of the Araphaho Pass Trail, reconstructed in 2005, is in good shape with an abundance of steps, log corridors across wet areas, and other improvements. Eventually, the trail steepens to climb along a more moderate grade. The route reaches the first of two trail junctions in the first mile. A trail to the left continues around the head of the drainage to reach Diamond Lake, a popular destination for backpackers and day hikers alike. Take the trail to the right, which continues on for another mile to the Fourth of July Mine. Set in an area of krummholz growth just below timberline, this mine dating to the 1870s produced some silver before eventually petering out. Unscrupulous promoters of the mine then devised a scheme to convince investors that there was still a large

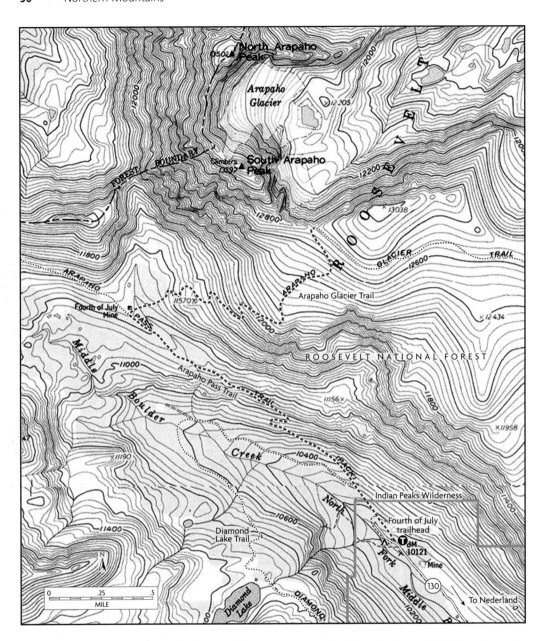

deposit of copper to be unearthed and millions of dollars in worthless stocks were sold to unsuspecting investors. Today, the Fourth of July Mine features some old machinery, a pile of decaying timbers, and a large tailings pile.

A second trail junction is reached at the Fourth of July Mine. The trail that heads north-west travels about 1 mile to 11,900-foot Arapaho Pass, while the trail that branches to the right continues on to the Arapaho Glacier overlook. Climbing steadily along a mostly moderate grade, the remaining 1.5 miles gain another 1500 feet to reach a high point of 12,700 feet. In short order, this route leaves the last vestiges of timber

Arapaho Glacier below South Arapaho Peak

behind to enter alpine tundra. Vistas of the Front Range to the south come into view as you climb, with Pikes Peak and Mount Evans included in the panorama.

Upon reaching the overlook, you can see the eastern plains stretching beyond the foothills. You can also peer into the head of North Boulder Creek, where the Arapaho Glacier spans the rocky cirque below. You might notice bluish ice in places, along with cracks and crevasses that stretch across some portions. These crevasses provide evidence that the glacier is actually in motion, albeit ever so slowly. While this hike turns back at this point, it is possible to continue following this high alpine ridge eastward along

what is sometimes called the Glacier Rim Trail. This route reaches the Rainbow Lakes trailhead in 6 miles. It is also possible to scramble up 13,397-foot South Arapaho Peak, which rises just north of the overlook.

Because much of this hike crosses exposed terrain, be wary of afternoon lightning storms. Water is available along the way, but it should be treated before drinking. Permits are required for overnight stays in the Indian Peaks Wilderness from June 1 to September 15. Stay on the trail, especially above timberline. Keep in mind that the Fourth of July trailhead is an extremely popular entry point for the Indian Peaks Wilderness, especially on weekends.

14 EMERALD LAKE

Distance: 3.6 miles round-trip
Difficulty: Moderate
Hiking time: 3 hours
Elevation: 9475 to 10,080 feet
Management: Rocky Mountain National Park
Wilderness status: None
Season: June to October
Map: USGS McHenrys Peak

Getting there: From Estes Park, drive west a short way on US Highway 36 to the park headquarters. Continue through the Beaver Meadows entrance station and turn left onto

Miner's lettuce blooming near Emerald Lake

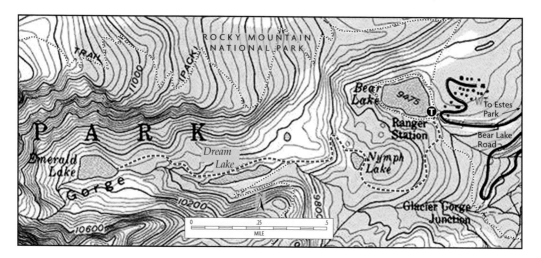

Bear Lake Road. The trailhead is at the road's end. To help alleviate traffic congestion, a free shuttle operates along the Bear Lake Road during the summer.

With more than 350 miles of backcountry trails, Rocky Mountain National Park offers hikers an incredible variety of routes from which to choose. While some take several days to complete, others are comparatively short and easy. Regardless of the length of any of these wilderness excursions, however, they all feature spectacular mountain scenery and a plentiful supply of natural wonders. One short but popular hike climbs from Bear Lake Road to Emerald Lake in the eastern portion of the park.

Climbing a little more than 600 feet in 1.8 miles, the trail to Emerald Lake is not particularly difficult or hard to follow. From the trailhead, the route sets out through a forest of lodgepole pine, Engelmann spruce, and subalpine fir. Before encountering diminutive Nymph Lake about 0.5 mile out, the route intersects a trail that heads southwest to Glacier Gorge. Beyond Nymph Lake, the route continues to climb to reach larger Dream Lake 1.1 miles from the trailhead. Perfectly reflecting Hallett Peak and Flattop Mountain, which rise to the west, Dream Lake is thought to be the most photographed lake in the park. It also marks the turnaround point for many hikers, especially those with small children.

From Dream Lake, the trail climbs another 250 feet in the final 0.75 mile of the hike to reach the east shore of Emerald Lake. Some beautiful scenery opens up along this last segment, especially to the east. At Emerald Lake itself, the stunning geology of Rocky Mountain National Park really unfolds. The mountains of Rocky Mountain National Park, part of the Front Range, serve as textbook examples of faulted anticlines—elongated blocks of Precambrian rock that were uplifted between 40 million and 65 million years ago. What really shaped this mountain landscape, however, were the large glaciers that covered the region a million years ago. The park's many lakes, the classic U-shaped valleys, the moraines, and the rugged east and north faces of such summits as nearby Hallett Peak all owe their existence to the sculpting action of these bygone sheets of ice. Some small glaciers still exist in the park above the 11,000-foot level.

Where the wildlife of the park is concerned, you might glimpse such impressive creatures as bighorn sheep, elk, and moose along this busy trail, but you are more likely to spot the marmots and pikas that haunt the upper elevations of the park.

Water can be found along this hike, but it should be treated before drinking. Lightning strikes are common in the area, especially during afternoon thunderstorms. To avoid the crowds that venture to Emerald Lake, you might want to save this hike for after Labor Day.

15 FLATTOP MOUNTAIN

Distance: 8.8 miles round-trip
Difficulty: Strenuous
Hiking time: 6 hours
Elevation: 9475 to 12,324 feet
Management: Rocky Mountain National Park
Wilderness status: None
Season: June to October
Map: USGS McHenrys Peak

Getting there: The start of the Flattop Mountain Trail is at the same trailhead used for the hike to Emerald Lake (Hike 14). Drive west from Estes Park a short way on US Highway 36 to the park headquarters. Continue through the Beaver Meadows entrance station and turn left onto Bear Lake Road. The trailhead is located at the road's end. To help alleviate traffic congestion, a free shuttle operates along Bear Lake Road during the summer.

Most visitors to Rocky Mountain National Park reach timberline by way of the paved Trail Ridge

Road. A good alternative for hikers interested in visiting the higher, treeless reaches of the park is the 4.4-mile Flattop Mountain Trail. Climbing steadily most of the way, this popular route accesses some incredible views and pristine alpine tundra.

At the trailhead, head right at the immediate junction (the left-hand route goes to Emerald Lake) and continue north along the shore of

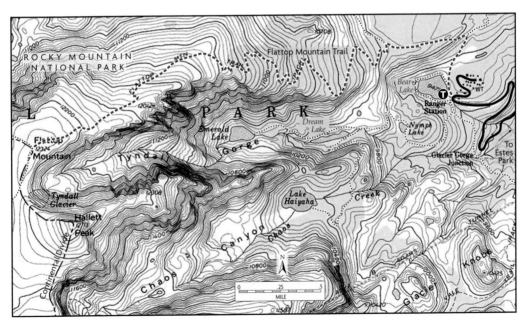

Mountain scenery along the trail to Flattop Mountain

Bear Lake. At a second trail junction near the north end of the lake, turn right again to begin the climb to Flattop Mountain. The route climbs easily on a wide and well-defined trail to a third trail junction less than 0.5 mile from the trailhead. Here a right turn will lead to Bierstadt Lake. For Flattop, turn left and continue west for about 0.5 mile to a fourth and final trail intersection. Bearing right will take you to Odessa and Fern Lakes, while a left turn leads up to the Flattop summit. The last 3.2 miles of the hike climb along easy-to-moderate grades (a few short stretches might be considered strenuous) through a number of switchbacks. Keep in mind that cutting switchbacks is not permitted and can damage the fragile montane environment.

Although the forests are thick along the lower portion of this hike, two views worth noting reveal Dream Lake and then Emerald Lake below. Use caution near these vistas located at switchbacks along the precipitous canyon's edge. Around the halfway point of the hike to the top, the route breaks free of the last trees to continue the rest of the way above timberline. The views are spectacular along this stretch and the opportunities to spot pikas, marmots, and a variety of wildflowers are considerable.

True to its name, the summit of Flattop is broad and nearly level. The top, and turnaround point for this hike, is marked by a trail junction. A right turn to the north will take you along the Continental Divide Trail to the western side of the park, whereas the left-hand route also drops into the west end of the park along the North Inlet Trail. This route is used by climbers continuing on to Hallett and Otis Peaks, which rise to the south. Hallett is the sharply rising summit just south of Flattop. Longs Peak is visible to the southeast. Trail Ridge Road and the Mummy Range stretch along the northern horizon. The Never Summer Range is west, as is Mount Zirkel (barely visible in the distance). And the rugged Gore Range rises in the distance to the southwest.

Take care when close to drop-offs. Bring plenty of water and watch for lightning in exposed areas, especially during the frequent summer thunderstorms. Keep in mind that this trail receives a lot of use.

16 LITTLE YELLOWSTONE

Distance: 9.4 miles round-trip
Difficulty: Moderate
Hiking time: 6 hours
Elevation: 9000 to 10,100 feet
Management: Rocky Mountain National Park
Wilderness status: None
Season: May to October
Map: USGS Fall River Pass

Getting there: This hike begins at the Colorado River trailhead, which is located about 9.5 miles north of Rocky Mountain National Park's western entrance, north of Grandby on US Highway 34 (Trail Ridge Road, inside the park). Because this is a popular hike, be prepared to see many other hikers, especially along the first few miles of the trail.

The hike to Little Yellowstone follows the Colorado River upstream through the mountain-ringed

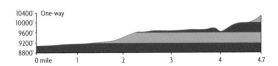

Kawuneeche Valley in the west end of Rocky Mountain National Park. Along the way, it serves up an interesting geological feature of the park, a surprising bit of history, and an up-close look at the headwaters of the Colorado River.

From the trailhead, the hike follows the

Colorful geology of Little Yellowstone

A young Colorado River along the hike to Little Yellowstone

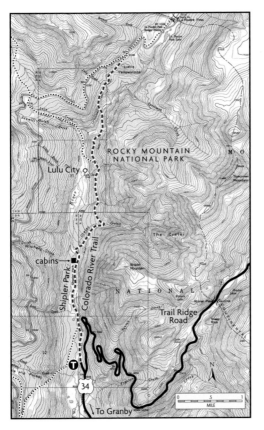

river, here—only a few miles from its start—it is a gently flowing stream. Lodgepole pine, spruce, fir, and aspen are common. There are also open meadows in which you might spy a moose or perhaps a small herd of elk. While these animals have lost much of their shyness in the park, they still prefer to visit these open areas in the early morning and late evening.

A little more than 2 miles from the trailhead, the route reaches Shipler Park, which features a pair of old cabins in disrepair. Like those at Lulu City farther on, these structures represent a bygone era of get-rich-quick schemes and failed dreams. The trail continues another 1.2 miles beyond the Shipler cabins to reach Lulu City. Now the trail climbs an easy grade among a forest of mostly lodgepole pine before dropping back to the river and the Lulu town site.

The remains of Lulu City are proof that the feverish search for gold and silver during the late nineteenth century touched many corners of the Colorado Rockies. First established in 1879, Lulu City (named after the daughter of probable town founder Benjamin Franklin Burnett) soon grew to a "Saturday-night population" of 500. One hundred blocks were platted, and although not all were developed, the town did boast four lumber mills, an elegant hotel, a post office, and more. Although some gold, silver, and lead were unearthed in the nearby mountains, the town was virtually abandoned by 1884. All that is left of this once-bustling city are a few rotting log foundations and some old stories.

Continuing another mile up the Colorado River drainage, the trail then reaches the Little Yellowstone area, a severely eroded section of white and yellow rock reminiscent of Yellowstone Canyon in Yellowstone National Park. This colorful substrata dates to a volcanic eruption that occurred some 28 million years ago. Although this marks the turnaround point for this hike, it is possible to continue beyond Little Yellowstone to reach the Continental Divide at La Poudre Pass beyond.

Water is plentiful along this hike, but it should be treated before drinking. Regulations for hiking within a national park prohibit dogs in the backcountry. A backcountry permit is required for an overnight stay.

Colorado River Trail north to where it soon climbs a short, moderately steep switchback. It then levels off to continue along level or easy grades most of the way. The trail reaches a junction near the 0.5-mile mark. The trail to the left crosses the Kawuneeche Valley before climbing to the Grand Ditch, which traverses the slopes of the Never Summer Range to the west. Dug by hand around the turn of the twentieth century, the Grand Ditch still collects water on the west slope of the Continental Divide and carries it east to cities and farmlands along the Front Range. In so doing it saps the Colorado River of some of its strength before it even gets started. The right-hand trail leads to Little Yellowstone.

Beyond this intersection, the trail continues due north for the remainder of the hike and passes within a few feet of the fledgling Colorado River in places in this first section. While the Colorado is often thought of as a mighty

17 MIRROR LAKE

Distance: 12.2 miles round-trip
Difficulty: Moderate
Hiking time: 8 hours
Elevation: 10,070 to 11,025 feet
Management: Roosevelt National Forest, Rocky Mountain National Park
Wilderness status: Comanche Peak Wilderness Area
Season: July to September
Maps: USGS Chambers Lake, Comanche Peak

Getting there: From Fort Collins, drive west on Colorado Highway 14 toward Cameron Pass. About 5 miles before the pass, turn left onto Long Draw Road (Forest Road 156) and drive 8.5 miles to the signed Corral Creek trailhead. Across the road from the trailhead is an information center administered by both the Forest Service and the Park Service.

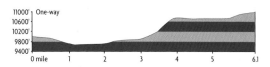

Nestled in the isolated northwest corner of Rocky Mountain National Park, Mirror Lake is an exceptionally memorable destination for day hikers and backpackers alike.

This hike heads out on the Corral Park Trail to enter the Comanche Peak Wilderness in 0.25 mile. In another 0.75 mile, it reaches the southern end of the Big South Trail, which heads north to follow the Cache La Poudre River downstream to a trailhead on Colorado Highway 14. The hike drops about 300 feet in this first mile. After turning right at the junction with Big South, follow the Poudre River Trail across La Poudre Pass Creek, which is usually swollen by waters carried across the Continental Divide by the Grand Ditch. Up to this point, the route traverses lands administered

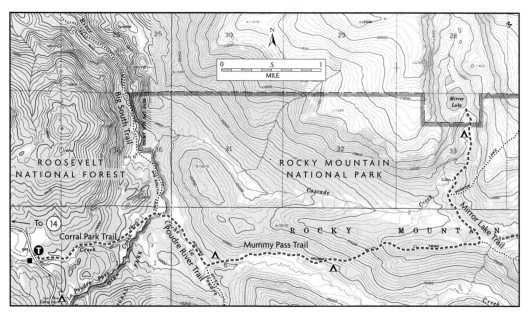

Beautiful Mirror Lake

by the Roosevelt National Forest. The remainder of the hike beyond this creek crossing falls within Rocky Mountain National Park.

About 0.5 mile beyond the park boundary, the Poudre River Trail reaches the start of the Mummy Pass Trail. While the Poudre River Trail turns right to follow the Cache La Poudre River south for 9 miles to Milner Pass on the Continental Divide, the Mummy Pass Trail crosses the Cache La Poudre River before heading east toward its namesake pass and the destination of this hike, Mirror Lake. Just east of the Cache La Poudre River is the Hague Creek campsite. Overnight campers in Rocky Mountain National Park must spend the night in designated backcountry sites, most of which include a primitive privy. Beyond the campsite, the trail climbs slightly to reach the west end of an expansive open park. Located at the edge of this park are two more backcountry campsites, Desolation and Flatiron.

After skirting the edge of the meadow, the Mummy Pass Trail begins ascending along a more moderate grade. The lion's share of the hike's 1300-foot climb is in the next 2.5 miles. This section of the hike, among pristine stands of lodgepole pine, is quite beautiful. Nearly 3 miles beyond the Cache La Poudre River crossing, the Mummy Pass Trail connects with the Mirror Lake Trail. From this junction, a right turn leads nearly 2 miles to Mummy Pass, while a left turn takes you 1.6 miles north to Mirror Lake. Most of this last stretch is level, with a few small climbs. As the trail nears the lake, a number of signs add some confusion. Each sign points left to different backcountry campsites, all of which are named Mirror Lake. Since these signs do not mention that they are campsites, it is easy to think that they are pointing the way to Mirror Lake itself. To find the actual lake, keep right at each of these junctions.

Nestled near timberline, Mirror Lake is surrounded by stunted spruce forests along with some areas of krummholz trees. Rising some 1200 feet above the lake to the northwest is a rugged, beautiful, but unnamed peak, while 12,702-foot Comanche Peak sits off to the northeast. A steep trail branches off from the Mirror Lake Trail and eventually accesses Comanche Peak, which rises along the border between the park and Roosevelt National Forest. Trout fishing is good at Mirror Lake, but as with the streams and rivers encountered along the way, anglers are allowed to use flies and artificial lures only.

Lightning can pose a danger along this high-country hike, although the route does not cross any particularly exposed areas. All water found along the route should be treated before drinking, and overnight visitors must first obtain a permit from Rocky Mountain National Park. Fires are prohibited in the park's backcountry; be sure to bring a stove for cooking.

18 CALYPSO CASCADES

Distance: 3.6 miles round-trip
Difficulty: Easy
Hiking time: 3 hours
Elevation: 8500 to 9200 feet
Management: Rocky Mountain National Park
Wilderness status: None
Season: June to October
Map: USGS Allens Park

Getting there: From Estes Park, drive about 12 miles south on Colorado Highway 7 to the signed turnoff for Wild Basin. Turn west and drive 0.4 mile to the park entrance. Continue

another 2.3 miles beyond the entrance on a good but extremely narrow (watch for oncoming traffic) dirt road to the Wild Basin Ranger Station and trailhead at road's end. Parking is limited.

An area known as Wild Basin constitutes the southeast corner of Rocky Mountain National Park. Whereas the broad and well-developed hiking trails here do not correspond to the character this moniker implies, the tumbling and frothy nature of area streams certainly do. A short but memorable hike here leads to one of the more impressive aquatic descents, Calypso Cascades.

The trail remains mostly in thick forested sections of the drainage bottom as it follows the riotous North St. Vrain Creek for most of the 1.8 miles to the Cascades. Species of trees include lodgepole pine, spruce, fir, and aspen. Ferns and wildflowers are also plentiful in spots. Within 0.3 mile from the trailhead, the route encounters Copeland Falls, a set of short but noisy drops in the creek. Farther on, additional cascades are encountered, the best of which can be enjoyed from a bridge that crosses to the south side of North St. Vrain Creek.

After crossing the bridge, the trail climbs the final 0.3 mile or so along Cony Creek to reach Calypso Cascades. A noticeable portion of the hike's 700-foot climb is achieved in this last section, but most if not all grade changes are easy in nature.

Tumbling 100 feet or so in a series of small falls and pour-offs fanned across a forested mountainside, Calypso Cascades typifies the picturesque nature of North St. Vrain Creek and its tributaries. Two bridges that span the creek just below the cascades offer good viewing. Photographers

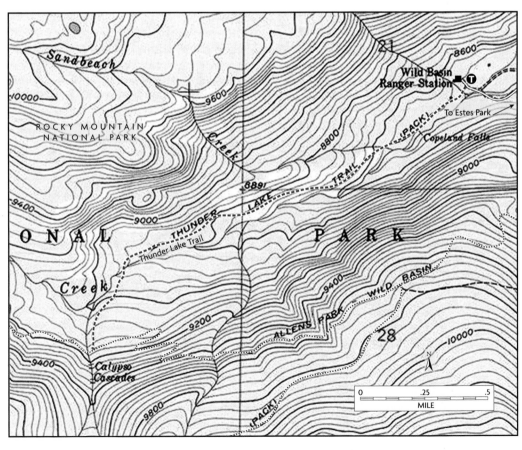

Detail of Calypso Cascades

interested in capturing the beauty of this spectacle may want to bring a tripod for slow exposures. This will allow the water to blur as it tumbles over boulders and logs.

The trail splits here. The left-hand route eventually accesses Finch and Pear Lakes within the Cony Creek drainage, while a right turn will take you to Ouzel Falls and Ouzel, Bluebird, Thunder, and Lion Lakes beyond. Ouzel Falls is an additional 0.9 mile, while the lakes are 3 to 5 miles beyond. Situated along the eastern foot of the Continental Divide, these lakes lie between 10,000 and 11,000 feet in elevation and are quite scenic.

Use caution around waterfalls and cascades, as rocks and logs are slippery. All water found along the route should be treated before drinking, and overnight visitors must first obtain a permit from Rocky Mountain National Park. Watch for oncoming autos while driving to the Wild Basin trailhead.

19 MOUNT McCONNEL

Distance: 5-mile loop
Difficulty: Moderate
Hiking time: 3 hours
Elevation: 6520 to 8010 feet
Management: Roosevelt National Forest
Wilderness status: Cache La Poudre Wilderness Area
Season: March to November
Map: USGS Big Narrows

Getting there: This hike begins at the Mountain Park Campground, about 26 miles west of Fort Collins along Colorado Highway 14.

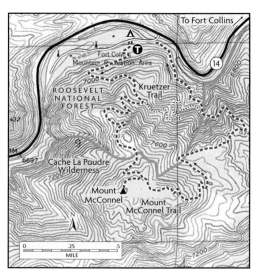

Detail of an old ponderosa pine stump

At 9380 acres, the Cache La Poudre Wilderness is one of the smallest wilderness areas in the state. Nevertheless, hikers who reach the summit of Mount McConnel will be rewarded with breathtaking views and pristine timberlands.

This hike starts out by following the nearly 2-mile Kruetzer Trail. Built by the Civilian Conservation Corps (CCC) in 1936, this trail is named after William Kruetzer, the first official forest ranger in the United States. Working in a forest preserve in the central part of the state, Kruetzer became the supervisor of the Colorado National Forest, now known as the Roosevelt National Forest. The Kruetzer Trail climbs 800 feet as it winds its way up the north slope of Mount McConnel. Interpretive signs along the way identify and describe some of the area's flora, including lodgepole and ponderosa pine. Some interesting outcrops of igneous rock are also encountered along the way. Views of the Cache La Poudre River below add to the hike's pleasurability.

From the upper end of the Kruetzer Trail, turn right onto the Mount McConnel Trail, which continues on to the summit. Grades along the remaining 0.5 mile are moderate to strenuous in difficulty as the trail ascends another 500 feet to the top. Upon reaching the 8010-foot summit of Mount McConnel, you can enjoy incredible views of the Mummy Range to the south.

From the summit, continue along the Mount McConnel Trail, which drops east and then north to hook back up with the Kruetzer Trail. After reconnecting with the Kruetzer Trail, continue northwest to return to Mountain Park Campground. Whereas the first part of the descent from the Mount McConnel summit is rocky and steep in places, the second half along the Kruetzer Trail is better defined.

No water is available along the hike to Mount McConnel. Lightning strikes are possible, given that the mountain is a high point in this region of the Roosevelt National Forest.

20 EMMALINE LAKE

Distance: 11.6 miles round-trip
Difficulty: Moderate
Hiking time: 7 hours
Elevation: 9000 to 11,000 feet
Management: Roosevelt National Forest
Wilderness status: Comanche
Season: July to October
Maps: USGS Comanche Peak, Pingree Park

Getting there: From Fort Collins, drive 35 miles west on Colorado Highway 14 to Pingree Park Road. Turn south and continue 15.8 miles to Forest Road 145. Turn right and drive 0.3 mile to a small parking area.

Stretching across the northern border of Rocky Mountain National Park, the Mummy Range varies from rugged granite faces to gently rolling alpine terrain. This dichotomy of landscapes resulted from the geologic makeup of the range and the persuasive carving action of past glaciers. A good place to enjoy this picturesque topography is Emmaline Lake at the foot of Comanche Peak.

The Emmaline Lake Trail begins by following a former 4WD road for a couple of miles to where it ends at the north end of the highly scenic Cirque Meadows. Along this first segment of the hike, you will encounter the turnoff for the Mummy Pass Trail (Hike 17), which heads southwest into the park and over its namesake. Upon reaching Cirque Meadows, the Emmaline Lake Trail crosses Fall Creek and continues

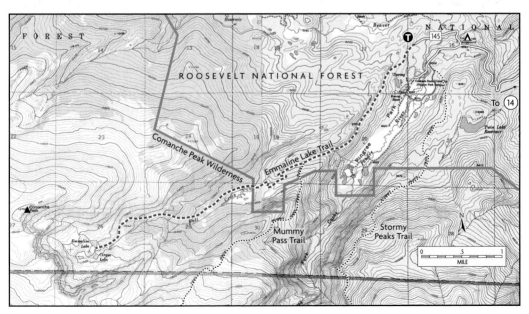

Rugged summits above Emmaline Lake

upstream the rest of the way to Emmaline Lake. The first 1.25 miles following the creek crossing climb along mostly easy grades through forests of lodgepole pine, spruce, and firs. Remnants of the 1994 Hourglass Fire are also encountered along this stretch.

Eventually, the trail then takes up a moderately difficult grade as it gains the upper reaches of the Fall Creek drainage. Around the 10,800-foot level, the Emmaline Lake Trail leaves the taller timber behind in favor of stunted krummholz growth. Soon after, it passes by a beautiful waterfall and a short distance farther climbs one final pitch to reach its destination—Emmaline Lake. In the 3 miles from Cirque Meadows to the lake, the Emmaline Lake Trail gains 1200 feet.

Rimmed by high cliffs to the south and west, Emmaline Lake lies in a classic glacial cirque.

Large mountain glaciers that covered the higher terrain of the Rocky Mountains about a million years ago etched this circular escarpment out of granite. Contrasting with the rugged cliffs are the much gentler western slopes of these same peaks. Named for their resemblance to reclining mummies, the Mummy Range formed as the result of faulted anticlines that were uplifted about 65 million years ago. The tallest summit in the area, 12,702-foot Comanche Peak, rises east of Emmaline Lake. Although Emmaline Lake is the largest lake in the basin, nearby Cirque Lake is equally beautiful.

This trail can see lightning activity in July and August, when afternoon thunderstorms are common, although it is not particularly exposed. All water found along the hike should be treated before drinking.

21 RAWAH LAKES

Distance: 18.5-mile loop
Difficulty: Strenuous
Hiking time: 3 days
Elevation: 8560 to 11,220 feet
Management: Roosevelt National Forest
Wilderness status: Rawah Wilderness Area
Season: July to September
Maps: USGS Boston Peak, Rawah Lake

Getting there: From Fort Collins, drive west on Colorado Highway 14 along the Cache La Poudre River to Chambers Lake. Turn right onto Laramie River Road (County Road 103)—a well-maintained gravel road that is passable to all vehicles—and continue 6 miles north to the developed West Branch trailhead, which is 0.25 mile north of the Tunnel Campground. As the large parking lot at the trailhead indicates, this hike is very popular.

The Rawah Wilderness in the southern Medicine Bow Range encompasses some memorable mountain areas. At the heart of this wilderness, the Lakes District offers a string of sky-blue lakes along the crest of the range. It is possible to visit

Twin Crater Lakes at dusk

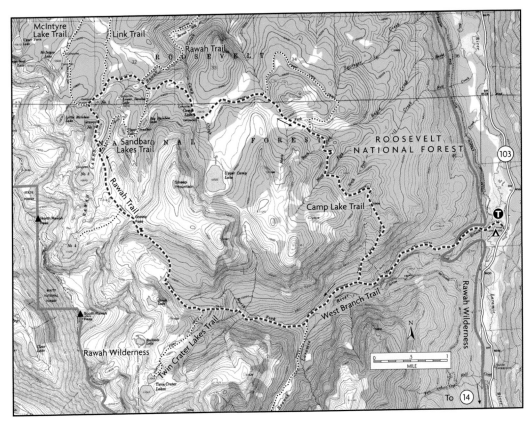

many of these lakes in a multiday hike along several different trails.

From the trailhead, follow the West Branch Trail for 3 miles as it heads upstream along the West Branch of the Laramie River. About 2 miles in, this route reaches the lower end of the Camp Lake Trail, which is the return leg for this hike. In another mile, the West Branch Trail reaches the south end of the Rawah Trail. From the trailhead to this junction, the West Branch Trail climbs about 1000 feet along mostly easy grades. Several stands of aspen dot the first 2 miles of this hike, but expect to see mostly lodgepole pines, Engelmann spruce, and subalpine firs as you gain elevation.

At the West Branch Trail and Rawah Trail intersection, turn onto the Rawah Trail. The trail climbs along a mostly easy grade for another 0.5 mile to reach a set of switchbacks. Taking up a more strenuous ascent from this point, the route climbs 700 feet in a mile to reach the next trail junction.

A left turn at this intersection leads 1.5 miles up the Twin Crater Lakes Trail to Twin Crater Lakes. Situated at 11,000 feet, the Twin Crater Lakes area features extensive krummholz growth. Clearly visible to the northwest is 12,644-foot South Rawah Peak. From Twin Crater Lakes, South Rawah Peak is a relatively nontechnical climb.

Beyond the Rawah and Twin Crater Lakes trail intersection, the Rawah Trail continues to climb northwest toward 11,220-foot Grassy Pass. This ascent is easy at first, but the trail climbs through a couple of steep switchbacks in the last 0.5 mile to the pass. After cresting the pass, the route descends slowly to reach the Rawah Lakes area. The four lakes are scattered along the northeastern base of 12,473-foot North Rawah Peak. Two lakes are located at trailside, while the other two are accessible via short side hikes. In the vicinity of the Rawah Lakes, the Rawah Trail intersects the McIntyre Lake Trail, which heads north. About 4 miles from the turnoff for

Twin Crater Lakes, the Rawah Trail reaches the upper end of the Camp Lake Trail. While the Rawah Trail continues northeast for another 9 miles to a trailhead on Laramie River Road, this hike bears right to follow the Camp Lake Trail east and south before eventually rejoining the West Branch Trail. From the junction with the Rawah Trail, it is 2 miles to Lower Camp Lake—a nice place to spend the night. A side trail climbs a couple of hundred feet in about 1 mile to reach Upper Camp Lake to the south. Lower Camp Lake is situated among trees, while Upper Camp Lake is closer to timberline and features some interesting subalpine growth.

From Lower Camp Lake, the Camp Lake Trail soon follows an old water ditch that is no longer in use. About a mile from the lake, a shortcut cuts southeast from the ditch to cross a low ridge before reuniting with the ditch on the far side. This shortcut saves about a mile and, while the trail can be faint in places, it is not difficult to find your way, especially with the help of a topographic map. Back at the ditch again, the Camp Lake Trail continues for another couple of miles south along a steady grade before dropping nearly 1000 feet back into the West Branch of the Laramie River drainage. From the intersection with the West Branch Trail, it is 2 miles back to the trailhead. Fishing is good in many of the lakes along this hike, and, given some added time, you might want to bag a peak or two.

Water is readily available along this hike, but it should be treated before drinking. Lightning can present a hazard in the higher terrain. Forest Service regulations require that dogs be kept on a leash at all times.

22 BAKER PASS

Distance: 12 miles round-trip
Difficulty: Strenuous
Hiking time: 8 hours
Elevation: 8940 to 11,253 feet
Management: Arapaho National Forest, Rocky Mountain National Park
Wilderness status: Never Summer Wilderness Area
Season: July to September
Maps: USGS Bowen Mountain, Mount Richthofen, Grand Lake

Getting there: The Baker Gulch Trail begins on the west side of Rocky Mountain National Park. From the park's west entrance, drive 6.4 miles north on Trail Ridge Road (US Highway 34) to the turnoff for the Bowen and Baker trailhead.

Nestled up to the western border of Rocky Mountain National Park, the Never Summer Mountains got their name from the Arapaho Indian word *Ni-chebe-chii* or "No Never Summer." Although the range does seem to be gripped by winter for much of the year, it is probably no more so than other comparable mountain ranges in northern Colorado. Nevertheless, the name does have a certain mystique, as do the mountains hemselves. A nice day hike—or perhaps an overnight excursion—into the Never Summers follows the Baker Gulch Trail for 6 miles to the drainage's headwaters at 11,253-foot Baker Pass. Because the pass lies at the heart of the range, and because the Never Summers are not well known, the chances of finding solitude along this hike are great.

After following a dirt road, normally closed, for its first 0.75 mile, this hike takes up a foot trail once it reaches the forest boundary. Shortly

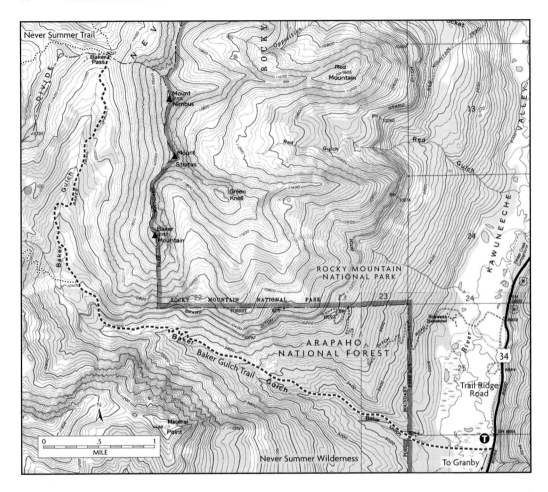

beyond this point, the route begins climbing out of the Kawuneeche Valley along Baker Gulch Creek. Ascending a mostly easy-to-moderate grade most of the way, this first half of the trail includes some steep switchbacks as it passes through forests of lodgepole pine, aspen, spruce, and fir. About 4 miles from the trailhead, the Baker Gulch Trail crosses the Grand Ditch and its service road. This water development constructed in the 1890s enjoys a permanent easement across the northwest corner of the park so that it can siphon water from the Pacific side of the Continental Divide to cities and farms along Colorado's Front Range. Shortly after, the trail heads in a more northerly direction as it rounds 12,397-foot Baker Mountain. About 0.5 mile north of the ditch is the turnoff for the trail to

Parika Lake. The lake, situated at an elevation of 11,400 feet, lies a mile or so west and is 1000 feet higher than this point.

Continuing north from the trail junction, the Baker Gulch Trail maintains a mostly easy ascent as it heads toward the pass. In the last 2-mile stretch from the ditch to the pass, the route climbs about 800 feet, spending much of the time in open meadows that span the gulch's bottom. Exposed areas such as these are good places to spot deer, elk, and other fauna that inhabit the Never Summers. One species of note is the Rocky Mountain bighorn sheep, which prefers the higher terrain above.

Upon arriving at the pass, admire the view of the Cloud Range—a trio of peaks (Mount Stratus, Mount Nimbus, and Mount Cumulus) that carry

Wilderness sign near Baker Pass

the Continental Divide along the western border of the park. Heading north from the pass is the Never Summer Trail—a 9-mile route that runs the length of its namesake mountains. A side trail leads 1 mile west to the end of the 4WD Jack Creek Road.

Because lightning wracks the Never Summers throughout much of the summer, plan to be off the higher terrain by noon or shortly after. Be prepared for deteriorating weather conditions. Water is available along this hike, but it should be treated before drinking.

23 RED DIRT PASS

Distance: 15 miles round-trip
Difficulty: Moderate
Hiking time: 2 days
Elevation: 8480 to 11,400 feet
Management: Routt National Forest
Wilderness status: Mount Zirkel Wilderness Area
Season: July to September
Map: USGS Mount Zirkel

Getting there: From Steamboat Springs, drive 2 miles west on US Highway 40 to the Elk River Road (County Road 129). Turn right and drive 18 miles north to Seedhouse Road (Forest Road 400). Turn right again and follow this route for 12 miles to its end at the Slavonia trailhead. Although graveled, Seedhouse Road is well maintained and passable to all vehicles. Upon arriving at the trailhead, do not be surprised to see a lot of cars as it accesses the most popular area of the Mount Zirkel Wilderness.

Beginning at the Slavonia trailhead, this hike takes you past the popular destination of Gold Creek Lake to access a beautiful mountain valley and a high pass beyond. The rewards of this 2-day trip include the remains of an old mine, wonderful flower-filled meadows, and that top-of-the-world feeling to be had on 11,400-foot

Red Dirt Pass. Add to all this the opportunity to climb nearby Mount Zirkel and you have all the makings for a memorable overnight trip.

From the trailhead, begin by following the Gilpin Trail for 0.25 mile to a trail junction. Turn right to take up the Gold Creek Lake Trail. In the next 5 miles or so the Gold Creek Lake Trail climbs 1700 feet along easy-to-moderate grades, with a few sections that could be considered strenuous. At the 4-mile mark, Gold Creek Lake serves as the turnaround point for many day hikers. To protect the fragile areas around the lake, camping and campfires are not permitted within 0.25 mile of this popular destination. Beyond Gold Creek Lake, the trail intersects the

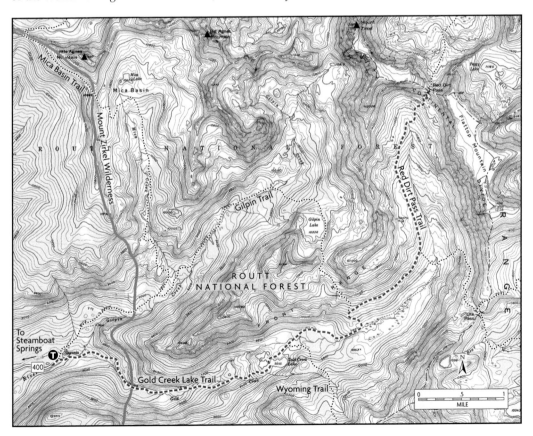

Dilapidated cabin at the Slavonia Mine

Wyoming Trail (Hike 24) and then the upper end of the Gilpin Trail, which covers 6.1 miles before arriving back at the Slavonia trailhead. The chief attraction along this route is Gilpin Lake, which, like Gold Creek Lake, is very popular. Similar camping restrictions apply there, as well.

Along the way you might notice numerous downed trees. This destruction occurred in October 1997 when winds topping 120 miles per hour buffeted the west slope of the Park Range and uprooted trees in a 5-mile-by-30-mile swath. While trail crews have cleaned up major trails in the area, hikers should be wary of hazardous conditions in the form of unstable standing trees and leaning downfall.

From the Gold Creek Lake and Gilpin trail junction, the Gold Creek Lake Trail continues east to eventually top Ute Pass. About 0.5 mile east of the Gilpin Trail, however, this hike turns left to take up the Red Dirt Pass Trail, which follows Gold Creek to its headwaters just below Red Dirt Pass. Contouring along the west face of this classic, glacially carved canyon, the trail passes the ruins of the old Slavonia Mine—little more than scattered piles of lumber, a few pieces of machinery, and some rotting log foundations. Beyond the mine, the trail eventually breaks out of the Engelmann spruce and subalpine fir forest

to continue above timberline for the remainder of the hike. Watch for wildflowers in these open meadows. Although some marshy areas might be encountered along this portion of the trail, the route is fairly evident.

As the trail approaches the head of the Gold Creek drainage, the final 1000 feet climb a series of moderately to strenuously steep switchbacks to reach Red Dirt Pass. Situated on the Continental Divide, Red Dirt Pass provides some wonderful views—especially of the Gold Creek drainage and Ute Pass to the south, and Fryingpan Basin, which opens up beyond the pass. While this hike turns around at Red Dirt Pass, it is a relatively easy traverse northwest to reach 12,180-foot Mount Zirkel, the namesake of this wilderness and the highest point in the Park Range. Mount Zirkel was named for a geologist who visited the area as part of the King Survey, which explored the 40th parallel in 1871. The climb from Red Dirt Pass to the summit ascends 800 feet in 1.5 miles.

Water is found along this hike, but it should be treated before drinking. Lightning can pose a hazard on Red Dirt Pass and in other high locations. Be mindful of Forest Service regulations concerning camping near lakes in the area. If crowds are a concern, you might want to plan your hike for a weekday.

24 WYOMING TRAIL

Distance: 20 miles one-way
Difficulty: Moderate
Hiking time: 3 days
Elevation: 10,300 to 11,880 feet
Management: Routt National Forest
Wilderness status: Mount Zirkel Wilderness Area
Season: July to September
Maps: USGS Buffalo Pass, Mount Ethel, Mount Zirkel

Getting there: The hike begins at Buffalo Pass, east of Steamboat Springs. From downtown Steamboat, turn north onto Seventh Street and follow the signs for Buffalo Pass. Outside the city turn right onto County Road 38 (Forest Road 60). Follow this road 11.3 miles to the trailhead on top of the pass. Forest Road 60 is gravel, but passable to most vehicles.

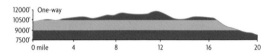

Following the Continental Divide for most of its 20-mile length, this hike along the Wyoming Trail offers a memorable multiday excursion across beautiful alpine terrain. Running north from Buffalo Pass to the Wyoming border, the

Along the high Wyoming Trail

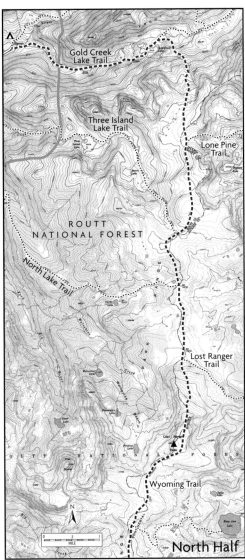

Wyoming Trail covers nearly 50 miles in all. This hike takes in the highest portion of the route as it traces the Divide through the southern half of the Mount Zirkel Wilderness. This segment of the Wyoming Trail is also part of the interstate Continental Divide Trail.

From Buffalo Pass, the Wyoming Trail begins by following an old jeep road for 4 miles along the crest of the Park Range. This portion of the hike traverses mostly rolling terrain with a few short descents and climbs along easy grades. The many open parks enhance the beauty of the area. Such areas are good places to spot deer, elk, and other species of wildlife that call the Mount Zirkel Wilderness home. These meadows become quite colorful in July and early August when a variety of alpine wildflowers are in full bloom. Tree species of the area include Engelmann spruce and subalpine fir. More nice scenery opens up as the Wyoming Trail continues north. The expansive

North Park stretches to the east and the Rabbit Ears and Never Summer mountain ranges rise in the southeast.

About 2 miles from Buffalo Pass, the Wyoming Trail intersects the upper end of the Newcomb Creek Trail, a secondary route that climbs up from the eastern side of the range, gaining some 2000 feet in 5 miles. Nearly 7 miles in, the Wyoming Trail picks up the upper end of the Luna Lake Trail, which climbs from the Swamp Park Trail, running along the west side of the mountains. A side excursion of less than 2 miles along this route leads to Lake Elbert and Luna Lake.

Beyond this trail intersection, the Wyoming Trail passes just west of 11,924-foot Mount Ethel. Bagging this summit would involve very little extra energy, as it is less than a mile away and only 300 feet higher than the Wyoming Trail itself. Beyond Mount Ethel, the route continues north along the crest of the Park Range for another 2 miles to reach the upper end of the 7.5-mile Rainbow Lake Trail, which climbs from a trailhead that lies at the eastern base of the range. Two miles later, the Wyoming Trail reaches its high point of 11,880 feet as it skirts a short distance east of 11,932-foot Lost Ranger Peak. The Lost Ranger Trail connects with the Wyoming Trail

about 1.5 miles north of the peak and the North Lake Trail is intersected a mile north of that. The Lost Ranger Trail approaches the Wyoming Trail from the east, while the North Lake Trail ascends the west side of the range.

In the next few miles, two more trails intersect the Wyoming Trail. The first of these, the Three Island Lake Trail, begins near Seedhouse Campground to the west. The second route—the Lone Pine Trail—climbs up from the North Park (east) side of the wilderness. A short distance beyond the Lone Pine intersection, the Continental Divide veers northeast while the Wyoming Trail continues due north and eventually drops into the Gold Creek drainage. Sections of this portion of the trail can be difficult to find, so a topographic map will help with any necessary routefinding. Generally speaking, the Wyoming Trail descends due north to reach the Gold Creek Lake Trail, which is a short distance northeast of the lake. Upon reaching the Gold Creek Lake Trail, turn left and continue 4.5 miles west to the Slavonia trailhead (see Hike 23).

Because much of this hike is near timberline, the threat of lightning is very real, especially in the summer. Water is found along the way, but it should be treated before drinking. Expect to see a lot of other hikers near both ends of this route.

25 SARVIS CREEK

Distance: 11.6 miles one-way
Difficulty: Moderate
Hiking time: 8 hours
Elevation: 7000 to 9240 feet
Management: Routt National Forest
Wilderness status: Sarvis Creek Wilderness Area
Season: June to October
Maps: USGS Blacktail Mountain, Walton Peak, Lake Agnes

Getting there: The hike begins at the lower end of the Sarvis Creek Trail, west of the wilderness boundary. To reach this trailhead, drive south from Steamboat Springs on US Highway 40 to Colorado Highway 131. Turn right and drive 4.25 miles to County Road 18.

Early morning along the Sarvis Creek Trail

Turn left and drive 6.7 miles south to the signed left turn for the Sarvis Creek trailhead. It is another 0.4 mile to the end of the road and the start of this hike. To reach the upper trailhead at the end of the hike, from Rabbit Ears Pass on US Highway 40, drive south on Forest Road 100 to Buffalo Park.

Spanning the width of the Sarvis Creek Wilderness Area, the Sarvis Creek Trail offers an excellent introduction to the northern portion of the Gore Range. Gentle in comparison to the southern half, this end of the Gores manifests as rolling mountains covered with timberlands. The Sarvis Timber Company logged portions of this region between 1912 and 1916. The 47,140-acre Sarvis Creek Wilderness Area was established as part of the Colorado Wilderness Act in 1993.

The Sarvis Creek Trail begins by following the right side of its namesake through an interesting little canyon. Spruce and fir trees are common, as are lodgepole pines. Some aspens are also encountered as the trail gains about 800 feet in the first 1.5 miles along easy-to-moderate grades. After this point, the route levels off a bit before crossing a bridge at 2 miles. The route follows the north side of the creek for the next several miles, though it disappears for a few hundred yards in one rocky area. Farther on are the remains of the Sarvis Timber Company's operations, including an old logging flume. Beyond that is a dilapidated cabin on the south side of the creek. The trail then crosses a series of small meadows. Up to this point the trail has covered 6 miles.

A little more than 7 miles from its start, the trail begins heading southeast, away from Sarvis

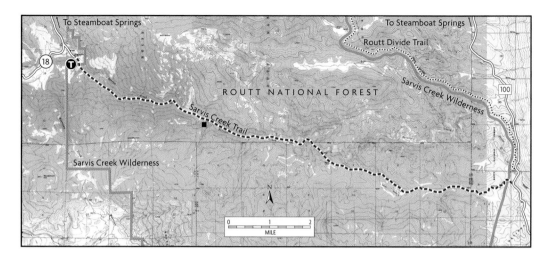

Creek. From here, the route climbs another 500 feet over the next 1.5 miles before leveling off again. Along the last portion of the hike, beautiful forests of lodgepole pine are a real treat to walk through. The Sarvis Creek Trail eventually reaches a dirt road that continues east for less than a mile before intersecting with Forest Road 100 at Buffalo Park.

Water is available along much of this hike, but it should be treated before drinking. Thick timber beyond the trail corridor can make it difficult to find a legal campsite (at least 100 feet from streams and trails) along much of this hike. Because the lower trailhead is located on Colorado Division of Wildlife land, you must first obtain a Conservation Certificate from the agency before parking at the trailhead. The nearest office is in Steamboat Springs.

26   LOST LAKES–DEVILS CAUSEWAY

Distance: 19.5-mile loop
Difficulty: Moderate
Hiking time: 3 days
Elevation: 10,280 to 11,928 feet
Management: Routt National Forest, White River National Forest
Wilderness status: Flat Tops Wilderness Area
Season: July to September
Maps: USGS Devils Causeway, Trappers Lake

Getting there: This hike begins at the Stillwater Reservoir trailhead. To reach it, drive 17 miles west of Yampa on County Road 7 (Forest Road 900), all the way to its end at the Stillwater Reservoir.

With 167 miles of trails, the Flat Tops Wilderness is conducive to long-distance hiking excursions.

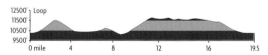

One particularly nice trip that accesses some of the most memorable topographical features of the area heads north from the Stillwater Reservoir to Lost Lakes. It then climbs west to pick up a high route that continues south toward the trailhead. The hike also encounters one of the most dramatic and unusual landmarks in the northern mountains of Colorado—the Devils Causeway. This 3-foot-wide, 1500-foot-high gangplank is a real thrill to traverse.

From the trailhead, follow the East Fork Trail southwest for 0.8 mile to the first trail intersection. The Bear River Trail, which is the end of this loop hike, continues straight at this junction to eventually climb up and over to Trappers Lake, while this hike turns right to follow the East Fork Trail in a more northerly direction. The route enters the Flat Tops Wilderness less than 0.5 mile past the junction and shortly beyond passes close to Little Causeway Lake. From the lake, the trail

ascends along mostly moderate grades to reach an 11,600-foot saddle situated between the Bear River drainage and the Williams Fork drainage to the north. The route has climbed 1300 feet in 1.6 miles.

At the saddle, a steep trail climbs a few hundred feet to the left to reach the Devils Causeway about 0.25 mile west. Hikers who are not particularly bothered by heights can save the visit to this unusual feature for the end of the trip. If you do suffer from acrophobia and think you might want to forgo crossing the causeway, leave your pack at the saddle and make the quick side trip now. Whether or not you cross it, this interesting landform should not be missed.

From the saddle, the East Fork Trail continues

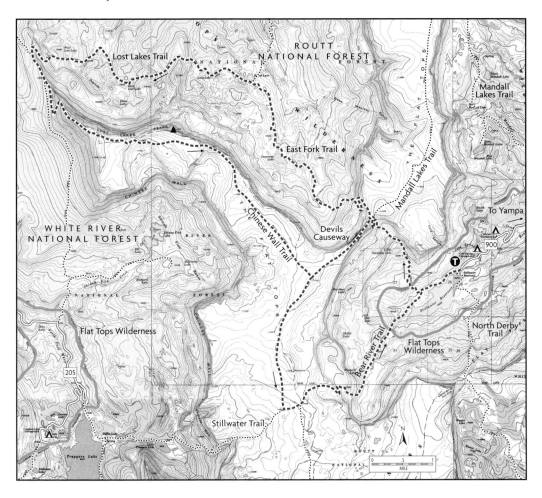

Along the East Fork Trail

north to drop into the head of the East Williams Fork drainage. As the route descends, it returns to the spruce and fir forests typical of the drainages of the Flat Tops. Here, as in many places across the wilderness, you can see countless spruce trees that died as a result of a beetle infestation in the 1940s.

A little more than 5 miles from the trailhead, the East Fork Trail reaches Causeway Lake. After that—near the 6.5-mile mark—the route reaches Round Lake, where the next trail junction is encountered. The East Fork Trail bears right to continue for another 7.5 miles to a trailhead north of the wilderness, while this hike turns left onto the Lost Lakes Trail. Within the next mile, it passes Long Lake and then makes a steep but short ascent to the top of a 10,720-foot divide. From there, the Lost Lakes Trail drops to reach East Lost Lake. The forest along this segment of the hike still bears scars from a severe fire around 1900.

Past East Lost Lake, the route enters a burn area from the 5000-acre Lost Lakes Fire of 2002. Another trail junction is encountered 2.6 miles beyond the turnoff at Round Lake. Keeping left on the West Lost Lakes Trail, the route now climbs 700 feet in 1.4 miles to reach the divide that separates the Williams Fork drainage from the White River drainage. This divide also forms

the boundary between the Routt and White River national forests. The climb ascends along moderate to strenuous grades, with several switchbacks in the last 0.5 mile to tops out at an elevation of 10,720 feet. Here, the West Lost Lakes Trail intersects the Chinese Wall Trail, which runs north to south. Turn left at this junction to begin the return leg of this hike.

Beyond the junction, the route along the Chinese Wall Trail climbs some more before continuing southeast for 6 miles along broad headlands of alpine tundra. There is something special about hiking across this treeless terrain; it constantly seems as if you are looking down upon the rest of the world. Although this segment of the hike crosses 11,928-foot Lost Lakes Peak (the high point of the entire hike), the grades are easy throughout. The trail is faint or nonexistent in places as it crosses this alpine terrain, however, so you will need to watch for the widely spaced rock cairns and trail posts that mark the way.

After 6 miles on the Chinese Wall Trail, the hike again reaches a turnoff for the Devils Causeway. If you want to cross the causeway, turn left here and continue northeast for a mile to the narrow passage. Epitomizing the unusual geology of the Flat Tops, the Devils Causeway resulted from a protective cap of volcanic rock that has prevented the erosion of material underneath. The Flat Tops as a whole were formed in this manner as volcanic activity some 35 million years ago spread lava across the White River Plateau. From the opposite side of the causeway, continue east for 0.25 mile to the East Fork Trail and follow it south for 1.6 miles to the trailhead.

If you decide not to cross the Devils Causeway, continue south on the Chinese Wall Trail for another 2 miles to the Stillwater Trail. Turn left and follow it a short distance east to where it becomes the Bear River Trail at the White River and Routt national forest boundary. From this point, it is 3 miles to the Stillwater Reservoir trailhead.

Bypassing the causeway adds a little more than 2 miles to the hike's total distance.

Bring plenty of water, especially for the section of the hike that follows the Chinese Wall Trail. Water drawn from lakes and streams along the rest of the hike should be treated before drinking. Because of the possibility of lightning along the higher reaches of this route, try to plan your hike so that you will traverse the higher alpine areas early in the day. Be wary of falling snags in forested areas devastated by beetle kill and forest fires. The Devils Causeway is a very popular destination for day hikers, and most of the lakes along this route are popular camping sites.

27 UPPER CATARACT LAKE

Distance: 10.2 miles round-trip
Difficulty: Moderate
Hiking time: 8 hours
Elevation: 8600 to 10,756 feet
Management: White River National Forest
Wilderness status: Eagles Nest Wilderness Area
Season: July to October
Map: USGS Mount Powell

Getting there: From Silverthorne, drive 16 miles north on Colorado Highway 9. Turn left onto Heeney Road (County Road 30) and continue 5.3 miles northwest to Cataract Creek Road (County Road 1725). Turn left again and drive 2.3 miles to the Surprise trailhead.

Although by no means the highest of Colorado's mountain chains, the Gore Range is considerably more rugged than many. As a faulted anticline range, these mountains rise abruptly to form an impressive collection of jagged peaks. Exploring these mountains is surprisingly easy, however, given the plentiful number of trails that penetrate them from the east and west. This is also a Colorado mountain range where a mining boom never really materialized, so the Gores are comparatively untouched by pick and shovel. This all-day hike into the Gore Range

begins near Lower Cataract Lake and climbs steadily to Upper Cataract Lake in the northeast portion of the mountains.

This hike starts by following the 2.6-mile Surprise Trail to Surprise Lake. Climbing steadily in places, the trail winds its way through aspen groves and spruce-fir forests. Just before reaching Surprise Lake, the Surprise Trail intersects the Gore Range Trail, which runs 54.5 miles along the eastern foot of its namesake mountains. If you are looking for a weeklong hike, the Gore Range Trail is ideal, as it accesses several side trails that, in turn, climb higher into the mountains.

The hike to Upper Cataract Lake turns right onto the Gore Range Trail and follows it for 0.5 mile before turning left onto the Upper Cataract

Upper Cataract Lake

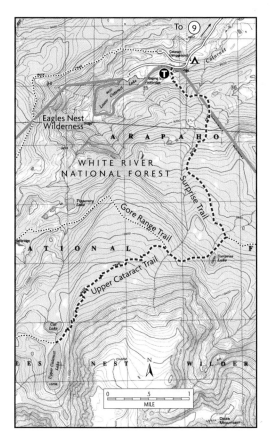

Trail. Shortly after taking up the Gore Range Trail, the route reaches Surprise Lake, which, in comparison to other lakes in the Gore Range, is small and unremarkable.

Shortly beyond Surprise Lake, turn onto the Upper Cataract Trail and follow it another 2 miles to Upper Cataract Lake. A much larger body of water than Surprise Lake, Upper Cataract is nestled just below beautiful 13,432-foot Eagles Nest Peak. Rising just south of Eagles Nest Peak is Mount Powell, named for Major John Wesley Powell, who climbed the summit in 1868. The Gore Range itself was named after Sir Saint George Gore, a rich nobleman who traveled west in 1855 on a hunting safari. It was reported that he bagged 2000 bison, 1600 deer and elk, 100 black bears, and untold numbers of smaller game.

Although Upper Cataract Lake is the turn-around point of this hike, the Upper Cataract Trail continues for another 1.5 miles to Mirror Lake. True to its name, Mirror Lake reflects an impressive cirque of rocky summits, including Eagles Nest Peak. The Upper Cataract Trail then passes by Mirror Lake and eventually crosses Elliot Ridge to the west side of the range.

Water is available along this hike, but it should be treated before drinking. Lightning is a potential hazard, although the hike to Upper Cataract Lake is not especially exposed.

28 ECCLES PASS

Distance: 10 miles round-trip
Difficulty: Moderate
Hiking time: 8 hours
Elevation: 9400 to 11,900 feet
Management: White River National Forest
Wilderness status: Eagles Nest Wilderness Area
Season: July to October
Maps: USGS Frisco, Vail Pass

Getting there: The hike to Eccles Pass begins at a trailhead just north of Frisco. After turning off Interstate 70 at the Frisco exit (exit 203), turn northwest and drive a short distance to a roundabout. Turn onto a gravel

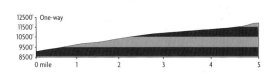

Scenery from Eccles Pass

road just to the right of the Interstate 70 westbound entrance. Follow this road to its end and the signed trailhead. Camping is not permitted within 0.25 mile of the interstate.

Located in the southern end of the Gore Range, 11,900-foot Eccles Pass makes a great destination for hikers, both for the scenery along the Meadow Creek Trail and for the sheer pleasure of reaching this high point.

The Meadow Creek Trail begins by climbing moderate grades along an old jeep road through thick stands of lodgepole pine and glades of aspen. Near the 2-mile mark, the route levels off a bit and begins to parallel Meadow Creek as it breaks into more open terrain and passes through a series of subalpine meadows to reach timberline less than a mile from the pass. Soaked by runoff from melting snows in early summer, some sections of the trail can be boggy in places, but the plethora of wildflowers that grows here is well worth the trouble. Be sure to stay on the trail to avoid damaging fragile meadow areas.

Within the last mile of the hike, the Meadow Creek Trail intersects the Gore Range Trail, which runs along the eastern side of the Eagles Nest Wilderness. Turn right onto the Gore Range Trail and continue north up a short series of switchbacks to reach Eccles Pass, where you are treated to wonderful views in all directions. To the south, the Gore Range continues for a few more miles before giving way to the Ten Mile Creek drainage and the Mosquito Range beyond. The Williams Fork Mountains rise to the east. Looking north, the vista takes in the South Willow Creek drainage, Red Peak, and Buffalo Mountain.

From Eccles Pass, the Gore Range Trail drops into the South Willow Creek drainage. About 1 mile north of the pass, the Gore Creek Trail branches west to climb up and over Red Buffalo

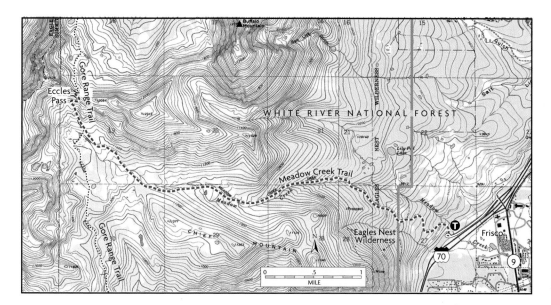

Pass before dropping down Gore Creek to a trailhead east of Vail. Red Buffalo Pass was once considered as a possible route for Interstate 70. Fortunately, the freeway was instead built around the southern tip of the Gore Range.

Water is plentiful along this hike, but it should be treated before drinking. Watch for lightning in open areas and on the pass itself, and be prepared for rapidly deteriorating weather conditions, even in midsummer.

29   HANGING LAKE

Distance: 2.4 miles round-trip
Difficulty: Strenuous
Hiking time: 2 hours
Elevation: 6100 to 7250 feet
Management: White River National Forest
Wilderness status: None
Season: Year-round
Map: USGS Shoshone

Getting there: This hike begins at the Hanging Lake rest stop along Interstate 70 in Glenwood Canyon, through which the Colorado River flows. Westbound travelers must exit a few miles farther west at the Grizzly Creek exit and double back on the eastbound lane to the Hanging Lake exit. Eastbound travelers can drive east from Glenwood Springs directly to the Hanging

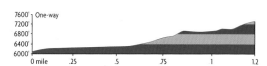

Lake exit. The return access to Interstate 70 from Hanging Lake is westbound only, so drivers who want to continue east on Interstate 70 must travel west to the Grizzly Creek exit to get back on track after the hike.

True to its name, Hanging Lake is tucked away on a high ledge in a narrow canyon. Scenic, to say the least, this precious jewel of a lake offers a just reward for all who hike the steep but short trail up.

From the Hanging Lake Rest Area, this hike begins by following the paved bicycle path east, or upstream, for about 0.25 mile to a narrow side canyon. Upon turning left up this drainage, the route climbs a mile on a mostly strenuous, rocky grade that does not quit until it reaches the lake, having ascended some 1000 feet. About a third of the way up, the trail intersects the Dead Horse Creek Trail, and then steepens to climb through a cliff area in the last 0.3 mile. Metal handrails provide some safety along this last stretch of the hike, where there are drop-offs of 100 feet or more. The trail in this portion also climbs a roughed-in staircase that is extremely steep but short.

While the hike to Hanging Lake is strenuous, it is also quite beautiful and well worth the effort. As the trail climbs along Dead Horse Creek, it passes through a wonderful riparian plant community that is home to such shady deciduous trees as box elders and cottonwoods, and an interesting variety of undergrowth can be found at trailside. Perhaps most alluring are the many ferns that grow along the streambed. Their presence, along with moss-clad boulders, attests to

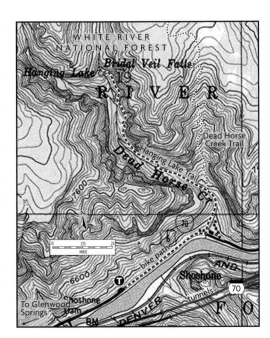

Wild rose blossom

the humid conditions of this ecological niche. Benches along most of the route provide nice rest spots from which to enjoy the canyon.

Upon reaching 1.5-acre Hanging Lake, hikers are immediately rewarded with its secretive, Eden-like ambience. Walled in by limestone cliffs and leafy cottonwoods, Hanging Lake resulted from the collection of water in a geologic fault. Because the lake's fragile shore has been built up from travertine deposits, visitors are required to stay on the boardwalk that rings the south shore. Bridal Veil Falls, a small but beautiful cascade of water, drops into the lake's north end. Of special interest are the schools of trout that swim in the lake's clear waters. Because of the fragile nature of this lake, swimming and fishing are prohibited. Follow a short side trail just west of the lake to visit nearby Spouting Rock, a waterfall that has cut a passage through solid limestone.

Water along this hike should be treated before drinking. Treat the dangerous drop-offs at the top of the trail with respect. You can expect to see many other hikers making the trip up from the popular rest stop. Dogs are prohibited along this route.

Opposite: An old quarry in Red Rock Canyon

CENTRAL MOUNTAINS

Most of Colorado's highest summits, including thirty-one of the state's fifty-four "fourteeners," are framed by Interstate 70 and US Highway 50. Many of these lofty peaks are found within the Sawatch Range, but others top the Mosquito and Front Ranges, and a handful are found in the vicinity of Aspen. While exploring this "roof" of Colorado's mountain terrain is the goal of several hikes in this section, other excursions reveal hidden treasures interspersed in between. Hikers visiting this region will enjoy plenty of the impressive scenery that Colorado is so famous for, and they will also discover a number of singular geological oddities, historical relics, and natural wonders.

30 ROXBOROUGH STATE PARK

Distance: 2.25-mile loop
Difficulty: Easy
Hiking time: 2 hours
Elevation: 6200 to 6000 feet
Management: Roxborough State Park
Wilderness status: None
Season: Year-round
Map: USGS Kassler

Getting there: From Denver, drive south on US Highway 85 to Titan Road, which is about 4 miles south of Colorado Highway 470. Turn right and drive west for 3.4 miles to where the road turns south and becomes the North Rampart Range Road. Continue south for a little more than 3 miles to Roxborough Park Road. Turn left, then make a right soon after the West Metro Fire Station. Follow this road south for about 2 miles to the park visitor center.

Given Roxborough State Park's wealth of geologic features, its ecological diversity, and its scenic beauty, you might find it hard to believe that this unique area is so close to Denver. But Roxborough State Park proves that natural wonders and large metropolitan areas can coexist. It is designated as a Colorado Natural Area and as a National Natural Landmark and National Archeological District. Of the park's five hiking trails, the Fountain Valley Loop Trail cuts to the chase where these natural wonders are concerned.

Begin at the visitor center, where you can purchase or borrow a trail guide that corresponds to numbered features along the route. From there, the Fountain Valley Loop heads north along a wide, dirt trail. The going is easy throughout, with little grade change. Within a short distance you can take in a view of the terrain ahead from a vista point located west of the main trail. Looking north from here, you see several geologic formations angling upward. The most colorful of these is the red sandstone that constitutes the Fountain Formation. This layer of rock was deposited some 300 million years ago in a streambed that carried sand and gravel down from the ancestral Rocky Mountains. Next in line is the yellowish sandstone of the Lyons Formation, which resulted from sand dunes and stream deposits along the shoreline of an ancient sea. Farther east is the Dakota Hogback, a pronounced formation of gray and buff-colored rock that was deposited along floodplains 135 million years ago. Sedimentary in origin, these three formations were once horizontal but were subsequently tilted upward when the present-day Rockies were uplifted beginning 65 million years ago. The oldest rocks in the area are the gneisses and granites

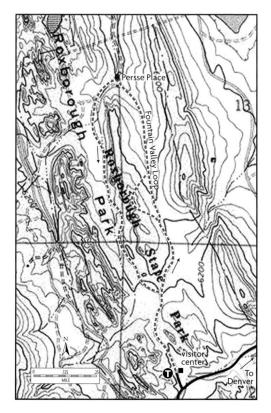

that make up the foothills of the Rockies along the western end of the park. They date back 1.2 billion years to Precambrian times.

From the vista point, continue north to where the loop splits. Stay right here to follow the loop counterclockwise. A bit farther north is an expanse of grasslands. In addition to its unique geology, Roxborough State Park encompasses an interesting ecological transition zone. Touted as a place where the plains and the mountains meet, the park features the grassland community of the Great Plains, which spread eastward, and the shrub and forest communities of the Rocky Mountains to the west. This interface is easily noted: prairie grasses grow in many open areas, while Gambel oak, ponderosa pines, and Douglas-firs inhabit the foothills and nearby summits.

Because of this ecological variety and the fact that Roxborough State Park has remained pristine, a wide variety of wildlife inhabits the area. Among the smaller creatures that live here are pocket gophers, rock squirrels, and prairie rattlesnakes. The larger species include mule deer, elk, coyotes, black bears, and mountain lions. If you are lucky, you might spot a golden eagle soaring on the thermals above.

Red-rock formations in Roxborough State Park

As you continue north along the east side of the loop, a short side trail less than 0.5 mile in length climbs easily to the left to reach the Lyons Overlook. From this vantage, you gain views to the north and west, plus an up-close look at the Lyons Formation, upon which you are standing. Because this side trail drops back to the Fountain Valley Loop without backtracking, it adds little distance to the hike's overall length.

At the north end of the Fountain Valley Loop is an old stone house known as the Persse Place. Dating to the turn of the twentieth century, this restored abode was built by Henry S. Persse, who lived here in the summer. His dream was to turn this area into a resort, but fortunately that scenario never materialized.

From the Persse Place, the Fountain Valley Loop heads south to lead back to the visitor center. This final stretch of the hike encounters a number of small ecosystems the trail guide describes in some detail. These include a riparian community of cottonwood trees, a sedge meadow, an aspen grove, and more. After passing some pinnacles of Fountain Formation sandstone, the trail eventually reaches the close of the loop and the short return trip to the visitor center.

Bring water, since none is available along the hike. Watch for rattlesnakes and keep in mind that park regulations prohibit leaving the trail, collecting any natural materials, rock climbing, pets, and bikes.

31 MOUNT FALCON

Distance: 1.9-mile loop
Difficulty: Easy
Hiking time: 2 hours
Elevation: 7700 to 7851 feet
Management: Jefferson County Open Space
Wilderness status: None
Season: April to November
Maps: USGS Morrison

Getting there: Mount Falcon Park is situated in the foothills of the Front Range. From Denver, drive west on US Highway 285 toward Conifer. Take the Indian Hills exit and drive north on the Parmalee Gulch Road to the Picutis Road about 2.8 miles from US Highway 285. Follow the Picutis Road another 2.2 miles to its end. Signs for the park lead the way.

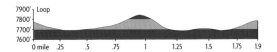

Owned and operated by the Jefferson County Open Space, Mount Falcon Park is home to numerous trails that lead to a number of historical and scenic treasures. This hike follows a short but interesting loop in the park's higher section.

Of the two entrance points to Mount Falcon Park, this hike takes advantage of the western trailhead, situated in the highest reaches of the park. From the trailhead, the Castle Trail drops gently along a broad ridge top. This trail, along with most others in the park, follows old roadways still utilized by park service vehicles. The trail passes among scattered ponderosa pine to reach a broad and scenic meadow in less than 0.5 mile. Here, the Castle Trail intersects with the Meadow Trail, which this hike follows straight ahead to an intersection with the Tower Trail a short distance beyond. Bear right onto the Tower Trail and follow it to the Eagle Eye Shelter. Perched on the edge of cliffs, the Eagle Eye Shelter provides great views toward the west and southwest. The Tower Trail then leads to a small

Pine cones along the hike to Mount Falcon

tower on top of Mount Falcon, the highpoint of the park.

Beyond the tower, the Tower Trail connects back up with the Meadow Trail 0.6 mile from where it turned off of the Meadow Trail and 1 mile from the trailhead. Turn left onto the Meadow Trail and follow it 0.5 mile back to its intersection with the Castle Trail. From this point, it is 0.4 mile to the trailhead, thus completing the hike.

With a bit of extra time, you might want to follow the Castle Trail less than 0.5 mile east of its intersection with the Meadow Trail to the old homestead of John Brisben Walker. Built in the early twentieth century, this large stone foundation speaks of Walker's life on Mount Falcon. Owning 4000 acres here, he envisioned and even began building a summer home for the president of the United States. But the construction never

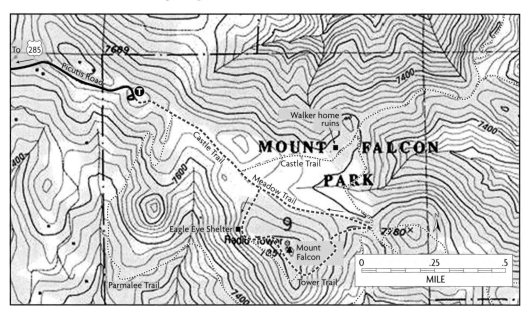

continued beyond foundation work and Walker's dream was never fulfilled. What remains is located farther east along the Castle Trail.

Bring plenty of water, as none is available along this hike. Watch for lightning during periods of thunderstorm activity. Watch for mountain bikes on the trails. Dogs are permitted but must be kept on a leash.

32 DEVILS HEAD

Distance: 2.8 miles round-trip
Difficulty: Moderate
Hiking time: 3 hours
Elevation: 8800 to 9748 feet
Management: Pike National Forest
Wilderness status: None
Season: June to October
Map: USGS Devils Head

Getting there: From Sedalia, drive about 10 miles west on Colorado Highway 67 to the Rampart Range Road (Forest Road 300). Turn south and drive 8.5 miles to the Devils Head Campground and Picnic Area. The Devils Head Lookout Trail begins at the picnic area. Watch for heavy traffic (including motorcycles) on the winding Rampart Range Road.

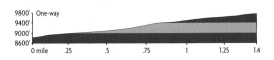

Mounted along a rocky highpoint of the Rampart Range, the Devils Head Lookout offers hikers fantastic views of the foothills that drop away to the east and higher terrain to the west. This moderately difficult hike located so close to the Denver metropolitan area receives up to 20,000 visitors annually.

From the trailhead, the 1.4-mile Devils Head Lookout Trail begins by climbing gently along a drainage bottom graced with aspen stands. It soon turns east, however, to begin climbing a broad ridge east of the drainage. Large, rounded outcrops of granite along the way typify the geology of the area. Such formations also hint at the structure of the Devils Head itself.

Continuing on, the route begins switchbacking to steadily gain elevation. At one point, a side trail leads a short distance to the Zinn Overlook. Signs point out this destination, and also warn against cutting switchbacks. With so many visitors along this trail, it would not take long for

Aspen growing among boulders along the trail to Devils Head

Stairs to the Devils Head lookout

serious erosion to result from hikers leaving the established trail.

Upon topping a summit of sorts, the Devils Head Lookout Trail encounters a cabin and work area for personnel staffing the lookout tower. It then leads a short distance to a series of steps that climb the granite outcrop that is the Devils Head. The first lookout to grace the top of this handy panoramic point was built in 1912, while the current structure was constructed in 1951 with the help of 100 men and 72 mules from nearby Fort Carson. Today it stands as the only operating fire lookout in the Front Range. Forest Service personnel occupy the tower from mid-May to mid-September and are usually happy to explain the workings of the facility. The number of visitors in the tower is limited to ten at any one time and it is important to avoid climbing the stairs during thunderstorm activity. Also, use caution on the stairs as they are steep and a fall could be disastrous.

Bring water as none is found along the way. Do not cut switchbacks and use caution when climbing the steps to the lookout. It is best to avoid the summit area when lightning is a possibility.

33 RESTHOUSE MEADOWS

Distance: 13 miles round-trip
Difficulty: Moderate
Hiking time: 8 hours
Elevation: 10,600 to 11,800 feet
Management: Arapaho National Forest
Wilderness status: Mount Evans Wilderness Area
Season: June to October
Maps: USGS Idaho Springs, Harris Park

Getting there: The Resthouse Meadows Trail begins at the Echo Lake Campground, which is reached by driving 14 miles south from Idaho Springs on Colorado Highway 103 to Colorado Highway 5. The trailhead is near the campground restrooms. Parking is available on the left side of the road. Do not park in the campground itself.

Thanks to its proximity to Denver, the Mount Evans Scenic Byway is a very popular driving route, especially on weekends. Hikers can leave the crowds behind, however, in favor of a quiet trail through the forests and alpine areas of the Mount Evans Wilderness. One of these backcountry routes is the 6.5-mile Resthouse Meadows Trail, which leads to an isolated park surrounded by stunning mountain scenery.

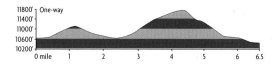

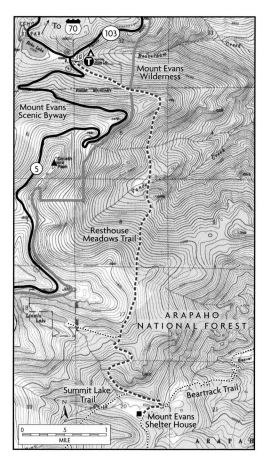

From the trailhead, the Resthouse Meadows Trail climbs steadily up an easy grade through a beautiful forest of Engelmann spruce and sub-alpine fir for the first mile. At the 1-mile mark, the route tops a ridge, then begins dropping along an easy-to-moderate grade into the Vance Creek drainage. Because this section of the trail crosses a south-facing slope, the added exposure to the sun allows for the addition of lodgepole pine to the spruce-fir mix.

About 1.5 miles out, the Resthouse Meadows Trail crosses perennially flowing Vance Creek. A small meadow in the vicinity provides a nice place to stop for lunch. Beyond Vance Creek, the trail begins the first of several easy climbs over the next 1.5 miles. Like the first portion of the hike, this section travels through a forest of mostly spruce and fir trees. About 4 miles from the trailhead, the route reaches a large burn area. Thought to have been ignited by a careless camper's fire in 1964, the Resthouse Fire swept across 1000 acres before it was finally extinguished. In the decades since, grasses, wildflowers, and some shrubs have taken hold in the burn, but the forest itself is still just a ghostly collection of sun-bleached tree trunks. Where the trail first enters this area, the dead snags are mostly the tall, straight trunks of spruce and firs, but in another 0.25 mile the twisted and gnarled remains of bristlecone pines are also apparent. Years of weathering have made these old trunks picturesque and you might see a variety of birds, given the abundance of nesting sites.

Nearly 0.5 mile into the burn area, the trail first reaches the hike's high point of about 11,800 feet, and then a right-hand turnoff soon after for Lincoln Lake. Situated at 11,600 feet, Lincoln Lake lies at timberline less than a mile up the side trail. If you visit the lake, be sure to scan the rocky slopes above for mountain goats. The Resthouse Meadows Trail turns left at this signed intersection and soon begins dropping toward the route's namesake. The trail descends nearly 1000 feet in this last 0.5-mile segment of the hike.

An old burn area near Resthouse Meadows

As you hike down to the meadows, you can see a number of beaver ponds strung along the creek bottom. Large patches of willows and some aspen groves turn bright yellow in the fall.

While the Resthouse Fire scorched timber on all sides of Resthouse Meadows, scattered stands of trees within the meadows were spared from the flames. Within the Resthouse Meadows area, you first pass the turnoff for the 4-mile Summit Lake Trail, which climbs west to its namesake on the upper end of the Mount Evans Highway. The Resthouse Meadows Trail then intersects the Beartrack Trail. Turn right at this junction and continue less than 0.25 mile to reach the ruins of the Mount Evans Shelter House and the turnaround point for this hike. Like the surrounding forests, this structure perished in a fire some years ago. All that remains today is a stone chimney and some of the foundation.

A free wilderness permit (available at the trailhead) is required to enter the Mount Evans Wilderness. Dogs must be on a leash while in the Mount Evans Wilderness. Water is available along this hike, but it should be treated before drinking. Some weekends see heavy use along the first couple of miles of the trail. Although this hike is not very exposed, lightning poses an occasional hazard.

34 MOUNT GOLIATH RESEARCH NATURAL AREA

Distance: 3 miles round-trip
Difficulty: Easy
Hiking time: 2 hours
Elevation: 11,550 to 12,150 feet
Management: Arapaho National Forest
Wilderness status: None
Season: July to September
Map: USGS Idaho Springs

Mount Goliath Research Natural Area • 97

Getting there: From Idaho Springs, drive 14 miles south on Colorado Highway 103 to Echo Lake. Turn right onto the Mount Evans Scenic Byway (Colorado Highway 5) and drive another 2.9 miles to a large parking area on the left. The M. Walter Pesman Trail begins at the south end of the parking lot. A fee is charged to drive up the Mount Evans Scenic Byway.

This short and mostly easy hike accesses one of the more interesting ecological features of the Colorado Rockies: an extensive forest of bristlecone pine. Given this forest's uniqueness, it is now the centerpiece of the 1-square-mile Mount Goliath Research Natural Area.

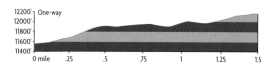

From the parking area, the 1.5-mile M. Walter Pesman Trail climbs through patches of willow before angling up a somewhat steeper grade along the east face of Mount Goliath. Within the first 0.5 mile, the trail completes most of its 600-foot climb in a few moderately steep switchbacks. The trail then levels off for the next 0.5 mile or so, giving hikers incredible views that stretch east across the Front Range to the Great Plains beyond. Visitors also encounter examples of this

Bristlecone pines in the Mount Goliath Research Natural Area

natural area's premier attraction. The bristlecone is a member of the limber pine family, and some specimens elsewhere in the country are as old as 5000 years. While the oldest of the Mount Goliath trees dates back a "mere" 1600 years, many of the larger ones are nevertheless picturesque. Sculpted over the years by the elements, these trees have been framed in the viewfinders of many a camera. Given this stand's extensive size, it is no wonder that scientists conduct studies here. You might also notice some Engelmann spruce intermingled among the bristlecones.

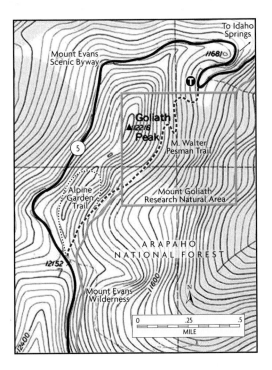

The M. Walter Pesman Trail eventually contours around a more southerly facing slope, where it leaves the last of the bristlecones, and a few final krummholz stands of spruce, behind. It then climbs a bit through arctic-alpine tundra to reach the upper trailhead. A stark contrast to the forests below, this tundra ecosystem features plants that are only a few inches high. Among the animals that live in this extremely cold and windy region are pikas, marmots, ptarmigans, bighorn sheep, and mountain goats. The upper end of the trail connects with the 0.5-mile Alpine Garden Trail at the turnaround point.

Bring water on this hike, as none is available along the way. Watch for the frequent lightning storms that cross this exposed area, and keep in mind that gathering wood, rocks, or any other natural material is prohibited within the Mount Goliath Research Natural Area. Dogs must be kept on a leash.

35 WIGWAM PARK

Distance: 13.2 miles round-trip
Difficulty: Moderate
Hiking time: 8 hours
Elevation: 9500 to 10,250 feet
Management: Pike National Forest
Wilderness status: Lost Creek Wilderness Area
Season: June to October
Maps: USGS Windy Peak, Topaz Mountain

Getting there: From Fairplay, drive 13 miles northeast on US Highway 285 to Lost Park Road (Forest Road 127). Turn right and follow this good dirt road east for 20 miles to its end. The trailhead is located just east of the Lost Park Campground.

Along the Wigwam Trail

Spanning the Kenosha and Tarryall Mountains, the 120,000-acre Lost Creek Wilderness Area encompasses an interesting mix of forests, open meadows, creek bottoms, and alpine ridges. Because of its size and the fact that no 14,000-foot peaks are found within its boundaries, this wilderness offers a considerable amount of solitude throughout. One seldom-used route—the Wigwam Trail—follows the area's namesake creek east for a couple miles before continuing on to beautiful Wigwam Park, one of several natural parks found within the Lost Creek Wilderness.

From the trailhead, the Wigwam Trail heads southeast across an open marshy area to reach a short stretch of narrow canyon. The trail enters East Lost Park at about 1 mile and continues inside it for 2 more miles. This naturally treeless area is partly the result of deep, finely textured soils more suitable for grasses, sedges, and willows than for the lodgepole pines, Engelmann spruce, and subalpine firs that constitute the nearby forests. Other influences, such as moisture levels, also contributed to the formation of such meadows. The end result is a beautiful open park where deer and elk might be spotted during the early morning and evening.

About halfway through East Lost Park, and 3 miles from the trailhead, Lost Creek turns south, away from the trail, to eventually reach an area where it occasionally disappears from view beneath boulder fields. The Wigwam Trail continues east to reach the far end of East Lost Park. It then begins an easy climb of about 300 feet to cross into the Wigwam Creek drainage. From this low saddle, the Wigwam Trail drops about 600 feet in the next mile to reach Wigwam Park, which features a number of beaver dams, some nice camping spots, and two trail intersections. The first is with the Rolling Creek Trail, which heads 6.4 miles north to the Wellington Lake area; the second is with the Goose Creek Trail, which continues nearly 10 miles south along the eastern end of the Lost Creek Wilderness Area.

While Wigwam Park is the turnaround point for this hike, you could extend your hike for many miles. The Wigwam Trail continues east for another 3.5 miles to a trailhead just beyond the wilderness boundary. Or you might explore

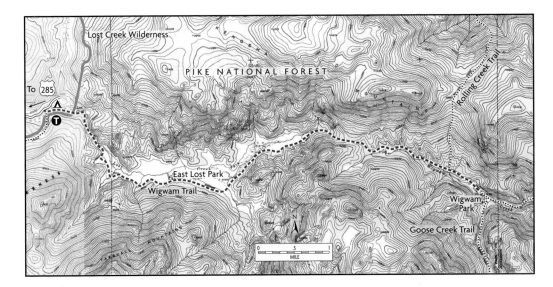

the Rolling Creek and Goose Creek Trails, which access their respective trailheads on the eastern side of the wilderness. If you're interested in a three- to five-day loop hike, you could follow the Goose Creek Trail south to the McCurdy Park Trail, turn right, and go west to the Brookside- McCurdy Trail. After turning right again, you would then continue north to return to your car at the Lost Park Campground.

All water found along this hike should be treated before drinking. Lightning is not too prevalent, but be mindful of it just the same.

36 RED ROCK CANYON

Distance: 2.1-mile loop
Difficulty: Easy
Hiking time: 2 hours
Elevation: 6160 to 6400 feet
Management: City of Colorado Springs
Wilderness status: None
Season: Year-round
Map: USGS Manitou Springs

Getting there: From downtown Colorado Springs, drive west a short distance on US Highway 24 (Cimarron Street). Turn south onto Ridge Road and take an immediate left into the developed trailhead area. Ample parking spaces attest to the area's popularity.

A 2003 addition to the city of Colorado Springs' docket of open spaces, Red Rock Canyon and adjacent ridges and mesas offer in-town hiking at its best. This hike follows a trio of easy trails to offer a good introduction to the geological wonders of the area.

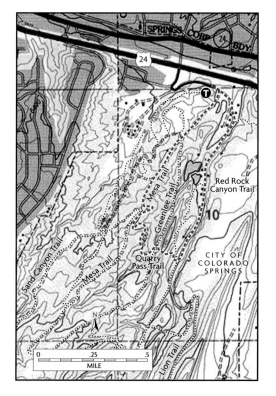

From the trailhead, begin by following the Red Rock Canyon Trail around the north end of a small rise of sandstone and into its namesake drainage. Because this trail, like many others in the area, follows an old road, the going is particularly easy. All trail intersections are well marked so the possibility of getting lost is nil. A little less than 0.5 mile in, the trail encounters a small reservoir and the remains of some stone buildings. A previous landowner, John George Bock, devised grandiose plans for a resort community, convention center, high-rise buildings, and a golf course. Fortunately, the city of Colorado Springs was able to purchase the land before much of this came about. Beyond the resevoir, this hike continues up the Red Rock Canyon Trail for another 0.4 mile to its intersection with the Quarry Pass Trail.

Upon turning right onto the Quarry Pass Trail, continue up and over the red-rock ridge directly in front. As the name suggests, this trail finds access through the stone ridgeline via an old quarry. Sliced along vertical planes, the stone cut from this quarry was used in various regional structures in the 1880s. A little less than 0.25 mile from the Red Rock Canyon Trail, the Quarry Pass

Giant stone stairsteps in an old quarry in Red Rock Canyon

Trail intersects the Greenlee Trail, which runs north and south through a shallow valley. From this intersection, continue on the Quarry Pass Trail as it winds about 0.5 mile along a contour to the sloping mesa top to the west. This segment of the hike follows a single-track trail.

About 1.5 miles from the hike's start, the Quarry Pass Trail intersects the Mesa Trail. Turn right at this point and follow the Mesa Trail 0.6 mile to the trailhead. The Mesa Trail slopes gently downhill on an old road. Along the way, it intersects four side trails, including the bottom end of the Greenlee Trail.

Popular with hikers, the Red Rock Canyon Open Space is also favored by rock climbers. Regulations prohibit bouldering, however, and technical climbers must first register at nearby Garden of the Gods Park. Dogs are permitted on the trails but must be on a leash at all times. Bring water, as none is available along the way.

37 NORTH CHEYENNE CAÑON

Distance: 4 miles one-way
Difficulty: Moderate
Hiking time: 3 hours
Elevation: 6250 to 7300 feet
Management: City of Colorado Springs
Wilderness status: None
Season: April to November
Maps: USGS Colorado Springs, Manitou Springs

Getting there: North Cheyenne Cañon Park is located southwest of downtown Colorado Springs. From downtown, drive southwest on Cheyenne Boulevard to the park entrance and the Starsmore Discovery Center. The Columbine Trail begins behind the center and follows the North Cheyenne Cañon west. To reach the upper end of the Columbine Trail, drive up the North Cheyenne Cañon Road to just past the Helen Hunt Falls.

Encompassing 1600 acres within its deep and scenic namesake, North Cheyenne Cañon Park is traversed by the 4-mile Columbine Trail. Because this route explores both the canyon's bottom and its upper slopes, it offers hikers a comprehensive introduction to the drainage's varied ecosystems. Whereas a shuttle will facilitate hiking the entire route, segments of the trail can be explored from each of its three trailheads. This hike follows the entire route from bottom to top.

Setting out from the Lower Columbine trailhead behind the Starsmore Discovery Center, the Columbine Trail begins by following North Cheyenne Creek up canyon. After passing a reservation-only picnic facility, the trail then takes up the riparian zone at creekside. Among the riotous greenery that typifies this area are willows, cottonwoods, and poison ivy. With the paved road that climbs North Cheyenne Cañon never far away, traffic noise is noticeable, but so too is the babbling creek at your feet. You might also catch a glimpse of some of the many bird species that inhabit the canyon. About 0.75 mile from its start, the trail enters the White Fir Botanical Preserve, a small grove of stately evergreens that is a pleasurable place to visit.

One mile into the hike, the Columbine Trail reaches the Mid Columbine trailhead. The trail takes on a second persona beyond this access point as it begins climbing along the drier slopes of the canyon's north face. Plant life along this section of the hike includes ponderosa pine,

The scenic upper end of North Cheyenne Cañon

Douglas-fir, and Gambel oak. Climbing steadily for 500 feet or so, the Columbine Trail eventually accesses dramatic views of the 1000-foot-deep canyon. The trail then levels out a bit to contour high above the canyon bottom and well out of earshot of traffic noise below.

About 3 miles from the Mid Columbine trailhead and 4 miles from the start of the hike, the Columbine Trail reaches its end at the Upper Columbine trailhead located at a bend in the road just past Helen Hunt Falls. Beyond this trailhead, the North Cheyenne Cañon Road intersects the Gold Camp Road to contour along the slopes of the higher peaks to the west.

Water is available along North Cheyenne Creek, but it should be treated before drinking. No water is available beyond the Mid Columbine trailhead. Watch for flash floods in the canyon bottom and lightning higher up. Horses and bicycles are permitted on the Columbine Trail so practice proper trail etiquette. Dogs are permitted but must be leashed at all times. North Cheyenne Cañon is home to black bears and mountain lions; use caution to prevent unwanted encounters.

38 WALDO CANYON

Distance: 7-mile loop
Difficulty: Moderate
Hiking time: 5 hours
Elevation: 7050 to 8100 feet
Management: Pike National Forest
Wilderness status: None
Season: April to November
Map: USGS Cascade

Getting there: From Colorado Springs, drive west on US Highway 24 for about 9 miles to the signed trailhead and large parking area on the north side of the road. The trailhead is about 3.5 miles west of Manitou Springs.

In the vicinity of Pikes Peak (and along its entire eastern face), the Front Range abruptly rises from the Great Plains as a wall of rugged mountains. The Waldo Canyon Trail explores a portion of this beautiful area with an easy and rewarding

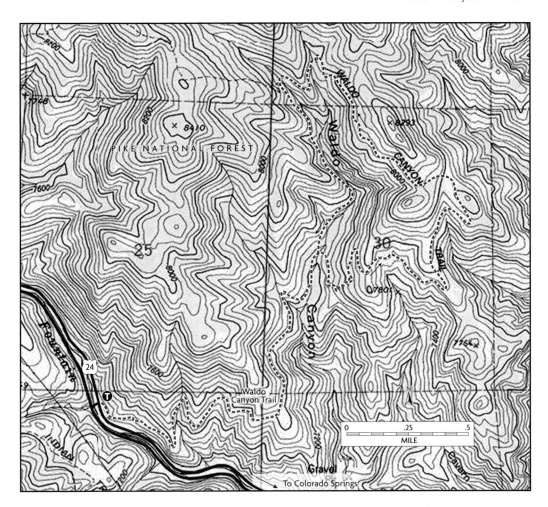

hike that begins just a few minutes from downtown Colorado Springs. Because of its accessibility, the Waldo Canyon Trail is extremely popular. In fact, Pike National Forest statistics show that this is the most heavily used trail in the Pikes Peak region.

From the trailhead, the route climbs immediately up a number of stairs before leveling off to ascend a mostly easy grade. It then begins contouring along the mountainside toward the east for about 1 mile. The trail then heads north into Waldo Canyon itself. Along this first segment of the hike, the trail is wide and well established, and the grades are mostly easy. Views are also nice, especially those of Fountain Creek Canyon (through which US Highway 24 runs) and the

Colorado Springs area down canyon. At one point, you can see the handful of tall buildings in the downtown section of the city. Because the first mile of trail traverses warm and relatively dry south-facing slopes, vegetation along the way includes junipers, pinyon pines, Gambel oaks, mountain mahogany, some yuccas and grasses, and a few ponderosa pines scattered about. In the second mile, the route encounters Douglas-firs as the canyon becomes more sheltered. The trail climbs 450 feet in this first segment.

Nearly 2 miles from the trailhead, the Waldo Canyon Trail drops slightly into the main portion of the canyon. Here it enters a small meadow that was once home to the Waldo Hog Ranch. Some camping sites are found in this meadow. Although

Rock formation along the hike into Waldo Canyon

the stream that usually flows through Waldo Canyon occasionally dries up after periods of no rain, there is sufficient ground moisture to support a variety of trees, including large ponderosa pines and Douglas-firs, some Colorado blue spruce, a few cottonwoods, and even some aspens.

A short distance above the meadow area, the trail reaches a fork where the two ends of a 3-mile loop join together. From this junction, you can travel in either direction to complete the loop. If you turn left, you will follow along the Waldo Canyon bottom for about a mile to reach the 8000-foot level. The trail then contours to the east and south to reach a ridgeline. After following this ridge for a short distance, the trail begins

dropping back into the canyon by way of a series of short switchbacks. From the bottom of the loop portion to its high point, this section of the trail climbs about 600 feet. Turning left at the junction and following the trail clockwise allows you to encounter easy-to-moderate grade changes. No matter which way you turn, you will enjoy a number of nice vistas, especially those taking in Pikes Peak to the south. And you might even spot some of the wildlife that inhabits the canyon, such as mule deer, elk, and bighorn sheep.

Water is not always available along this trail, so bring your own. Watch for mountain bikes. Because of the hike's popularity, you might want to plan your visit for a weekday.

39 THE CRAGS

Distance: 5 miles round-trip
Difficulty: Easy
Hiking time: 4 hours
Elevation: 10,100 to 10,800 feet
Management: Pike National Forest
Wilderness status: None
Season: June to October
Maps: USGS Pikes Peak, Woodland Park

Getting there: From Colorado Springs, drive 24 miles west on US Highway 24 to the small town of Divide. Turn left and drive 4.3 miles south on Colorado Highway 67 to County Road 62, which becomes Forest Road 383. Turn left and drive 3.2 miles on this somewhat rough but passable road to the Crags Campground. The trail starts at the campground's upper loop.

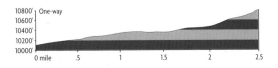

Rising more than 14,000 feet, Pikes Peak captures the imaginations of all who spy its impressive summit. Among its more interesting features are the many pink-colored outcrops of Pikes Peak granite found throughout the massif. Dating back to Precambrian times, Pikes Peak granite formed as part of a batholith, a large intrusion of molten rock deep within the earth. The rock then cooled very slowly. Perhaps nowhere are these

formations more fascinating than in the area known as The Crags. Located on the back, or west, side of the mountain, these fantastical spires of rock are accessible via a short, easy trail.

From the trailhead, the Crags Trail travels northeast for most of the way as it follows Four-mile Creek to its headwaters. The trail is in very good condition and grade changes are either nonexistent or easy for the first 2 miles. Along the way, the route encounters forests of Engelmann spruce and subalpine fir, aspen glades, and a few natural meadows. These open areas make for good wildlife watching in the early morning

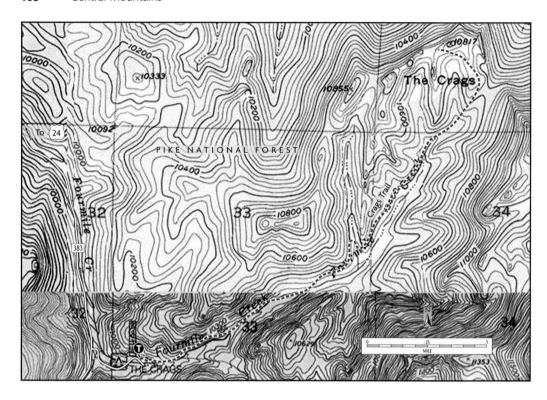

Formations at The Crags

and evening hours. Some picturesque pools and cascades can also be enjoyed along Fourmile Creek. A number of granite outcrops add interest to the hike after the first mile, but these are just a taste of what is to come.

In the last 0.5 mile, the trail begins to climb along a more moderate grade. Upon reaching the head of Fourmile Creek, the trail picks its way northwest for about 0.25 mile along a rocky ridge. Interesting rock formations are scattered along this last segment of the hike, but The Crags themselves are best enjoyed from the trail's end at a high point along this ridge. From this vantage, the striking pinnacles of Pikes Peak granite are visible in almost all directions. Well worn after countless centuries of erosion, these formations exude an organic quality, much like abstract sculptures. From this vista, you can also enjoy some fine scenery. To the north is the Rampart Range, while a look west reveals nearby Florissant Fossil Beds National Monument. And rising abruptly to the east are the treeless reaches of Pikes Peak itself. You might also notice a number of interesting bristlecone pines growing in the immediate vicinity. Some are still alive, while others have died to become snags of wildly twisted wood.

Water is available along this trail, but it should be treated before drinking. Watch for lightning at the exposed top end of the Crags Trail.

40 BOULDER CREEK

Distance: 3.2-mile loop
Difficulty: Easy
Hiking time: 2 hours
Elevation: 8400 to 8550 feet
Management: Florissant Fossil Beds National Monument
Wilderness status: None
Season: Year-round
Map: USGS Lake George

Getting there: To reach Florissant Fossil Beds National Monument, drive 35 miles west from Colorado Springs on US Highway 24 to the small town of Florissant. Turn south onto County Road 1 and drive 2.4 miles to the signed turnoff for the national monument visitor center.

Known for its fossilized tree stumps, insects, and such, Florissant Fossil Beds National Monument also features some nice hiking routes, all of which can be enjoyed by hikers of any age. This hike heads west from the visitor center past some interesting ecological communities to Boulder Creek.

Like most routes within Florissant Fossil Beds National Monument, the hike to Boulder Creek begins at the visitor center—the facility's back door, to be exact. From here, walk through the outdoor exhibit area. This short stretch of paved trail passes a selection of fossilized stumps, the remnants of a now-extinct species of giant sequoia tree that once grew along an ancient stream. These trees, like a variety of other plants and insects, were buried by a massive mudflow that originated from a volcano 15 miles to the southwest. The end result of this process is an unusually well-preserved look at what life was like some 34 million years ago.

At the end of the exhibit area, the trail reaches an intersection of two graveled paths. Follow the Ponderosa Loop Trail for 0.1 mile to a sign that points the way to the Boulder Creek Trail. From this junction, the route heads west along

Fossilized tree trunks

a level grade for 0.2 mile to reach another trail junction. Turn right again before dropping gently into a broad valley to the north. Note how the ponderosa pines that grow in the vicinity of the visitor center give way to open meadows. Parks like this are ideal places to spot deer, elk, coyotes, and other species of wildlife that inhabit the area. These meadows are filled with flowers in the summertime; appropriately, *florissant* is French for "flowering."

After crossing Boulder Creek, the trail turns left at the intersection with Hornbek Wildlife Loop to continue west for 1 mile along a meadow's edge. This segment of the hike encounters a small stock pond and some fragile wetlands along the stream to the left. Some scattered aspens and Colorado blue spruce trees inhabit the edges of this meadow. At the head of this valley, the trail reaches a pile of house-size granite boulders, which early settlers erroneously named The

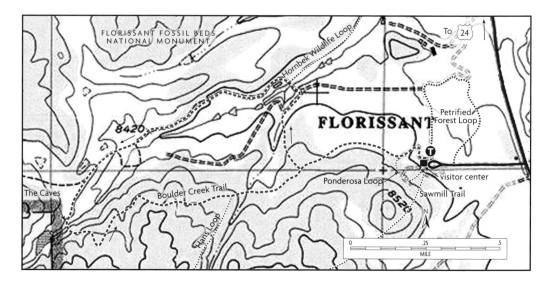

Caves. Visitors can explore the passageways here, and picnicking is permitted.

From here, it is 1.6 miles back to the visitor center by way of a return trail that climbs a low ridge to the east. This last stretch of the hike encounters forests of Douglas-firs, ponderosa pines, blue spruces, and aspens. About 0.6 mile from the visitor center, the trail intersects the Hans Loop. Turn left here. (The right-hand route follows the Sawmill Trail, which loops south through the woods before eventually returning to the visitor center.) In another 0.2 mile, the route rejoins the first segment of the hike, thereby completing a loop. From here, it is about 0.4 mile back to the visitor center.

Because any water found along this hike should be treated before drinking, it is best to bring your own. Keep in mind that fossil collecting in Florissant Fossil Beds National Monument is strictly prohibited.

41 FRENCH PASS

Distance: 7.6 miles round-trip
Difficulty: Moderate
Hiking time: 5 hours
Elevation: 10,500 to 12,046 feet
Management: Pike National Forest
Wilderness status: None
Season: June to October
Map: USGS Boreas Pass

Getting there: The French Pass Trail begins along the Michigan Creek Road at the north end of South Park. From Fairplay, drive northeast on US Highway 285 to the small enclave of Jefferson. Turn left or north on Michigan Creek Road (Forest Road 400) and drive to the Michigan Creek Campground. Continue another 2.25 miles on this graveled road to where the road crosses French Creek. Park just before the creek on the left side and look for a trail sign just inside the nearby forest.

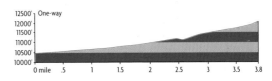

Alluding to the presence of nineteenth-century French trappers in the Colorado Rockies, French Pass provided one of the easier crossing points over the Continental Divide between South Park and the Blue River drainage to the north. Today, the little known French Pass Trail offers hikers moderately easy access to the Divide and to some memorable montane scenery.

From the small parking area on the left side of the Michigan Creek Road, the 3.8-mile French Pass Trail begins by following an old wagon road that serviced some turn-of-the-century mines above. Climbing gently most of the way, this section of the route is easy to follow as it cuts a wide swath through sporadic forest cover for about 2.4 miles, staying south of French Creek as it continues west.

Shortly beyond where the wagon route turns northwest, the French Pass Trail diverges right to drop into the drainage bottom. After crossing French Creek, it climbs a couple of hundred feet up the other side. Beyond this turnoff point, which is marked by some branches piled across the wagon road, the remaining 1.4 miles of the hike follows single-track trail.

After crossing French Creek and climbing up the far side of the drainage (there is one steep but short section in this ascent), the trail breaks out of the forest for good. Some stands of bristlecone pine and krummholz spruce populate this

At the summit of French Pass

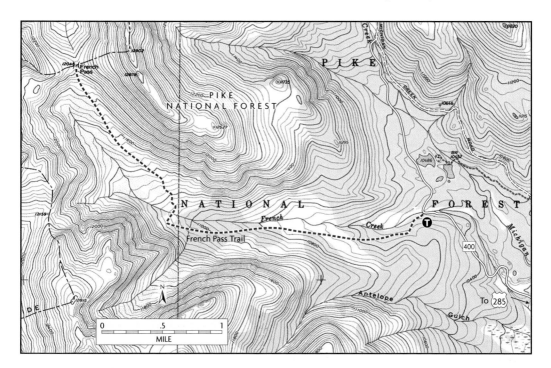

transition zone to alpine tundra. Beyond timber-line, the trail climbs easy-to-moderate grades toward its namesake pass. Although the lofty summits of Boreas and Bald Mountains were visible earlier in the hike, the treeless upper section of the trail provides unobstructed views of the peaks.

Boasting an elevation of 12,046 feet and situated at the northern end of the French Creek drainage, French Pass is marked by a large stone cairn and a sign. Vistas to the north take in Mount Guyot farther up the Continental Divide and into the upper reaches the Blue River drainage, home to Keystone, Breckenridge, and Frisco. The "French" in French Creek refers specifically to one early trapper, French Pete, who worked trap lines on both sides of the Divide.

Water is found in French Creek, but it should be treated before drinking. Watch for lightning and quickly deteriorating weather conditions in the higher reaches of this hike.

42   MOUNTS DEMOCRAT, LINCOLN, AND BROSS

Distance: 8.8-mile round-trip
Difficulty: Strenuous
Hiking time: 6 hours
Elevation: 12,000 to 14,286 feet
Management: Pike National Forest
Wilderness status: None
Season: July to September
Maps: USGS Climax, Alma

Getting there: The hike begins at Kite Lake. From Fairplay, drive nearly 6 miles north on Colorado Highway 9 to the town of Alma. Turn left in downtown Alma at the sign for Kite Lake and County Road 8, and follow this gravel road for 5.5 miles to the lake. The last 0.25 mile is steep enough that some cars might not make it. A day-use fee is charged at the trailhead. There is an overnight fee at the campground at Kite Lake, reputed to be the nation's highest-elevation campground.

Hiking to the top of three of Colorado's elite "fourteeners" in one day seems like a major undertaking, suitable only for a seasoned mountaineer. The summits of this lofty trio, however, are close enough to one another that a hiker of average strength and ability can do just that. Linked together by relatively straightforward ridge walks, Mount Democrat, Mount Lincoln, and Mount Bross are the crowning jewels of the Mosquito Range, which rises between the towns of Fairplay and Leadville.

Because Kite Lake is situated at 12,000 feet, hikers have a jump on this hike before they even leave their vehicles. From the trailhead, a well-used trail heads around the east side of the lake toward an alpine basin to the north. Within the first 0.5 mile, the route climbs past an old miner's cabin that is still fairly intact. It then angles northwest to begin switchbacking up to a saddle that connects Mount Democrat and Mount Cameron. After a mile of climbing, the route reaches the

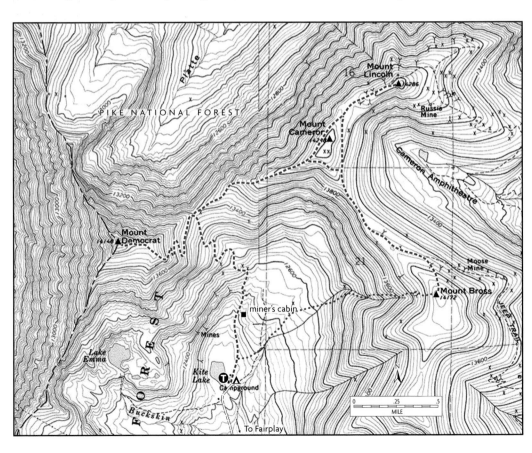

13,400-foot saddle, where it turns south to climb along the northeast ridge of Democrat. Many routes ascend this ridgeline—the result of thousands of climbers who have tackled the peak. Choose the one that looks best to you—they will all get you to the top. Within the 0.5 mile from the saddle to the 14,148-foot summit of Mount Democrat, you first reach a false summit, from which it is a short climb west to the top.

As evidenced by the remains of the fallen-down building near Democrat's summit, the Mosquito Range has been subject to heavy mining activity for many decades. Beginning in the 1870s, miners have poked and prodded at these mountains in search of gold, silver, and other metals such as molybdenum, which is used to toughen steel alloys and in fertilizers, dyes, and enamels. From the summit, you can plainly see the giant Climax Mine to the northwest, which has produced more than half of the world's supply of molybdenum over the past seventy years. Other sights include nearby 14,036-foot Mount Sherman, the Sawatch Mountains, and even the distant Maroon Bells to the west. To the north are 14,264-foot Quandary Peak and the Gore Range. Two more fourteeners—Grays and Torreys Peaks—are visible to the northeast. Rising beyond the expansive South Park to the southeast is 14,110-foot Pikes Peak.

After you've had your fill of the views from Mount Democrat, backtrack down to the saddle before climbing some 800 feet to the 14,238-foot summit of Mount Cameron. The route follows a well-defined trail that picks its way up the southwest ridge of the peak. Because Mount Cameron is considered part of Mount Lincoln, it does not count as an official fourteener. It is an interesting peak, however, simply for its broad and relatively smooth summit.

From Cameron, the route drops a short distance to the north before making an easy climb of only a few hundred feet to the summit of 14,286-foot Mount Lincoln. Home to plenty of mining activity, the slopes of Lincoln are dotted with old excavations, tailings piles, a few roads, and even some structures clinging to the mountain's south and east faces. The name, of course, reflects nineteenth-century praise for our sixteenth president. It is believed that Mount Democrat gained

Hikers descend Mount Democrat.

its name from miners from the South who didn't care much for the Republican Lincoln.

Nearby Mount Bross—the third summit of this hike—was named after William Bross, a mine owner from nearby Alma. To reach the 14,172-foot summit of Mount Bross from Lincoln, return to Mount Cameron and follow the trail that skirts along its east face to the saddle connecting Cameron and Bross. You might notice a 4WD road that nearly tops this saddle before climbing up to the summit of Bross. (Yes, this fourteener is still accessible by vehicle, but you probably won't see many drivers making the attempt.) After climbing 300 feet from the saddle to the top of Bross, you can enjoy the broad and level countenance of this summit.

The quickest way to return to your car is to descend directly from Bross to Kite Lake by way of a steep trail that drops down a gully on the mountain's west face. Quite dramatic in its vertical descent—2200 feet in 1 mile—this loose and rocky route might be too difficult for some, and the Forest Service discourages its use. The Forest Service advises that you circle back around to Cameron and hike down to the saddle that accesses Democrat. This milder descent adds about 1.5 miles to your hike, but bypasses the really steep terrain.

Although all three mountains are accessed by trails, this hike is not without hazards. First and foremost is the weather—watch for lightning and incoming precipitation. It is best to begin your hike at dawn so that you are off the peaks by early afternoon. Second, bring plenty of water, as none is available along the way. With much of the route above 13,000 feet, altitude sickness can pose a problem for some. Although these summits are relatively gentle, there are still drop-offs in some places. Exercise caution in these areas. Additionally, because much of this hike traverses privately held mining claims, liability concerns have caused access to the summits to be closed off. The town of Alma, however, devised a plan that allowed hikers' access to resume in 2007.

43 BUFFALO PEAKS LOOP

Distance: 11.5-mile loop
Difficulty: Moderate
Hiking time: 8 hours
Elevation: 9950 to 11,500 feet
Management: Pike National Forest
Wilderness status: Buffalo Peaks Wilderness Area
Season: July to September
Maps: USGS South Peak, Jones Hill

Getting there: From Fairplay, drive 4.8 miles south on US Highway 285 to Weston Pass Road (County Road 5). Turn right onto this good gravel road and drive 7 miles to its intersection with County Road 22. Bear right and drive another 2.9 miles to the signed trailhead.

The Buffalo Peaks are the centerpiece of the 43,410-acre Buffalo Peaks Wilderness Area. Following a pair of scenic drainages across the north slope of these prominent 13,000-foot mountains, the Rich Creek and Rough and Tumbling Creek Trails can be combined to create one memorable loop hike.

From the trailhead, the Rich Creek Trail immediately crosses the South Platte River, after which it intersects with the lower end of the Rough and Tumbling Creek Trail. Turn right at this trail intersection to follow Rich Creek upstream for nearly 6 miles—the trail crosses the stream three times in its first mile. At about 1.25 miles, the trail intersects a 0.8-mile side trail that turns right to access the Weston Pass Campground; near the 2-mile mark it reaches the remains of an old cabin. The surrounding forest along this first segment of the hike includes a mix of lodgepole pine, Engelmann spruce, subalpine fir, and aspen.

After climbing along an easy grade for the first 2 miles, the Rich Creek Trail begins to ascend more steeply. Some interesting vistas along this section look back down the drainage. After 3 miles, the route levels off again as it reaches an open park that follows the creek for the next couple of miles. Characterized by waist-high willows, this area provides vistas of nearby treeless ridges leading up to the higher Buffalo Peaks. Beaver ponds in this area have covered some of the trail. During periods of low water it is

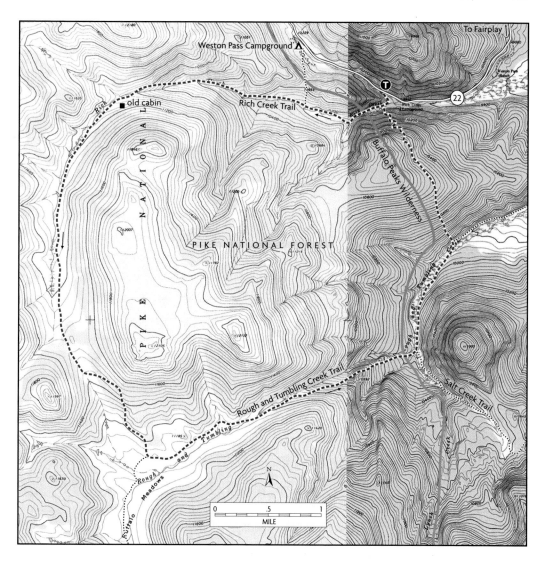

possible to cross the dams themselves. Otherwise you will need to cut through the thick willows to the other side. This open area is a good place to spot deer and elk in the early hours of the day. Other wildlife of the Buffalo Peaks area include bighorn sheep, which might occasionally be sighted around the higher reaches of the peaks.

After nearly 2 miles of easy climbing through this scenic valley, the Rich Creek Trail reaches the high point of the hike at an 11,500-foot saddle. From here, the trail drops easily into the upper portion of the Rough and Tumbling Creek drainage (named for a number of cascades and waterfalls found farther downstream), where it takes up the expansive Buffalo Meadows. The Rich Creek Trail ends at a junction with the Rough and Tumbling Creek Trail. While this hike turns left at this point, a right turn leads a couple of miles to a pass just west of the Buffalo Peaks.

Heading east from the Rich Creek Trail intersection, the Rough and Tumbling Creek Trail begins descending gently along its namesake drainage. The open environs of Buffalo Meadows eventually give way to timbered areas. About

The scenic Buffalo Peaks at sunset

2 miles past the Rich Creek Trail intersection, the Rough and Tumbling Creek Trail passes a right turn onto the Salt Creek Trail, which follows Lynch Creek upstream. Keep left at this junction as the route continues down Rough and Tumbling Creek before turning away from the stream to climb over a ridge to the north. In this ascent, the trail climbs moderately to gain about 400 feet in 1 mile. The trail then drops about 600 feet before intersecting with the start of the Rich Creek Trail and the trailhead.

Water is available along this hike, but it should be treated before drinking. Watch for lightning on the higher portions of this hike.

44 NOTCH MOUNTAIN

Distance: 10.6 miles round-trip
Difficulty: Strenuous
Hiking time: 7 hours
Elevation: 10,320 to 13,100 feet
Management: White River National Forest
Wilderness status: Holy Cross Wilderness Area
Season: July to September
Maps: USGS Minturn, Mount of the Holy Cross

Getting there: The hike to Notch Mountain begins at the Fall Creek trailhead, which is adjacent to the Half Moon Campground. From Vail, drive west on Interstate 70 to Minturn. Exit south onto US Highway 24, drive 4 miles to Tigiwon Road (Forest Road 707), turn right, and drive 8 miles to the trailhead at the end of this narrow, 2WD road. Because the Half Moon Trail (the route to the summit of Mount of the Holy Cross) also starts at this point, the parking lot can be crowded.

Mount of the Holy Cross may be the most fabled of Colorado's high mountain peaks. Featuring

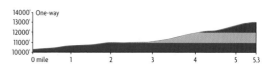

an enormous cross formed by two intersecting crevasses filled with snow for much of the year, this mystical mountain has attracted considerable interest for more than a century. While the 14,003-foot peak is a popular climb, the best place to actually view the cross is nearby Notch Mountain, which rises to the east.

This hike begins by heading south along the Fall Creek Trail, which traverses the eastern end of the Holy Cross Wilderness. Climbing along

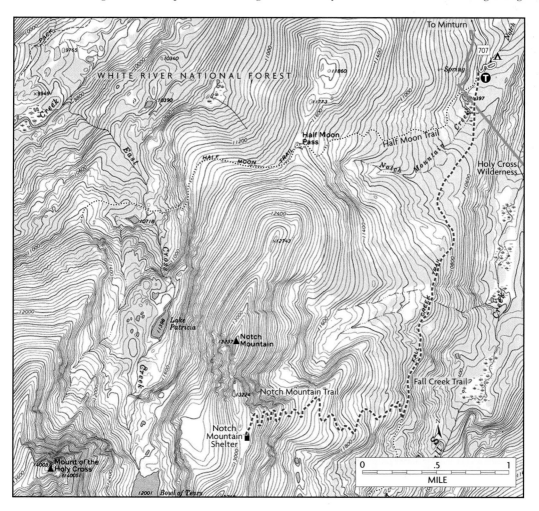

Stone cabin on the summit of Notch Mountain

easy-to-moderate grades, this first segment of the hike encounters nice forests of Engelmann spruce and subalpine fir. At the 2.5-mile mark, the Fall Creek Trail intersects the Notch Mountain Trail. After turning right at this junction, the route soon reaches timberline, beyond which it breaks into alpine tundra and continues up the east slope of Notch Mountain. Along this final segment of the hike, the route climbs strenuously to gain some 1900 feet in 2.8 miles. As you might expect, several switchbacks are encountered along the way. Be sure not to cut these switchbacks—damage to the fragile tundra can result.

Awaiting hikers at the trail's end is an unobstructed view of the east face of Mount of the Holy Cross. This singular scene has stirred a great many who have made the climb up Notch Mountain. From the time the first white men explored the Colorado Rockies, stories of this snowy cross spread. It was not until 1873, however, that excitement over the mountain really began to build. That was when nineteenth-century photographer William Henry Jackson reached the summit of Notch Mountain. The weather was cloudy that evening, so it was not until the following morning that he got his first glimpse of the cross. After snapping a now-famous photo, Jackson returned with concrete evidence that this incredible geologic feature actually existed. His photo has since spurred thousands to visit Notch Mountain, and religious pilgrimages and even tales of miraculous healings have continued into the twentieth century. A stone shelter was built in 1924 to accommodate visitors, and in 1929 the mountain gained national monument status. Although that designation was withdrawn in the 1950s, the shelter is listed on the National Register of Historic Places.

While the scene's natural beauty is an inspiration to visitors regardless of their religious beliefs, the views to the north, south, and east are equally stunning. Within this grand panorama you can see the rugged Gore Range, the Vail Ski Area (it looks puny from this high point), the Mosquito Range beyond the Leadville area, and the Sawatch Mountains as they stretch south through the Holy Cross Wilderness and on toward the Mount Massive and Collegiate Peaks Wilderness Areas beyond.

Lightning is a frequent hazard along the upper reaches of this hike and very little water is available, so be sure to bring plenty. Because of these factors, camping at the Notch Mountain shelter is discouraged. Dogs must be leashed at all times. A permit is required to enter the Holy Cross Wilderness, but there is no fee (as of 2007) and permits can be obtained when registering at the trailhead.

45 FANCY PASS

Distance: 8.8-mile loop
Difficulty: Strenuous
Hiking time: 6 hours
Elevation: 10,000 to 12,380 feet
Management: White River National Forest
Wilderness status: Holy Cross Wilderness Area
Season: July to September
Maps: USGS Mount of the Holy Cross, Mount Jackson

Getting there: From Minturn, drive 12 miles south on US Highway 24 to Homestake Road. Turn right and continue 7.8 miles to Missouri Lakes Road (Forest Service Road 704). Turn right again and drive 2.6 miles to

the signed trailhead. About 100 yards before reaching the Fancy Pass trailhead, you pass the Missouri Lakes trailhead, which marks the end of the trail portion of this hike.

The hike to Fancy Pass accesses some wonderful mountain terrain as well as a handful of pristine alpine lakes in the southern end of the Holy Cross Wilderness Area. A continuation of the route over nearby Missouri Pass adds miles and interest to the trip to make an 8.8-mile loop.

The 4.4-mile Fancy Pass Trail begins by climbing along a rerouted trail that eventually takes up the Fancy Creek drainage bottom. After 1.5 miles, the route levels off for a bit as it parallels Fancy Creek. Timber in the area includes lodgepole pines that grow side-by-side with Engelmann spruce and subalpine firs. Higher up, the forest becomes a strictly spruce-fir mix. Eventually, the trail climbs a moderate-to-strenuous grade to reach Fancy Lake 3.2 miles from the trailhead. Located at timberline, Fancy Lake offers a scenic respite before you tackle Fancy Pass above.

From Fancy Lake, the Fancy Pass Trail climbs a short distance to join an old road that heads over the pass itself. The old route to nearby Holy Cross City, this road is littered with the remains of nineteenth-century cabins, wagons, and an old mill. The Gold Park Milling and Mining Company built the road around the turn of the century. From the lake to 12,400-foot Fancy Pass is a climb of about 800 feet in about 0.5 mile. Beyond the pass the trail drops easily over the next 0.75 mile to the head of Cross Creek and the Treasure Vault Lake area. Here the route picks up the upper end of the 4.4-mile-long Missouri Lakes Trail, which in turn climbs a short distance—300 vertical feet in 0.3 mile—to 11,986-foot Missouri Pass.

From this second pass, the Missouri Lakes Trail drops steeply over the next 0.5 mile to reach the Missouri Lakes, which are scattered along the head of Missouri Creek. From here, the route drops down Missouri Creek along a mostly moderate grade. Some interesting cliff faces on the lower end of the trail add to the beauty of this hike. The route also passes several diversion pipelines that are part of the Homestake I water project. This development transfers water from Fancy and Missouri Creeks, as well as other streams, across the Continental Divide and on

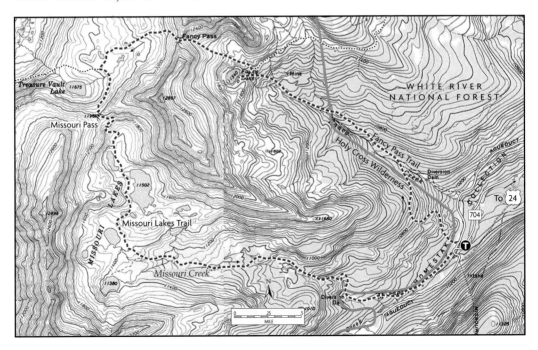

to thirsty residents of Front Range cities. Phase II of the Homestake project would tunnel farther west under the Holy Cross Wilderness to tap into the Cross Creek and Fall Creek drainages. It is thought that such a plan would dry up many wetland areas within the Holy Cross area, thereby compromising its wilderness characteristics. The Holy Cross Defense Fund is actively opposing Phase II of the Homestake project. After passing a diversion dam, the Missouri Lakes Trail soon parallels the Homestake aqueduct to return to a trailhead a short distance down the road from where you started.

Water is available along this hike, but treat it before drinking. Watch for lightning in the higher reaches, and be aware that snowfields often linger well into August along some stretches of trail. Use caution when crossing these places. Dogs must be leashed at all times. A permit is required to enter the Holy Cross Wilderness, but there is no fee (as of 2007) and permits can be obtained when registering at the trailhead.

Colorful Indian paintbrush blossoms

46 HAGERMAN TUNNEL

Distance: 5.5-mile loop
Difficulty: Easy
Hiking time: 3 hours
Elevation: 10,940 to 11,530 feet
Management: San Isabel National Forest
Wilderness status: Mount Massive Wilderness Area
Season: June to September
Maps: USGS Homestake Reservoir, Mount Massive

Getting there: This hike starts on Hagerman Pass Road near Turquoise Lake. From downtown Leadville, drive a few blocks west on US Highway 24. Turn right onto a paved road directly across from the entrance to the Colorado Mountain College. Follow this road west for 7.5 miles, past Turquoise Lake, to a rough but passable gravel road that bears left. This is Hagerman Pass Road (Forest Road 105); follow it 4.8 miles to the trailhead. Parking is available on the right and the trail takes off on the left.

For all their ruggedness, the Sawatch Mountains were far from impervious to man's endeavors during the nineteenth century. A good example of this is the old railroad grade that crosses the Continental Divide by way of the 2161-foot-long Hagerman Tunnel. Representing the labor of hundreds of immigrant laborers, this tunnel was

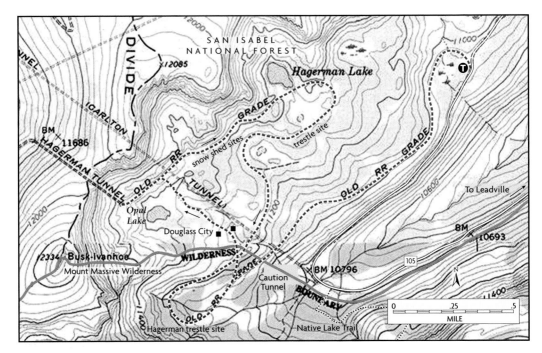

the highest railroad tunnel in the world at the time of its completion in 1887.

Be sure to read the interpretive sign at the trailhead, which describes the Colorado Midland Railroad and its successful attempt to cross the Continental Divide. Begun in the early 1880s, this was the first standard-gauge railroad to traverse the Colorado Rockies. With only 350 miles of track, however, the venture never made money. The trail to the tunnel follows the old railroad grade for part of the way. At the start, this means hiking through a lengthy cut in the bedrock. Old ties are strewn about, some still in place and others discarded to the side. In a little more than a mile, the grade reaches the first of two ravines that were once crossed by lengthy trestles. The Hagerman Trestle is no longer standing, but it is easy to visualize the 1100-foot-long, 84-foot-high structure as if it were still in place.

Where the trestle originally began, the main trail drops down to continue along the railroad route. Instead of following the trail, take a sharp right onto an old road that provides a shortcut to the next curve above. In 0.25 mile this shortcut trail crosses the railroad grade and then reaches the old townsite of Douglass City. Once a camp for

the mostly Italian workers who built the railroad and tunnel, Douglass City was as lively a community as any in the Rockies. Of course, it had its share of saloons—eight in all—and a dance hall, plus a post office. Today all that remains are some fallen-down log structures and scattered debris. From Douglass City, climb directly to the railroad route above. In this next 0.5 mile you pass Opal Lake to reach the final stretch of railroad, which approaches the tunnel entrance.

Like the trailhead and the Douglass City townsite, Hagerman Tunnel features an interpretive sign that explains the excavation's engineering and historical significance. Completed in 1887, the 2161-foot-long tunnel was in service for only a few years. It was replaced in 1891 by the much longer Busk-Ivanhoe Tunnel, whose entrance you drove past on the way to the trailhead. Interestingly, the Busk-Ivanhoe Tunnel was converted to auto traffic in 1922 and did not close until 1943. Vehicles now cross the Divide by way of Hagerman Pass a few miles beyond the trailhead. The Hagerman Tunnel entrance is partially blocked by rockslides, but it is still possible to enter. It is not advisable to do so, though, because of safety concerns. Looking in from the outside,

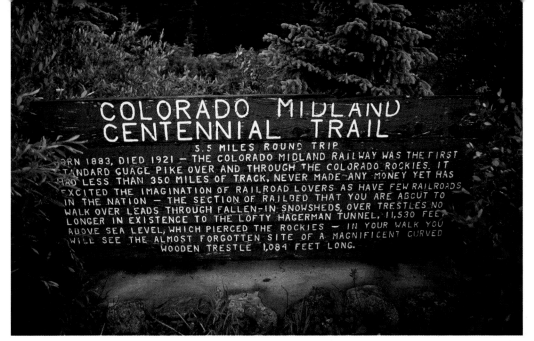

Interpretive sign along the hike to Hagerman Tunnel

you can see that snow and ice linger year-round in the tunnel's cool darkness.

So as not to miss other features of this hike, be sure to follow the railroad grade back down instead of taking the shortcut trail through Douglass City. Along the way the railroad passes beautiful Hagerman Lake and the sites of thirteen different snow sheds. These structures collapsed long ago, and little evidence of their existence remains. Farther on, the trail passes the site of a second trestle, which, like the Hagerman Trestle, has disappeared over the years. Within the next mile, the railroad grade meets the shortcut trail below Douglass City. Turn left and follow it down to the start of the Hagerman Trestle. At this point turn left again to return to the trailhead.

Water is available along this hike, but it should be treated before drinking. Lightning can be a problem, although this hike does not cross particularly exposed terrain.

47 MOUNT MASSIVE

Distance: 14 miles round-trip
Difficulty: Strenuous
Hiking time: 10 hours
Elevation: 10,100 to 14,421 feet
Management: San Isabel National Forest
Wilderness status: Mount Massive Wilderness Area
Season: July to September
Map: USGS Mount Massive

Getting there: From Leadville, drive 3 miles southwest on US Highway 24. Turn right onto County Road 300, drive 1.3 miles, and then turn left onto Halfmoon Creek Road (Forest

Road 110). Drive another 5.6 miles to the signed trailhead. Forest Road 110 is narrow and rough in places. Drive with caution.

Although Mount Massive is Colorado's second highest summit, with an elevation of 14,421 feet, it is readily accessible to hikers thanks to a 7-mile hiking route that climbs all the way to the summit. Like its neighbor, 14,433-foot Mount Elbert, the summit of Mount Massive provides some of the most impressive vistas to be found anywhere in the lower forty-eight. The hikes up both peaks begin at adjacent trailheads on Half-moon Creek Road.

The hike starts by following the much-touted Colorado Trail north for 3 miles, climbing 1100 feet on mostly easy grades. As the trail contours around to Mount Massive's east slope, it crosses a few minor drainages. Timbered areas of lodge-pole pine are common at the lower elevations. As the trail climbs, however, the forest changes to a mix of Engelmann spruce and subalpine fir. Shortly after reaching the 11,000-foot level, the Colorado Trail meets the 4-mile-long Mount Massive Trail, which this hike follows west to complete the final ascent to the top. Well defined after years of heavy use, the Mount Massive Trail climbs steeply, especially as it nears the

top. This second segment of the hike gains 3200 feet, mostly above timberline. Be sure to note the variety of low-profile plants that grow in these alpine tundra areas. Stay on the trail, as these areas are very fragile. As you near the top, it can be difficult to pick out the actual summit. Stretching across 3 miles, Mount Massive's crest includes several false summits. By sticking to the trail, however, you will eventually wind up on the tallest point of the mountain.

While nearby Mount Elbert is taller than Mount Massive, the two peaks were once at the center of a controversy that questioned their rankings as the state's tallest and second tallest peaks. Elbert eventually won out, but by only 12 feet. The views from Massive's summit are commanding, to say the least. To the east lie Leadville and the Mosquito Range with its 13,000- and 14,000-foot peaks. The Arkansas River Valley stretches south, as does the Collegiate Range. North is the Holy Cross Wilderness Area, and west is the Hunter–Fryingpan Wilderness. Of course, the vistas extend far beyond these locales as well.

Water is found in places along the first half of this hike, but it should be treated before drinking. Watch for lightning on the peak, especially on summer afternoons. To best avoid such hazards,

On the summit of Mount Massive

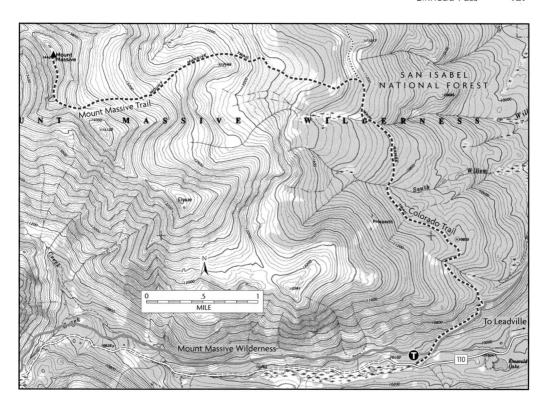

plan to complete your hike early. As is true for all fourteeners in Colorado, weather conditions can deteriorate rapidly on Mount Massive. Because this hike is popular, you might want to plan your trip for a weekday or after the Labor Day weekend.

48 ELKHEAD PASS

Distance: 9 miles round-trip
Difficulty: Strenuous
Hiking time: 7 hours
Elevation: 9660 to 13,220 feet
Management: San Isabel National Forest
Wilderness status: Collegiate Peaks Wilderness Area
Season: July to September
Maps: USGS Mount Harvard, Winfield

Getting there: This hike follows the Missouri Gulch Trail, which begins near the historic townsite of Vicksburg. To reach the trailhead, drive 19 miles south from Leadville on US Highway 24 to the turnoff for County Road

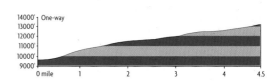

390, which becomes Forest Road 120. Follow this good graveled road west for 7.8 miles to the signed trailhead.

Elkhead Pass, the state's second highest saddle, is a real grunt of a hike—but worth every bit of the effort. Located on the north end of the Collegiate Peaks Wilderness, this route climbs to the head of Missouri Gulch, where it reveals some

spectacular views. Additionally, three fourteeners are located within the vicinity of the pass. While the round-trip distance listed in the information block above covers only the hike to the pass, it is a relatively simple matter to also scramble up two of these elite peaks, Mounts Belford and Oxford.

After crossing Clear Creek a short distance from the trailhead, the Missouri Gulch Trail begins

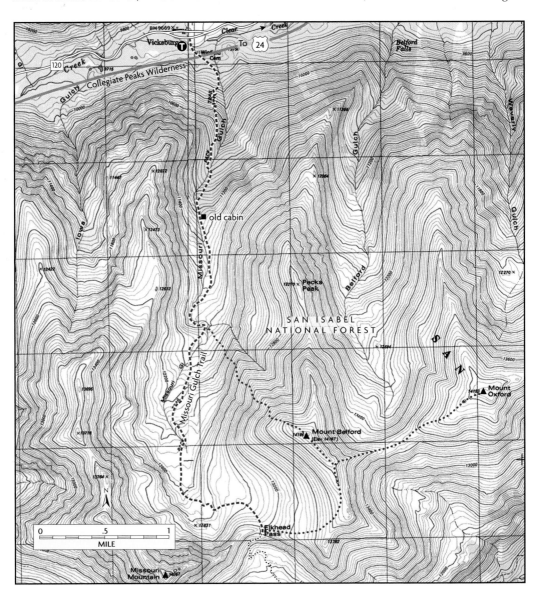

climbing strenuously up a series of switchbacks; the route climbs 1300 feet in the first 1.25 miles. The surrounding forest is a patchy mix of aspen, lodgepole pine, Engelmann spruce, and fir. The trail eventually levels off to climb along more moderate grades, and at about 2 miles in it crosses a creek where a trail sign points the way to the creek's left bank. The route then climbs up the bottom of the gulch, which has been regularly scoured by avalanches, and enters a thick stand of spruce and fir forest. As timberline draws closer, the trail encounters an old cabin. A relic of the region's mining heritage, this structure has fallen into disrepair. Nearby, you might spot some bristlecone pines.

Beyond the cabin, the trail soon breaks out into an open basin. While a few scattered pockets of krummholz trees lie ahead, the trail from here on out mostly crosses alpine tundra. After climbing easily through the first basin, the trail forks. While this hike turns right to continue up to Elkhead Pass, a left turn heads directly to the summit of Mount Belford. If your only goal is to bag the fourteener, and you do not mind extremely steep climbing, then take this route and forget about Elkhead Pass. However, most hikers who are intent on climbing the peak find it easier to get to the pass first and then head toward the summit from there.

From the trail junction, the Missouri Gulch Trail makes a short and somewhat strenuous climb to access the next basin. After this climb, the grade levels off for a while as the trail continues south toward the pass. It then climbs again, and again levels off for a bit. In this stair-step manner, the pass is eventually reached. You must look for cairns that mark the way in one rocky area, but the route is otherwise clearly visible.

Situated at 13,220 feet, Elkhead Pass separates Missouri Gulch to the north from Missouri Basin to the south. From the pass, you gain a commanding view not only of Missouri Basin, but also of a host of tall peaks to the south of the basin and north of the Clear Creek drainage. The Missouri Gulch Trail continues into the basin, where it turns east to drop down Pine Creek.

Despite its lofty altitude, Elkhead Pass is actually the low point of a ridge that includes three 14,000-foot peaks: 14,067-foot Missouri Peak,

The trail to Elkhead Pass

just west of the pass; 14,197-foot Mount Belford, less than a mile east; and 14,153-foot Mount Oxford, which is connected to Mount Belford by a ridge that runs to the east. Although climbing Missouri Peak from Elkhead Pass involves some scrambling, the climb up Mount Belford (and Mount Oxford beyond if you are so inclined) is a relatively easy endeavor: from the pass the route climbs about 1000 feet to reach the summit in only 1 mile. The breathtaking views from the summit take in the Maroon Bells–Snowmass Wilderness far to the west and Pikes Peak to the east.

Lightning poses a danger at the pass and on the nearby summits, so plan to complete your hike earlier in the day during the summer. Water is available along most of the Missouri Gulch Trail, but it should be treated before drinking. As evidenced by the summit register on Mount Belford, this hike is very popular, especially on holiday weekends.

49 BROWNS CABIN

Distance: 8.8 miles round-trip
Difficulty: Strenuous
Hiking time: 6 hours
Elevation: 9900 to 12,040 feet
Management: San Isabel National Forest, Gunnison National Forest
Wilderness status: Collegiate Peaks Wilderness Area
Season: July to September
Map: USGS Mount Yale

Getting there: The hike to Browns Cabin begins at the Denny Creek trailhead on Cottonwood Pass Road (County Road 306). From downtown Buena Vista, drive 12 miles west to the trailhead located about 1 mile beyond the Collegiate Peaks Campground.

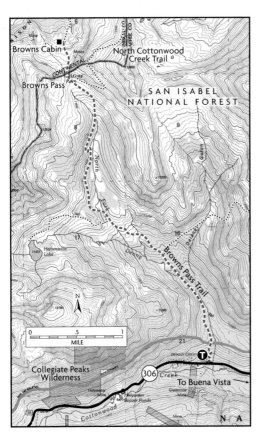

The hike to Browns Pass and nearby Browns Cabin offers a pleasurable way to enjoy the southern portion of the Collegiate Mountain Range. In addition to the incredible scenery you would expect to find among this collection of peaks, this excursion offers a vivid taste of Colorado's mining history.

Following the Browns Pass Trail for the entire way, this hike climbs steadily north for 4 miles to the 12,040-foot pass, then drops for a short distance into the Texas Creek drainage, where it reaches Browns Cabin. Small but beautiful Denny Creek runs alongside the trail for the first mile. Beyond the 1-mile mark, the route crosses the stream to continue north, while the creek itself bends to the northwest. The trail climbs along easy-to-moderate grades for the first 2 miles. Forests at this elevation include lodgepole pine, Engelmann spruce, and subalpine fir, along with a few stands of aspen. About 2 miles in, a side trail branches left to continue for another mile to Hartenstein Lake, a nice destination in its own right. Located at an elevation of 11,451 feet, the lake is close to timberline.

Beyond the turnoff for Hartenstein Lake, the Browns Pass Trail continues to climb—first at an easy pace, but soon along a moderately steep ascent. In the 2-mile stretch from the Hartenstein Lake Trail junction to the pass, the route climbs 900 feet. Timberline is reached around the 11,600-foot level, so much of this portion of the hike traverses alpine tundra. Many species

Detail of the historic Browns Cabin

of wildflowers grow here in late July and early August.

Once on top of the pass, which is on the Continental Divide, you can enjoy a grand view—especially to the north. Rising along the far side of the Texas Creek drainage are the Three Apostles—a trio of summits that top 13,900 feet. Also to the north is 14,420-foot Mount Harvard. Although it rises 2.5 miles southeast of Browns Pass, 14,196-foot Mount Yale is not visible from the hike. Heading east from Browns Pass is the North Cottonwood Creek Trail. After climbing some 500 feet above the pass, this route drops down the North Cottonwood Creek drainage to pass Kroenke Lake, situated at 11,500 feet, in a little more than 2 miles. About 6 miles from the pass, the North Cottonwood Creek Trail ends at a trailhead just east of the wilderness.

From Browns Pass, the Browns Pass Trail crosses north into the Gunnison National Forest, then drops easily—about 300 feet in less than 0.5 mile—to reach Browns Cabin. Nestled in the trees just below timberline, this two-story structure dates back to the mining boom of the late nineteenth century. Because it has been maintained over the years, the building still provides shelter for overnight hikers. This hike turns around at the cabin, although the Browns Pass Trail continues northward for a little more than a mile farther to reach the Texas Creek Trail, which follows its namesake west to east.

Water is available along this hike, but it should be treated before drinking. Watch for lightning in the vicinity of the pass and in other exposed areas.

50 WATERDOG LAKES

Distance: 4 miles round-trip
Difficulty: Strenuous
Hiking time: 3 hours
Elevation: 10,200 to 11,475 feet
Management: San Isabel National Forest
Wilderness status: None
Season: June to September
Map: USGS Garfield

Getting there: From the town of Poncha Springs, drive west on US Highway 50 for 15 miles. Park in a large pulloff area on the left and look for the signed trailhead located in the woods on the right side of the road. The trailhead is about 0.25 mile east of the turnoff for the Monarch Park Campground.

For a short but sweet hike in the Monarch Pass area, try the 2-mile trail to Waterdog Lakes. Located near timberline, these two lakes are surrounded by scenic alpine ridges. In addition, they offer some good fishing opportunities: Mackinaw trout are regularly stocked and brook trout are caught there as well.

The trail first follows a small creek upstream for a short distance before bearing left to contour along the hillside above the highway. Some beautiful old-growth spruce and fir trees line the creek. Upon turning onto the drier hillside, however, the trail enters a mix of lodgepole pine, Engelmann spruce, and fir. After paralleling the highway for about 0.3 mile, the trail turns right onto an old 4WD road that is now closed to vehicles.

Once the route turns onto this old road, it climbs along a mostly moderate grade for the

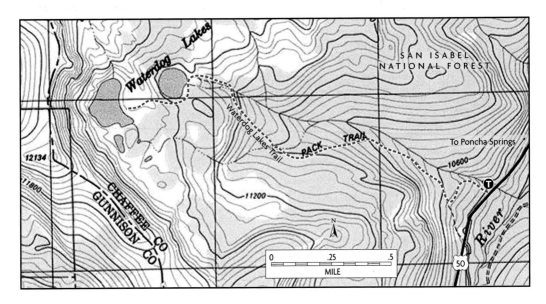

Waterdog Lakes

next 0.5 mile or so before leveling off. In this middle portion of the hike, the trail passes beneath a small powerline that is still in use. In its last 0.5 mile, the trail climbs a strenuous grade that is loose and rocky in places to reach the first of the two Waterdog Lakes. Upper Waterdog Lake is located about 0.3 mile beyond Lower Waterdog Lake. Because it is slightly higher, the upper lake features some krummholz growth along its shore. At this elevation of nearly 11,500 feet, the forest mix is strictly spruce and fir, with no lodgepole pines in sight. Forming the western and northern skylines above the lakes are some treeless alpine ridges that carry the Continental Divide northward.

Water is available along this hike, but it should be treated before drinking. Lightning can pose a threat, although this route is not too exposed.

51   LOST MAN LAKE

Distance: 8.8 miles one-way
Difficulty: Strenuous
Hiking time: 6 hours
Elevation: 11,500 to 12,800 feet
Management: White River National Forest
Wilderness status: Hunter–Fryingpan Wilderness Area
Season: July to September
Maps: USGS Mount Champion, Independence Pass

Getting there: To reach the start of the Lost Man Lake hike, from Aspen drive 18.5 miles east on Colorado Highway 82 to the upper trailhead. The end of the hike is located 14

miles east of Aspen on Colorado Highway 82, directly across from the Lost Man Campground.

Picking up where the Collegiate Peaks and Mount Massive Wilderness Areas leave off, the Hunter–Fryingpan Wilderness encompasses an 82,580-acre parcel of high mountain terrain along the western slope of the Sawatch Range.

In addition to a number of 13,000-foot peaks and timberlands, this wilderness includes many beautiful streams and lakes. The Lost Man Trail visits two of these lakes while exploring a pair of drainages. Stretching between two trailheads located along the highway leading over Independence Pass, this highly scenic hiking route covers 8.8 miles as it loops north through the heart of the Hunter–Fryingpan Wilderness.

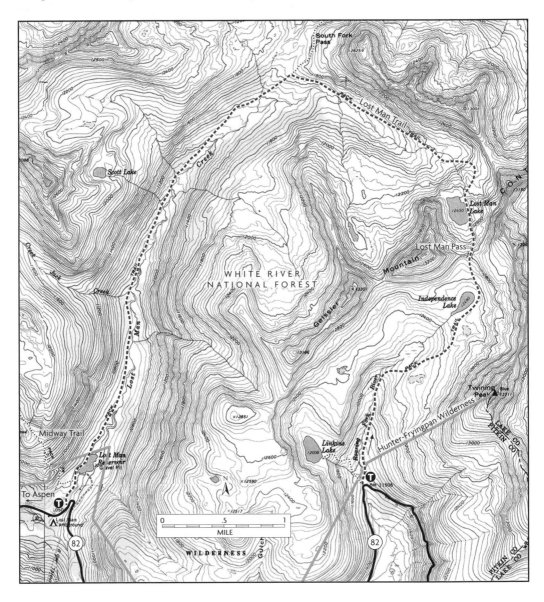

Along the Lost Man Trail

From the upper trailhead, the Lost Man Trail begins by following the Roaring Fork River—at this point a small stream—north through a scenic alpine valley. While most of this first segment of the trail is easy to follow, some stretches can be faint—look for rock cairns that mark the way in these areas. After climbing nearly 1000 feet in 2 miles, the trail reaches Independence Lake. The trail then climbs another 300 feet or so in less than 0.5 mile to reach Lost Man Pass. At 12,800 feet this pass is the highpoint of the hike. While the scenery is memorable all along this hike, the vistas from the pass are tremendous. At this point the Continental Divide is less than 0.5 mile to the east.

From Lost Man Pass, the Lost Man Trail drops some 350 feet in 0.5 mile to reach the hike's second alpine jewel, Lost Man Lake. Situated at an elevation of 12,450 feet, Lost Man Lake is nestled in an exceptionally scenic glacial cirque that is entirely above timberline. Several suitable camping sites can be found here, but remember to camp at least 100 feet away from the lake and the stream, and fires are not permitted. To avoid ecological damage, you might want to camp farther down in the trees. Fishing at the lake is reported to be good.

Beyond Lost Man Lake, the route takes up a creek by the same name, which it follows for 2 miles northwest to an intersection with the South Fork Pass Trail. This side route climbs a couple of hundred feet to the top of South Fork Pass. It then drops north to follow the South Fork of the Fryingpan River to reach Deadman Lake 2 miles from the Lost Man Trail junction. Situated near the 11,000-foot level, Deadman Lake is a nice destination should you want to extend your hike a bit. From there, the South Fork Pass Trail continues for another 3.5 miles before ending at a trailhead north of the wilderness.

After keeping left at the South Fork Pass trail junction, continue downstream along the Lost Man Trail for another 4 miles to the trailhead. Descending gently, this last stretch of the hike follows Lost Man Creek closely. Within the last 0.5 mile, the route passes the diminutive Lost Man Reservoir and the turnoff for the Midway Trail, which heads northwest over 11,841-foot Midway Pass before dropping to Midway Creek. Midway Creek, in turn, feeds into Hunter Creek in the western portion of the wilderness. The start of this hike is located 4.5 miles up Colorado Highway 82.

Water is found along this hike, but it should be treated before drinking. Watch for lightning during summer afternoons, especially above timberline.

52 SNOWMASS LAKE

Distance: 17 miles one-way
Difficulty: Strenuous
Hiking time: 2 days
Elevation: 9550 to 12,462 feet
Management: White River National Forest
Wilderness status: Maroon Bells–Snowmass Wilderness Area
Season: July to September
Maps: USGS Maroon Bells, Snowmass Mountain, Capitol Peak

Getting there: To begin this hike, drive 0.5 mile west from Aspen on Colorado Highway 82 to the roundabout. Go around it to Maroon Creek Road. Turn south and drive 9.5 miles to the trailhead at the upper parking lot. To reach the end of this hike, drive 6 miles west of Aspen on Colorado Highway 82 and turn left onto Brush Creek Road. Drive 5.5 miles to Divide Road. Turn right and follow the Divide Road to its end. A high-clearance 2WD vehicle may be required.

The Maroon Bells–Snowmass Wilderness is one of the most popular wilderness areas in Colorado, and for good reason. Several fourteeners highlight this 181,138-acre wilderness, including what are likely the most photographed peaks in the state—the Maroon Bells. A nice overnight hike that accesses the heart of this wilderness area visits Crater Lake before crossing west over Buckskin Gulch to Snowmass Lake. The route then drops north along Snowmass Creek to end near Snowmass Village.

From the trailhead on Maroon Creek Road, this hike follows the Maroon–Snowmass Trail southwest for 1.75 miles to scenic Crater Lake. In this first segment, the route passes Maroon Lake as it gains about 500 feet along a mostly moderate grade. Extensive stands of aspen in the area make this a colorful autumn excursion. Additionally, views of the stunning Maroon Bells, which rise about a mile southwest of Crater Lake, can be enjoyed throughout. Sometimes referred to as the Deadly Bells, these two 14,000-foot summits of crumbling sedimentary rock have served as the backdrop for fatal climbing accidents on

numerous occasions. For hikers following established trails, however, these mountains are anything but a threat. Their distinctive layers of purplish rock, combined with their rugged outlines, make them two of the most recognizable mountains in the nation.

Near Crater Lake, the West Maroon Pass Trail branches off to head south, while the Maroon–Snowmass Trail begins climbing west along Minnehaha Gulch toward Buckskin Pass—the highpoint of the hike. In the next 3 miles, the route climbs from an elevation of 9580 feet to 12,462 feet. Grades along this ascent are mostly moderate, although the trail becomes steeper as it draws closer to the pass. Less than a mile before reaching Buckskin Pass, the Maroon–Snowmass Trail intersects with the turnoff for Willow Pass. After topping Willow Pass, this trail drops to Willow Lake before traversing another saddle and entering the East Snowmass Creek drainage. Known as the East Snowmass Trail, that route eventually ends at Snowmass Falls Ranch.

The views from Buckskin Pass are outstanding. To the west stands 14,092-foot Snowmass Mountain, with its obvious snow-filled basin. Rising 2 miles to the north of Snowmass is 14,130-foot Capitol Peak. Like Snowmass, Capitol is easily recognizable from a distance. Characteristically light in color, this prism-shaped rock is unmistakable thanks to its steep slopes and pronounced summit. Named by the Hayden Survey, the peak was thought to resemble the

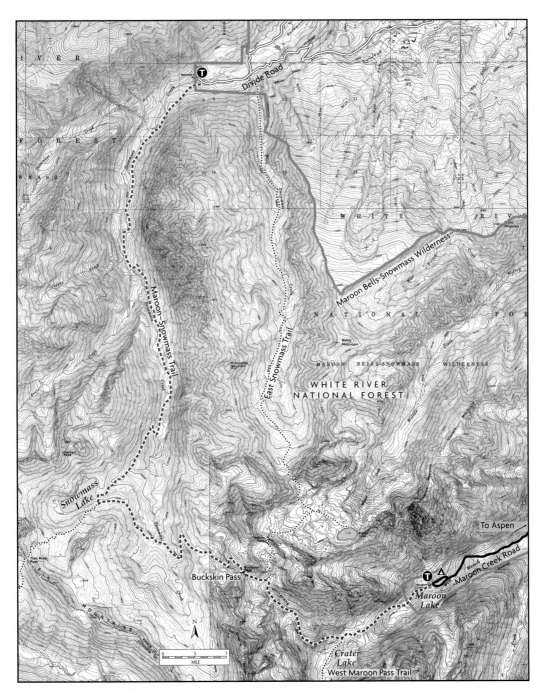

U.S. Capitol building. One of the most difficult fourteeners to climb, Capitol Peak was not conquered until 1909.

Beyond Buckskin Pass, the Maroon–Snowmass Trail drops 1600 feet over the next 3 miles to reach Snowmass Creek. After crossing the creek,

The Maroon Bells rise above Crater Lake.

the route climbs 200 feet over the next mile to reach Snowmass Lake, the largest of all lakes in the Maroon Bells–Snowmass Wilderness. Snowmass Lake is an incredibly popular destination for backpackers, and campfires are prohibited within 0.25 mile of its shores. Although stopping here for the night means sharing the area with plenty of other campers, the lake does mark the halfway point for this hike.

From Snowmass Lake, continue following the Snowmass Creek drainage north. About 2 miles north of Snowmass Lake, the trail passes a couple of beaver ponds where it crosses the creek via a ford just below a large logjam. From this point, the trail follows closely along the east side of the creek for the remaining 6.5 miles to the Snowmass Falls Ranch trailhead. In this last segment the trail drops 2600 feet along easy-to-moderate grades.

Watch for lightning in the vicinity of Buckskin Pass and along other high portions of this hike. Although water is found along much of the route, be sure to treat it before drinking. Given the popularity of this hike (the Forest Service claims this is one of the most heavily backpacked trails in Colorado), you might want to plan your trip for during the week or after Labor Day.

53 ELECTRIC PASS

Distance: 11 miles round-trip
Difficulty: Strenuous
Hiking time: 8 hours
Elevation: 9880 to 13,500 feet
Management: White River National Forest
Wilderness status: Maroon Bells–Snowmass Wilderness Area
Season: July to September
Map: USGS Hayden Peak

Getting there: From Aspen, drive 0.5 mile west on Colorado Highway 82 to the roundabout. Go around it to Castle Creek Road (Forest Road 102). Follow this paved route 12 miles south to a gravel road that turns right. Follow this route for 0.6 mile to the trailhead at the road's end.

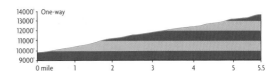

Accessing the summits of the Maroon Bells, Snowmass Mountain, and other lofty peaks in the Elk Mountains would be the subject of another book entirely, but it is possible to hike established trails to a variety of vantage points that put you on virtually the same level as nearby 13,000- and 14,000-foot summits. One such vantage point is 13,500-foot Electric Pass, considered Colorado's highest trail-accessible pass.

Setting out among beautiful aspen forests, this hike follows the Cathedral Lake Trail as it climbs along Pine Creek. Because this first stretch of the trail climbs 2000 feet in 3.2 miles, you can expect a variety of grade changes, as well as some level areas. The first mile of the route climbs at a mostly moderate pace to reach a basin where it then levels off somewhat. After breaking out of the aspens, the trail begins traversing open meadows and rockslide areas. After the 2-mile mark, it reaches the head of the first basin, where a series of short but very steep switchbacks climb to the basin above. Although there is much more climbing to come, this is by far the most difficult part of the hike.

The rugged Elk Mountains as seen from Electric Pass

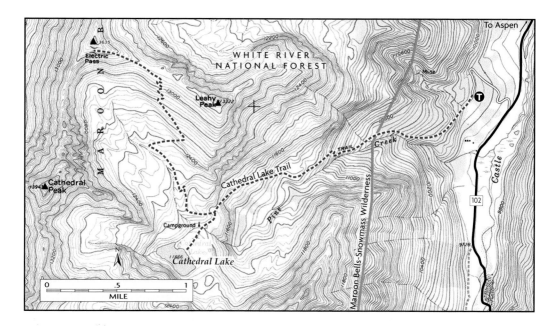

Shortly after topping the switchbacks, the trail reaches a signed fork in the trail. While the right-hand trail heads on to Electric Pass, the route to the left continues for another 0.4 mile to Cathedral Lake. Situated at an elevation of 11,866 feet, Cathedral Lake is a popular destination for day hikers and backpackers alike. Situated above treeline and surrounded by rugged summits—the most imposing of which is 13,943-foot Cathedral Peak—Cathedral Lake is a terrific destination in itself. Because of its popularity, however, campfires are prohibited within 0.25 mile of the lake.

Soon after turning right at the trail junction, the route to Electric Pass reaches timberline, then continues on through waist-high willows. Like the aspens below, the willow bushes put on a showy display of colors in the fall. After reaching a second turnoff for Cathedral Lake, the trail to the pass bends northward to head into a basin above. While the route climbs another 1600 feet in the next 1.5 miles, the going is surprisingly easy. As the trail makes its way toward Electric Pass, it passes beneath the crumbling summit of Cathedral Peak, below which is an extensive rock glacier. Eventually, the trail begins switchbacking up the east side of the basin, where it reaches a high ridge that extends southeast to 13,322-foot

Leahy Peak. From the ridge top, you can look into the American Lake area, which sits above the Castle Creek drainage to the east. From the north end of this ridge, the trail skirts along the rocky south face of 13,635-foot Electric Pass Peak to eventually reach Electric Pass.

From the pass you can look directly west into Cataract Creek, which is part of the Conundrum Creek drainage. Rising beyond this canyon is the unmistakable outline of the Maroon Bells. True to their name, these summits sport a purplish tint that characterizes the Maroon Formation. Beyond the Bells you can make out Snowmass Mountain with its extensive snowfield, as well as many other peaks. Cathedral Peak dominates the skyline directly south of the pass, obscuring the view of 14,265-foot Castle Peak, which sits directly behind it, though Castle Peak is visible along much of the trail leading up to the pass. Farther south, several slightly lesser peaks stand guard over passes that lead to the Crested Butte area. To the east you can make out the Sawatch Mountains, as well as numerous other ranges.

As the name suggests, lightning can pose an extreme danger on Electric Pass. All water along this hike should be treated before drinking. Expect some crowds on weekends and holidays.

54 LAMPHIER LAKE

Distance: 6 miles round-trip
Difficulty: Moderate
Hiking time: 4 hours
Elevation: 10,030 to 11,720 feet
Management: Gunnison National Forest
Wilderness status: Fossil Ridge Wilderness Area
Season: July to September
Map: USGS Fairview Peak

Getting there: From Gunnison, follow US Highway 50 east to Parlin—a distance of about 12 miles. Turn left and drive 8.5 miles northeast to Ohio City. Turn left again and drive 7 miles north on Forest Road 771 (this road is narrow and rough in places, so use caution) to the Gold Creek Campground. The trailhead is just north of the campground. A small parking area is provided.

Nestled just below timberline, Lamphier Lake is the destination of this nice hike into the 33,060-acre Fossil Ridge Wilderness Area. Not only is the lake particularly scenic, but the fishing can be good as well.

Following the South Lottis Trail, the hike to Lamphier Lake begins by entering the Fossil Ridge Wilderness and then ascending easily among timbered areas of lodgepole pine, Engelmann spruce, and subalpine fir. Nearly a mile in, the route crosses Lamphier Creek and continues along the west bank of the stream. This segment of the hike soon climbs at a more moderate rate as it ascends the drainage bottom. Near the halfway mark the route pulls away from the creek a bit and follows closely along the foot of the drainage's steep west side. This rocky face is actually the eastern end of 12,749-foot Fossil Mountain and Fossil Ridge, which stretches to the west. Consisting of limestone that was formed during the Paleozoic era, Fossil Ridge is true to its name.

Within the last mile to the lake, the South Lottis Trail crosses Lamphier Creek again, climbs a final pitch of moderately steep terrain, and turns west to reach the east shore of Lamphier Lake.

Nestled in a glacial basin, the lake is surrounded by 12,985-foot Square Top Mountain to the west and rocky ridges to the north and south. Cut precisely into the horizon just north of the lake is 12,167-foot Gunsight Pass. From Lamphier Lake, the South Lottis Trail climbs for another mile before topping Gunsight Pass. From there, it drops into its namesake drainage to reach the

Plant along the trail to Lamphier Lake

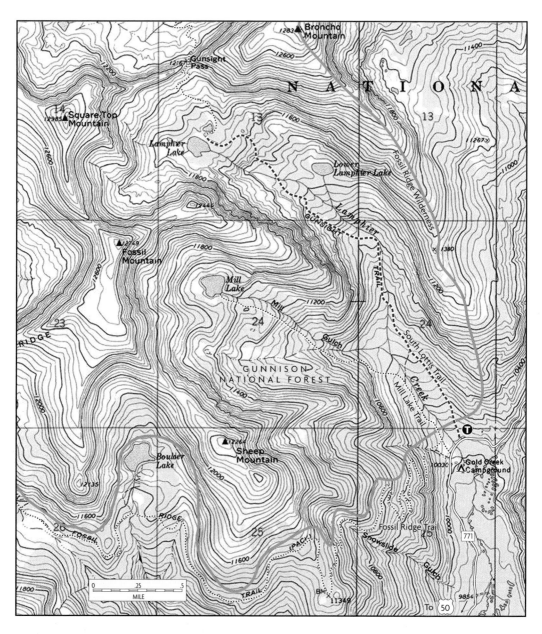

Lottis Creek Campground on Taylor River Road. From end to end, the South Lottis Trail covers 10 miles along the eastern end of the Fossil Ridge Wilderness.

Established with the passage of the Colorado Wilderness Act of 1993, the Fossil Ridge Wilderness encompasses part of a mountainous area long known to locals for its recreational opportunities. Because the area is popular with trail-bike enthusiasts as well as hikers, other portions of the Fossil Ridge area were set aside as the Fossil Ridge Recreation Management Area. Existing trails in the 43,900-acre management area are open to off-road vehicles, but it has been withdrawn from all future mining and timber harvesting activities.

Water is found along this hike, but it should be treated before drinking. Lightning can pose a threat during summer thunderstorms, although the hike never traverses especially exposed terrain. Should you plan to hike on to Gunsight Pass, however, the danger increases greatly.

55 SILVER BASIN

Distance: 13.5-mile loop
Difficulty: Moderate
Hiking time: 2 days
Elevation: 8640 to 10,250 feet
Management: Gunnison National Forest
Wilderness status: Raggeds Wilderness Area
Season: July to September
Maps: USGS Marcellina Mountain, Anthracite Range

Getting there: From Crested Butte, drive 11.5 miles west on Kebler Pass Road (County Road 12) to the signed turnoff for Horseranch Park. Drive north on this rough but passable dirt road for 0.3 mile to the trailhead at road's end.

Rising along the eastern end of the Raggeds Wilderness, the Ruby Mountain Range makes a colorful backdrop for this loop hike, which follows the Silver Basin and Dark Canyon Trails.

This hike begins by following the south end of the Dark Canyon Trail for 2 miles to its signed intersection with the Silver Basin Trail. Originally a 4WD road, this portion of the Dark Canyon Trail is easy to follow as it is well marked and mostly level. Because this trail encounters many nice aspen stands along the way, it is especially scenic in the fall. Nice views of Marcellina Mountain to the west and the Beckwith Peaks to the southwest can be enjoyed.

At the Dark Canyon and Silver Basin trail intersection, turn right to follow the Silver Basin Trail as it heads toward the foot of the Ruby Mountains. A short distance beyond this turn, the route enters the Raggeds Wilderness Area, and less than 0.3 mile from the junction, it reaches a second intersection. A right turn at this point leads south to Lake Irwin, while the Silver Basin Trail continues straight ahead and soon begins climbing along a more moderate grade. As the trail gains in elevation, additional views of the West Elk Wilderness to the south open up, as do vistas of the Ruby Range directly east. From this proximity, it is easy to see how these mountains got their name. Characterized by shades of deep red, the Ruby Range is composed of the same Maroon Formation that gives the Maroon Bells their distinctive color.

In the first 2 miles following the turnoff from the Dark Canyon Trail, the Silver Basin Trail climbs 1200 feet to reach this hike's high point of 10,250 feet. In this segment the route crosses two forks of Gold Creek that flow west from Gold Basin. It then reaches Silver Basin itself. Graced by numerous species of wildflowers, Silver Basin is made all the more scenic by the up-close views it affords of the Ruby Range directly east. The highest of these peaks is 13,058-foot Mount Owens, but several other summits in the range easily top the 12,000-foot mark. Of course, other portions of the Raggeds Wilderness are visible from Silver Basin as well. Of particular interest is the deep canyon to the west through which Ruby Anthracite Creek flows. Adding a historical footnote

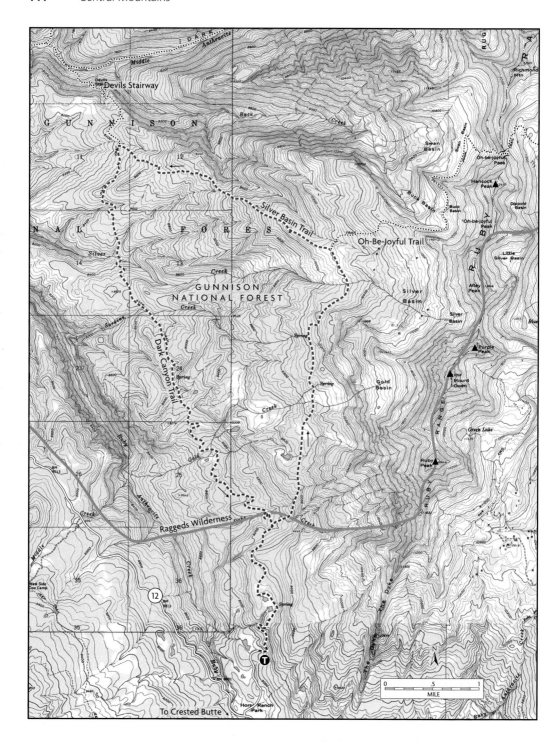

Golden aspen forest along the Silver Basin Trail

to the hike are the many tailings piles scattered about the surrounding mountain slopes. Silver Basin witnessed a fair amount of mining activity during the late 1800s.

Continuing north through the basin along a mostly level grade, the Silver Basin Trail eventually meets the west end of the Oh-Be-Joyful Trail about 5 miles from the start of the hike. Climbing moderate-to-strenuous grades, this side trail continues for nearly 3 miles to reach 11,740-foot Oh-Be-Joyful Pass. Continuing east from the pass, the Oh-Be-Joyful Trail then crosses into a 5500-acre tract of land that was added to the Raggeds Wilderness with the passage of the 1993 Colorado Wilderness Act. Just beyond the Oh-Be-Joyful trail junction, the Silver Basin Trail descends 1750 feet in 2.3 miles before reconnect-

ing with the Dark Canyon Trail. By turning right at this junction you can follow the Dark Canyon Trail north for 12.5 miles to reach a trailhead near the Erickson Springs Campground, just west of the wilderness. Along the way, the Dark Canyon Trail descends the Devils Stairway—a drop of 1200 feet in 0.75 mile. This hike turns left at the junction, however, and continues south for 6.5 miles to return to the Horseranch Park trailhead. The grades are mostly easy on this final section as the hike climbs from an elevation of 8640 feet to 9400 feet over a distance of about 6 miles.

Although water is found along much of this hike, it should be treated before drinking. Watch for lightning, especially during the afternoon thunderstorms that frequent this high country in the summer.

56 BECKWITH PASS

Distance: 5 miles round-trip
Difficulty: Easy
Hiking time: 3 hours
Elevation: 9640 to 9970 feet
Management: Gunnison National Forest
Wilderness status: West Elk Wilderness Area
Season: June to October
Map: USGS Anthracite Range

Getting there: from Crested Butte, drive 15 miles west on Kebler Pass Road to the turnoff for Lost Lake Slough (Forest Road 706). Then drive 2 miles south to the trailhead at the northeast end of the Lost Lake Campground.

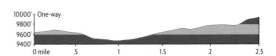

While the West Elk Wilderness is the stuff that memorable multiday hikes are made of, this nice little day hike accesses a great view of the extensive wilderness from its destination, 9970-foot Beckwith Pass.

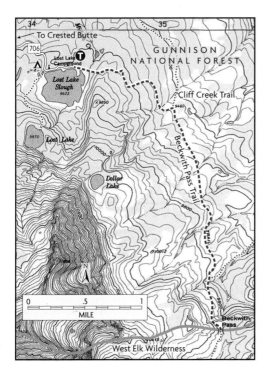

From the trailhead, the Beckwith Pass Trail heads east as it alternates between spruce and fir forests, aspen stands, and open meadows. While the route gains about 300 feet along its entire 2.5-mile length, the trail actually drops a couple of hundred feet in the first mile. After this low point, the trail then climbs along mostly easy grades to gain 500 feet in the remaining 1.5 miles of the hike. As it draws closer to the pass, the trail encounters open meadows with incredible views of nearby 12,432-foot East Beckwith Mountain. To the north, the Ruby Range rises along the eastern end of the Raggeds Wilderness. Just shy of the pass, the Beckwith Pass Trail intersects the Cliff Creek Trail that drops to the vicinity of Horseranch Park on Kebler Pass Road.

Upon reaching Beckwith Pass, the trail crosses through a gate to enter the West Elk Wilderness beyond. It then descends into the head of Cliff Creek. While the pass serves as the turnaround point for this hike, it is possible to continue south along the Beckwith Pass Trail for another 8 miles to its junction with the Castle Pass Trail. About 1.5 miles south of Beckwith Pass, the Lowline Trail branches left to head southeast over Swampy Pass.

From Beckwith Pass, you can look deep into the eastern side of the West Elk Range. Included in this panorama is a distant collection of pinnacles known as the Castles. Volcanic in origin, the West Elk Range formed as a broad dome that

Wildflowers at trailside

was covered with volcanic material during a fiery period some 35 million years ago. The dark rock of the West Elk Mountains, West Elk Breccia, has since been eroded into interesting formations that are widely scattered about the range. In addition to the unusual geologic features, this wilderness is also home to mule deer, elk, bighorn sheep, and the like.

Lightning is a very real threat along the upper portion of this hike and on Beckwith Pass. Some water is found along the route, but it should be treated before drinking.

57 TATER HEAP LOOP

Distance: 11.25-mile loop
Difficulty: Strenuous
Hiking time: 9 hours
Elevation: 7600 to 10,200 feet
Management: Gunnison National Forest
Wilderness status: West Elk Wilderness Area
Season: June to October
Map: USGS Mount Guero

Getting there: From the small town of Crawford, drive east on Forest Road 712, which heads up the Smith Fork. At a little less than 8 miles from town, Forest Road 712 turns right to skirt around a private ranch. The road becomes considerably rougher from this point, and a high-clearance vehicle might

be required. After about 9 miles, turn left onto a 4WD road and follow it for about 0.25

mile to the signed trailhead. A small parking area on the left just before this side road drops down a hill is a good place to park if you do not have a 4WD vehicle.

At 10,984 feet, Tater Heap is not the highest of peaks in the western end of the West Elk Wilderness. Nevertheless, this oddly named summit is quite a sight, thanks to its distinctive conical shape. A nice 11.25-mile hike connects three trails to loop around this memorable landmark. This hike can be completed in a long day, but an overnight excursion would allow for plenty of time to enjoy the scenery.

The first leg of the Tater Heap Loop follows the Throughline Trail north up the Trail Creek drainage. From the trailhead, the Throughline Trail begins by crossing South Smith Fork Creek (a log may be found a short distance upstream for crossing) where it then intersects the Sink Creek Trail, which is the return leg of this hike. After continuing straight at this intersection, the route climbs a ridge before dropping into the Trail

Creek drainage. Numerous livestock trails can be somewhat confusing up until the Throughline Trail crosses Trail Creek about 1.25 miles from the trailhead. Wood "trail" signs occasionally mark the way, however, and horse traffic may leave tracks that help point the way. The Throughline Trail becomes easier to follow beyond the creek crossing as it passes through open meadows and stands of Gambel oak. A little over 3 miles from the start, the Throughline intersects a trail that leads to Little Elk Basin. Keep right here and continue less than 0.5 mile to a signed right turn onto the Lone Pine Trail. To reach this point, the hike has climbed about 1000 feet in a little less than 3.5 miles.

Receiving considerably less use than the Throughline, the Lone Pine Trail is often overgrown and littered with deadfall, especially in the first mile where it climbs moderately through stands of diseased aspen trees. The trail becomes easier to follow, however, as it eventually enters healthier stands of aspen and then breaks across open mountain slopes. As the Lone Pine Trail

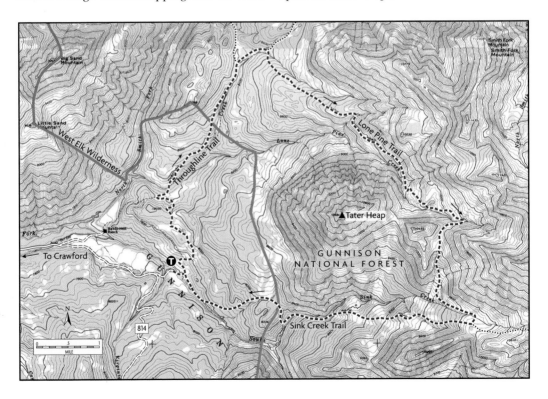

nears its 3-mile mark (or nearly 6.5 miles from the trailhead), it reaches a small, unnamed lake that is situated below a rocky ridge. This lake makes a great place to camp.

Just beyond the lake, the trail becomes very faint as it climbs an open ridge a short distance before dropping to cross a small creek to the right and then climbing to a low saddle beyond. If you lose the trail at this point, just keep your eyes on the saddle directly south. Upon reaching the saddle, the Lone Pine Trail becomes easy to find again. This unnamed saddle at 10,200 feet is the hike's highpoint. From this point, the Lone Pine Trail drops for about a mile into the Sink Creek drainage. It then climbs a short distance before crossing the creek itself and intersecting the third and final leg of this loop hike, the Sink Creek Trail.

Whereas the Lone Pine Trail continues upstream along Sink Creek, the 3.5-mile Sink Creek Trail turns right to follow its namesake downstream. Over the next 1.5 miles or so, this route follows along the south face of the drainage, where periodic views of Tater Heap to the north and of such landmarks as Saddle Mountain and the Grand Mesa to the northwest open up. As with much of the rest of this hike, the Sink Creek portion encounters numerous stands of aspen. It also drops quite steeply in several places as it descends more than 2000 feet. About halfway through, the Sink Creek Trail drops to cross Sink Creek, then climbs briefly but steeply—some 350 vertical feet—before resuming its descent to the trailhead. The route once again encounters expansive patches of Gambel oak in the last mile of the hike. At the intersection of the Sink Creek and Throughline Trails encountered earlier, turn left and continue a short distance to the trailhead.

Water is available in various places along this hike, but it should be treated before drinking. Because of occasionally rough terrain, a lot of deadfall and faded tread, this hike should not be attempted by beginning hikers. It is also best not to attempt it alone. Watch for lightning in the higher exposed terrain of this hike. Be sure not to cut switchbacks or create new trails.

Aspen along the hike around Tater Heap

58 CRAG CREST

Distance: 10-mile loop
Difficulty: Moderate
Hiking time: 7 hours
Elevation: 10,152 to 11,189 feet
Management: Grand Mesa National Forest
Wilderness status: None
Season: July to September
Map: USGS Grand Mesa

Getting there: From Grand Junction, drive 17 miles east on Interstate 70 to the turnoff for Colorado Highway 65—a paved route that climbs up and over Grand Mesa. Continue south on Colorado Highway 65 for 34.5 miles to Forest Road 121. Turn left and follow this paved route for 2.5 miles to where it splits. Bear left and drive another 0.9 mile to the trailhead for the Crag Crest Trail. Parking is available on the right side of the road; the trail begins on the left.

One of the largest flat-topped mountains in the world, Grand Mesa offers a great opportunity to learn about the complex geology of Colorado and to enjoy some truly unique scenery. The premier hiking trail on Grand Mesa is the Crag Crest National Recreation Trail, which loops for 10 miles over one of the highpoints along the mesa top. From this memorable route, hikers can enjoy sweeping panoramas of surrounding mountain ranges and relish the quiet solitude of pristine forestlands as well.

From the trailhead, the Crag Crest Trail climbs slightly to reach a junction less than 0.25 mile north. At this intersection, continue straight ahead on the middle trail. The route to the left is the trail you will return on, while the right-hand trail is a short side route unrelated to this hike. Beyond this junction the route continues to climb at an easy pace through forests of Engelmann spruce and subalpine fir. This combination is found all along the hike, although a few aspen trees are scattered among the steeper slopes above. After 0.75 mile, the route levels off as it passes Upper Eggleston Lake, and at about 1.25

miles out the route encounters Bullfinch Reservoir No. 1 and the signed turnoff for Butts Lake. Nearly a mile in length, Butts Lake is plainly visible from the crest above. After passing these two lakes, the Crag Crest Trail begins to climb again, but this time along a more moderate grade. As it ascends it draws closer to the rocky ridgeline of Crag Crest itself. The route climbs through several short switchbacks and crosses a few boulder fields before it finally reaches the top. The Crag Crest Trail climbs about 900 feet in this first 2 miles of the hike.

Upon reaching the top, the Crag Crest Trail follows its namesake westward for 3 miles or so. As it does, the geology of Grand Mesa reveals itself plainly. Capped by a 200- to 600-foot-thick layer of dark basaltic rock that originated from volcanic fissures some 10 million years ago, the layers of sedimentary rock that underlay Grand Mesa were spared a more rapid rate of erosion than might normally have occurred. When these softer underlayers did erode away along the edge of the mesa, parts of the basalt top subsequently dropped, often along a curved slip face. These chunks of caprock, in turn, tilted inward toward the center of the mesa. Eventually filling with water, these basins today form a string of elongated lakes along the base of Crag Crest. Other forces have been at work in the shaping of Grand Mesa as well. The entire mesa was uplifted over the last 10 million years

Butts Lake as seen from the Crag Crest Trail

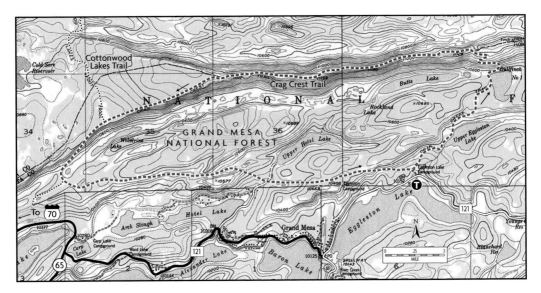

to its present height. And, over the last 100,000 years, intermittent glaciers have scoured the mesa's surface, leaving behind still more lakes, moraines, and such.

Geology lessons aside, Crag Crest is an interesting landform to hike along as the trail follows the summit of the crest the entire way. In some places the trail corridor is barely 4 feet wide, with sheer drop-offs on either side. Of course, the views from this high route are spectacular. Included in the panorama are the Raggeds and West Elk Wilderness Areas to the east and southeast, the entire western half of the San Juan Mountains far to the south, Battlement Mesa and the Roan Cliffs to the north, the Uncompahgre Plateau to the west, and—visible on an especially clear day—Utah's La Sal Mountains even farther west. Add to these faraway landmarks the mesa's highpoint—11,234-foot Leon Peak, which rises to the east—and you have vistas worth writing home about.

After following the narrow spine of Crag Crest, the trail eventually reaches the gentler western end of the landform. Here the route passes among a quiet spruce and fir forest

before dropping off to the south. Before doing so, however, it intersects with a trail that leads north to the Cottonwood Lakes. After turning left at this trail junction, continue for a mile to the next intersection, which is well signed. While a right turn at this point leads 0.5 mile to the west trailhead for the Crag Crest Trail, the route to the left returns you to your car at the east trailhead via the 3.5-mile return portion of the Crag Crest Trail. Along this last leg of the hike, expect to find more spruce and fir forests along with some open meadows. You also encounter some short climbs and drops along the way, but nothing too dramatic. Near the halfway mark of this last segment of the hike is an unsigned intersection that might cause some confusion. The trail running south to north accesses a nearby lake, but you must continue straight ahead (east) to complete this loop trip.

Bring a good supply of water, as none is available along most of this hike. Be wary of lightning along the exposed upper portion of this trail, and use plenty of caution near dangerous drop-offs. This is an extremely popular hike, so you might want to plan accordingly.

Opposite: Aspen growing along Goulding Creek

SOUTHERN MOUNTAINS

Standing sentinel over the southern portion of Colorado's eastern plains, the Spanish Peaks serve as a reminder of the broken terrain that typifies the state's southern mountains. Just as these twin cones rise steeply from surrounding flatlands, so too do a number of other peaks farther to the west. Beginning with the Spanish Peaks, hikes highlighted in this section penetrate the Sangre de Cristo Mountains and visit two interesting sections of the San Luis Valley. A great majority of these hikes, however, explore southwest Colorado's San Juan Mountains. The largest mountain range within the U.S. Rockies, this alluring chain of peaks twists and turns along the Continental Divide, revealing a variety of personalities unique to this corner of the state.

59 WEST SPANISH PEAK

Distance: 5 miles round-trip
Difficulty: Strenuous
Hiking time: 4 hours
Elevation: 11,005 to 13,626 feet
Management: San Isabel National Forest
Wilderness status: Spanish Peaks Wilderness Area
Season: July to September
Maps: USGS Cucharas Pass, Spanish Peaks, Herlick Canyon

Getting there: From Walsenburg, drive west on US Highway 160 for about 11 miles to the turnoff for Colorado Highway 12. Drive south 5 miles to La Veta and then another 17.5 miles to Cucharas Pass. Turn left onto Forest Road 46 and drive 6 miles on this good gravel road to 11,005-foot Cordova Pass. The trail begins on the north side of the pass. There is a fee for trailhead parking.

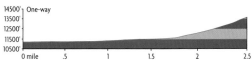

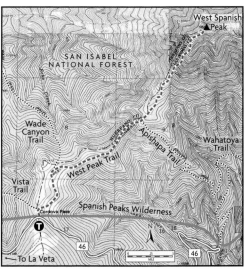

The Spanish Peaks have long served as important landmarks for all who pass within sight of them. The Indians called them Huajatolla, or "Breasts of the World." Early Spanish explorers used them as easily identifiable landmarks in their northern frontier. Today they provide modern-day motorists along Interstate 25 with one of the more stunning vistas in the state. Fortunately for hikers, the taller of the two peaks, 13,626-foot West Spanish Peak, is accessible via a steep but short hike.

From the start, the West Peak Trail heads northeast along a broad and gentle ridge for about 2 miles. Along this first section of the hike, grades are easy to nonexistent. Within this segment, the route encounters a variety of environments—forests of Engelmann spruce, corkbark fir, and limber pine; stands of aspen trees; and natural meadows. These open areas offer an exciting view of West Spanish Peak, which rises suddenly to the east.

Within a very short distance from the trailhead, the West Peak Trail encounters the Vista Trail, which heads left to a vista overlooking the Cucharas Valley. About 0.25 mile from the trailhead, the West Peak Trail then intersects the Wade Canyon Trail, which descends to the north. Seldom used, this side route is easy to miss. At the 1.4-mile mark, the West Peak Trail intersects the upper end of the Apishapa Trail, which heads south for 4 miles to reach Forest Road 46 south of Cordova Pass. Along the way, it also intersects the 12-mile Wahatoya Trail, which eventually tops the saddle between the two Spanish Peaks. Beyond the Apishapa Trail junction, the West Peak Trail climbs along a series of switchbacks through what remains of the forest. Among this final stand of trees you might notice the bleached trunks of bristlecone pines; these trees are especially picturesque this close to timberline.

After climbing easy-to-moderate grades for less than 0.5 mile from the junction with the Apishapa Trail, the West Peak Trail reaches timberline and the start of the real climb. Towering before you at this point is the bare, rocky summit of West Spanish Peak. Because this route ascends 2000 feet in about 0.5 mile, the task of climbing to the summit might seem rather daunting. Indeed, the climb is strenuous all the way to the top, but the going is not too bad. Although no official route leads to the summit, several bootleg trails lace their way up the peak's southwestern ridgeline. And, while the steep sides of this mountain are rocky, these rocks do not easily give way when stepped upon. Add to these pluses the fact that the scenery is tremendous all along the hike and the possibility that you might see some bighorn sheep skirting about the slopes, and you will find yourself on top in no time.

Upon reaching the top, you are treated to an incredible 360-degree view. Rising just east is East Spanish Peak, which, at 12,683 feet, is nearly 1000 feet lower than West Spanish Peak. Beyond it stretch the Great Plains. Although these prairie lands appear to be featureless, you might be able to pick out canyons, washes, and mesas. To the north is the Cucharas River Valley, and beyond it is 12,349-foot Greenhorn Mountain. To the northwest is La Veta Pass and 14,345-foot Blanca Peak beyond. Marching southward into New Mexico, the Sangre de Cristo Mountains can be seen a few miles to the west, just beyond the Cucharas Pass area. Included in this portion of the range is 14,047-foot Culebra Peak to the southwest.

Wildflowers below West Spanish Peak

Scattered all across the lower lands that surround the Spanish Peaks are dozens of volcanic dikes, which appear as vertical curtains of rock protruding from the surrounding terrain. A geologic anomaly, these impressive formations were developed as lava-filled fissures in sedimentary rock during the Tertiary period. The source of this lava was the Spanish Peaks themselves, which formed as massive intrusions of molten rock, or stocks. While the Spanish Peaks are impressive even today, it is believed that they once stood much higher. Given the unusual quantity of these volcanic dikes, the geologic scenario that the Spanish Peaks portray is indeed one for the textbooks.

Bring water, as none is found along this route. Because lightning is a very real threat on this exposed peak, plan your hike for the early morning hours—especially during the summer. Use caution when descending from the summit.

60 NORTH CRESTONE LAKE

Distance: 12 miles round-trip
Difficulty: Strenuous
Hiking time: 9 hours
Elevation: 8500 to 11,840 feet
Management: Rio Grande National Forest
Wilderness status: Sangre de Cristo Wilderness Area
Season: July to September
Maps: USGS Rito Alto Peak, Horn Peak

Getting there: From Saguache, drive 18 miles southeast to the small town of Moffat, and then another 12 miles east to Crestone, located at the base of the Sangre de Cristo Range. From Crestone, drive a little more than 2 miles north on Forest Road 950 to the North Crestone Creek Campground.

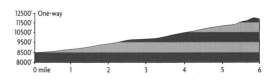

Forming a 70-mile-long crest of 13,000- and 14,000-foot peaks, the Sangre de Cristo Range encompasses some truly extraordinary mountain terrain. Nestled in glacial valleys on the steep western slopes of the range are numerous alpine lakes, most of which are accessible via established trails. North Crestone Lake, which is situated at the head of the Lake Fork of Crestone Creek, makes for a memorable day hike or overnight excursion.

From the North Crestone Creek Campground, the North Crestone Trail begins by following its namesake creek northeast for a little more than 2 miles to where the Lake Fork branches right. Climbing along easy-to-moderate grades, this first segment of the hike gains about 1000 feet.

Within a mile of the creek junction, the trail switchbacks up the north slope of the drainage to reach a level that is 200 feet or so above the creek bottom. The route meets the lower ends of the North Fork Crestone and Loop Trails, which branch to the left. These two routes climb toward the crest of the range, where two additional trails make a connection to form a loop over Venable Pass and Phantom Terrace.

After keeping right at this junction, the North Crestone Trail continues climbing for nearly 4 miles to reach North Crestone Lake, one of the largest lakes in the Sangre de Cristo Range. Although it maintains a moderate grade for most of the way, the trail does make a strenuous 600-foot climb up a steep headwall just below the lake itself. Fishing holes and beautiful little waterfalls appear along the Lake Fork of North Crestone

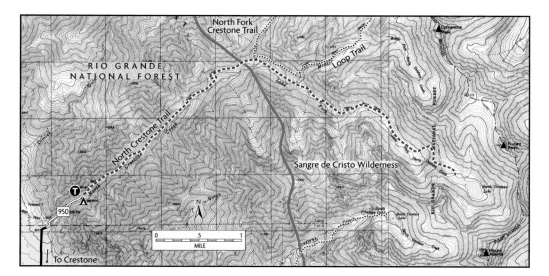

Creek. While the first half of this trail encounters expansive stands of aspen, its upper end climbs beyond the normal elevation range of the tree and instead passes through spruce and fir forests. North Crestone Lake is surrounded by several high peaks, including 13,931-foot Mount Adams directly south and 13,554-foot Fluted Peak to the northeast.

Used liberally in this part of the Sangre de Cristo Range, the name Crestone, which is Spanish for "Cock's Comb," alludes to the inherent ruggedness of these mountains and testifies to the early influence Spanish explorers had on the area. The name Sangre de Cristo, which translates to "Blood of Christ," is thought to have been assigned to the mountain range in 1647 when a

Along the North Crestone Trail

group of conquistadors camped near San Luis Lake and looked up to see the peaks bathed in the brilliant vermilion light of sunset. Interestingly, the remains of stone fortresses built by the early Spaniards have been found near 14,197-foot Crestone Needle, which is a few miles down range from North Crestone Lake. Additionally, an American expedition during the 1850s found a

skeleton dressed in Spanish armor stashed away in a cave.

Water is found along most of this hike, but it should be treated before drinking. Although not a persistent threat, lighting strikes are possible on the higher reaches of this hike. Forest Service regulations prohibit camping within 300 feet of North Crestone Lake.

61 GREAT SAND DUNES

Distance: 2 miles round-trip
Difficulty: Moderate
Hiking time: 2 hours
Elevation: 8050 to 8690 feet
Management: Great Sand Dunes National Park and Preserve
Wilderness status: Great Sand Dunes Wilderness Area
Season: Year-round
Map: USGS Zapata Ranch

Getting there: From Alamosa, drive 14 miles east on US Highway 160. Turn left onto Colorado Highway 150 and drive 19 miles north to reach the Great Sand Dunes National Park and Preserve visitor center. This hike begins at the parking area, which is about 1 mile north of the visitor center.

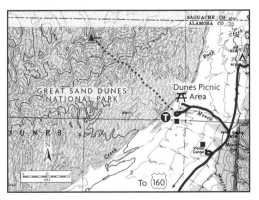

Great Sand Dunes National Park and Preserve encompasses a 30-square-mile dune field on the eastern edge of the San Luis Valley. These swells of sand towering nearly 750 feet above the valley floor are considered the tallest dunes in North America. For hikers of all ages, the Great Sand Dunes offer an enormous sandbox in which to explore. Because these sands are constantly shifting, no actual trails exist within the dunes. There is, however, a 1-mile route that climbs to one of the high points in the dunes.

From the parking area, cross the Medano creekbed (the stream is usually dry nine months a year) to reach the foot of the dunes in about 0.6 mile. From here, you can pick any of the dune crests, which ascend to the 8690-foot summit of what appears to be the tallest dune ridge in sight. The route climbs 650 feet along moderate-

to-strenuous grades to reach the top. Hikers should keep in mind that walking in soft sand is somewhat difficult and tiring. Of course, the return trip to the trailhead can be a matter of free-form bounding down the faces of the dunes. Some visitors have even taken to skiing the fall lines the dunes provide.

The Great Sand Dunes at sunset

Upon leaving the line of cottonwoods just north of the picnic area, this hike enters an environment unique in a number of respects. The first of the area's unusual features to be encountered is Medano Creek, which, in essence, dictates the dunes' eastern and southern boundaries by constantly eating away at the encroaching sands. Surfacing during spring runoff or after a summer rain, Medano Creek normally flows beneath the surface through the porous sand. Geologically speaking, the dunes were formed when sands blown across the expansive San Luis Valley were deposited at the foot of a low saddle in the Sangre de Cristo Mountains. This saddle effectively funnels the prevailing winds up and over the range.

Beyond Medano Creek, the loose sands support scattered tufts of Indian ricegrass, blowout grass, a legume known as the scurfpea, and prairie sunflowers. Reaching a surface temperature of 140 degrees in the summer and containing few nutrients, these shifting sands constitute an extremely harsh environment—not just for plants, but for animals as well. Although an occasional deer, coyote, or other animal might wander a short way into the dunes, the only mammal that successfully inhabits them is the kangaroo rat. The dunes are also home to seven species of insect found nowhere else on earth—the Great Sand Dunes tiger beetle and a species of circus beetle among them.

Drinking water is not available along this hike, so bring plenty. While it might be possible to walk barefoot, bring your shoes in case the sands become unbearably hot. Do not enter the dunes during thunderstorms, as lightning strikes the area with great frequency.

62 MOSCA PASS

Distance: 7 miles round-trip
Difficulty: Moderate
Hiking time: 4 hours
Elevation: 8200 to 9737 feet
Management: Great Sand Dunes National Park and Preserve
Wilderness status: Sangre de Cristo Wilderness Area
Season: June to October
Map: USGS Zapata Ranch

Getting there: To reach Great Sand Dunes National Park and Preserve, drive 14 miles east from Alamosa on US Highway 160. Turn left onto Colorado Highway 150 and drive 19 miles north to the visitor center. This hike begins at a trailhead just beyond the visitor center.

Constituting the "preserve" portion of the Great Sand Dunes National Park and Preserve are a string of summits within the Sangre de Cristo Mountains that tower over the dunes to the east. The 3.5-mile Mosca Pass Trail offers a nice introduction to the forested portions of these peaks. The Mosca Pass Trail begins by following the Montville Nature Trail east. This 0.5-mile guided loop trail explores the former town site of Montville. Once complete with an orchard, a store, some twenty houses, and a post office,

Montville was established in the 1880s. The post office closed in 1900 and a flash flood wiped out most structures in 1911 or 1912. More recently, in April 2000, a 3100-acre wildfire swept across the area, leaving stands of skeleton trees in its wake. Upon reaching an intersection 0.25 mile from the trailhead, the Mosca Pass Trail turns right to continue up the Mosca Creek drainage. For the next 0.5 mile or so, the route follows the canyon bottom, which is rich with riparian growth—chokecherry, maple, aspen, and some impressive Douglas-firs and white firs. A plethora of chirping birds and a babbling stream add to the allure of this section.

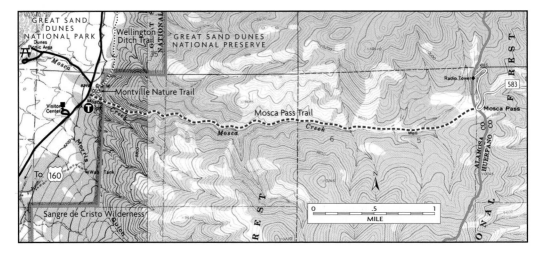

Riparian growth along Mosca Pass Trail

Beginning in the 1870s, Mosca Canyon provided a corridor for a toll road that ushered settlers into the San Luis Valley for several years. A single horse and rider was charged $1.00 to use the road while a wagon and team was charged $2.00. The road was eventually wiped out by flash floods and little of the road remains today.

After following along the canyon bottom for a bit, the Mosca Pass Trail then climbs a few hundred feet up the left canyon wall to escape the tight canyon bottom and to provide a bird's-eye view of the riparian growth below. Vistas also open up of the west end of the sand dunes framed by the canyon's mouth. Eventually, the Mosca Pass Trail draws back closer to the canyon bottom where the riparian community can once again be enjoyed up close.

About 2 miles from the trailhead, the canyon splits where the Mosca Pass Trail continues up the left fork. Although the route climbs fairly steadily within the first portion of the hike, the grades become somewhat easier as the drainage levels out a bit. Within the last mile of the hike, the trail enters the first of several meadows that are ringed by aspen and evergreen groves. And, as it nears the top, you may notice scattered limber pines and a stand or two of stately bristlecone pines. Eventually, the trail reaches a split-rail fence and some signs that mark the Sangre de Cristo Wilderness boundary. A dirt road, Forest Road 583, leads from this point a few hundred yards to 9737-foot Mosca Pass itself. The road climbs up from the east through the San Isabel National Forest and continues a short distance farther to reach a radio tower. Return to the trailhead by retracing the Mosca Pass Trail.

Water is available on this hike, but it is best to bring your own, as stream water must be treated first before consuming. Watch for lightning, especially in the higher reaches of this hike.

63   PENITENTE CANYON

Distance: 3 miles round-trip
Difficulty: Easy
Hiking time: 2 hours
Elevation: 8000 to 8450 feet
Management: Bureau of Land Management
Wilderness status: None
Season: Year-round
Map: USGS Twin Mountains SE

Getting there: From Del Norte, drive north on Colorado Highway 112 for 3.1 miles to the turnoff for County Road 33. Turn north and follow this good gravel road 9.5 miles to the signed left turn for Penitente Canyon. Drive 1 mile west to where the road forks in the developed camping area. Bear right and drive a short distance farther to the trailhead. Penitente Canyon can also be reached from the small village of La Garita, which is a couple of miles east of the canyon.

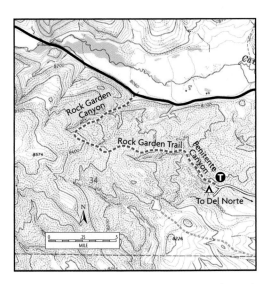

Since its discovery by rock climbers in 1985, Penitente Canyon has been visited by technical scramblers from as far away as Europe, Africa, and South America. Although relatively shallow, Penitente Canyon is enclosed by sheer cliff faces nearly 100 feet tall. Other areas, such as above the canyon's rim to the west, feature unusual rock formations and outcrops. A short and easy trail links both areas to create an interesting excursion for hikers.

From the trailhead, the route follows the canyon bottom northwest for 0.3 mile to where the canyon forks. While walking along this first section of the hike you can see a beautiful image of the Virgin Mary painted about 40 feet above on a canyon wall. This image attests to the canyon's longtime use as a place of worship by a little-known sect of the Catholic religion known as the Brothers Penitente. Founded during the early 1800s, the Penitente movement began when Spanish settlers in the Southwest were isolated from the Catholic Church in Europe.

Upon reaching the fork in the canyon, turn left to follow the sign that points west to the Rock Garden Trail. A short distance up this side canyon, the route follows rock cairns as it begins climbing to the north. A bit of scrambling is required, but none of it is very difficult. Upon reaching the canyon's rim, you get a nice look back into Penitente Canyon. Gazing out across the higher terrain to the west, you begin to see different species of trees growing in the area. Ponderosa pines and Douglas-firs are most evident, but junipers and pinyon pines are plentiful as well. In addition, several aspens can be found growing in protected places.

Once the trail climbs out of the canyon, it

Historic pictograph in Penitente Canyon

heads northwest across an area that features numerous outcrops of volcanic rock that have eroded into well-rounded shapes. This volcanic material originated in the San Juan Mountains to the west. The trail is not well established here, so you will need to follow the rock cairns, which are located at sporadic intervals. Less than 0.5 mile from where the route climbs out of Penitente Canyon, it turns east to drop into Rock Garden Canyon, the next canyon north. Descending about 75 feet in all, the trail follows this canyon a short distance east to its mouth and a rural road that follows Carnero Creek west. The mouth of Rock Garden Canyon marks the turnaround point for this hike.

While water is not found along the hike, you can fill your canteen at a pumphouse just outside of the campground entrance. Lightning can occasionally pose a danger during afternoon thunderstorms.

64 WHEELER GEOLOGIC AREA

Distance: 15 miles round-trip
Difficulty: Moderate
Hiking time: 2 days
Elevation: 10,800 to 12,000 feet
Management: Rio Grande National Forest
Wilderness status: La Garita Wilderness Area
Season: July to September
Maps: USGS Pool Table Mountain, Wagon Wheel Gap, Halfmoon Pass

Getting there: To reach the beginning of this hike, drive 7.3 miles southeast from Creede on Colorado Highway 149 to the Pool Table Road (Forest Road 600). Turn north and continue 9.7 miles along this good gravel road to the signed trailhead at the Hanson's Mill site. All that is left of the old mill is a large pile of sawdust. From Hanson's Mill, Forest Road 600 continues for another 13.7 miles northeast and then west to reach the Wheeler Geologic Area at the upper end of this hike.

Certainly one of Colorado's more unusual geologic formations, the Wheeler Geologic Area is also one of its most remote natural features. Volcanic in origin, the white tuff of the area has eroded into a variety of hoodoos, pinnacles, and canyons. So unusual are these formations that they captured the interest of the then chief of the U.S. Forest Service, Gifford Pinchot, and his boss, President Teddy Roosevelt, who made the Wheeler formations the centerpiece of a 300-acre national monument in 1908. Due to lack of access, however, the area was redesignated as a

geologic area in 1969 and its size was increased to 640 acres. Today a rough and lengthy 4WD road reaches the Wheeler Geologic Area, as do a number of hiking trails. This hike follows the shortest of these trails, the East Bellows Trail. Newer signs along the route refer to it as the Wheeler Trail.

From the trailhead, the East Bellows Trail sets out due north in a forest of Engelmann spruce and subalpine fir. The trail maintains a relatively level grade in the first 0.5 mile, and then begins to descend easily after it reaches the head of the East Bellows Creek drainage. The route continues to descend easily over the next 1.5 miles. Portions of this first segment traverse open meadows and briefly parallel the deep canyon of East Bellows Creek, which runs a short distance to the west. In the last 100 yards or so, the trail drops through a handful of short switchbacks before reaching the creek itself. Upon crossing the creek, the route

Formations in the Wheeler Geologic Area

222

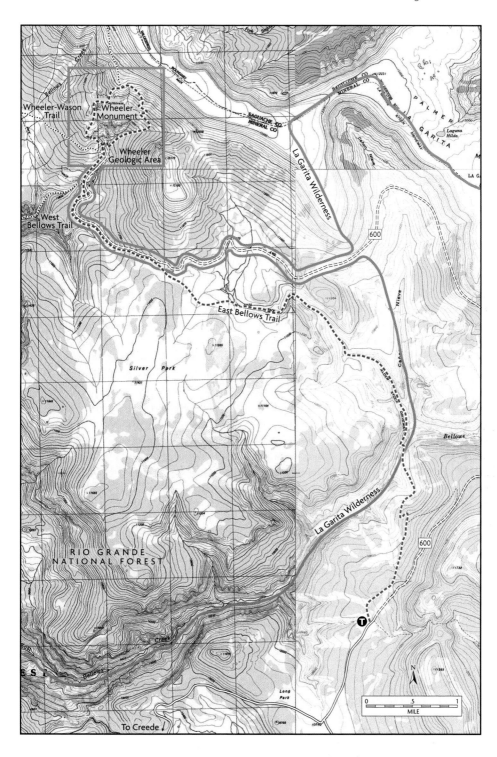

enters the La Garita Wilderness, which means mountain bikes must turn back.

A sizable stream at this point, East Bellows Creek is home to beavers and is also a favorite of anglers. It can be difficult to cross in the early summer when high waters prevail. Beyond the crossing, the East Bellows Trail continues north into an interesting little canyon known as Cañon Nieve. About 0.5 mile from the crossing, the trail turns left up a side canyon to head northwest. Following this drainage for the next 2 miles, the route climbs easily through open meadows to reach another patch of spruce and fir. Beyond this forest area, the trail enters expansive Silver Park, through which it continues for another mile. Here and in other open areas along the hike, you can gain some nice views of the surrounding alpine mesas, and you might spot deer or elk in the early morning hours. Running along the north side of the park is the 4WD road that snakes in and out of the trees as it accesses the Wheeler area. About 5.5 miles from the trailhead, the East Bellows Trail reaches the road, which it then follows for about a mile to the boundary of the geologic area. In this last mile, the route drops 350 feet into the head of West Bellows Creek. To the west you can see the rather deep canyon this drainage has carved for itself.

The 4WD road ends at a fence and signboard that mark the boundary of the Wheeler Geologic Area. (This road was "cherry-stemmed" out of the 25,640-acre Wheeler addition to the La Garita Wilderness mandated by the Colorado Wilderness Act of 1993, while the Geologic Area was added.) From the road's end, it is about a 0.5-mile walk to the formations. As you approach them, the trail splits at a signed intersection. The right-hand trail continues on to the base of the rocks and then to a small log structure known as the shelter house, beyond which it continues to climb north for another 2 miles or so to reach 12,700-foot Halfmoon Pass. The left-hand trail climbs along the western end of the formations, then circles around the north end to connect with the trail to Halfmoon Pass. This route also intersects the upper end of the 10.7-mile Wheeler-Wason Trail, which begins near Creede, and the slightly shorter West Bellows Trail, which travels north along its namesake creek. This latter route begins on private land below.

No matter which trail you take once you're inside the Wheeler Geologic Area, you will get a close-up view of these stunning rocks. Reminders of the San Juan Mountains' fiery past, these formations evolved after ash and debris blown from volcanic vents settled in the area to form a thick layer of tuff. In the millions of years since, this soft, light-colored rock has eroded into a seemingly endless variety of shapes and designs. While climbing about the formations is alluring, the Forest Service discourages it. These pinnacles are fragile and the rock itself is crumbly. Should you decide to spend the night at the Wheeler Geologic Area, you can find several suitable camping spots near the end of the road near the fence. Camping within the formations is prohibited.

Water is available in places along this hike, but it should be treated before drinking. Watch for lightning in the higher areas, especially during afternoon thundershowers.

65 POWDERHORN LAKES

Distance: 9 miles round-trip
Difficulty: Moderate
Hiking time: 7 hours
Elevation: 11,100 to 11,859 feet
Management: Bureau of Land Management
Wilderness status: Powderhorn Wilderness Area
Season: July to September
Map: USGS Powderhorn Lakes

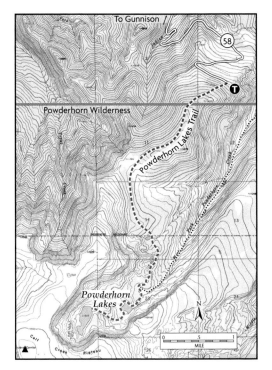

Powderhorn Lakes Trail begins climbing easily to gain 600 feet in the next 1.5 miles. This well-established route is easy to find throughout. At the 1.5-mile mark, the trail enters the upper end of a large meadow that features nice views to the southeast. Included in this vista is the eastern portion of the Powderhorn Wilderness, as well as several peaks that tower over 13,000 feet in the La Garita Wilderness beyond. This meadow is a great place to spot deer and elk in the early morning and wildflowers during midsummer months.

After crossing this meadow, the Powderhorn Lakes Trail follows the western edge of the opening for a short distance before continuing on toward the south through more spruce and fir

Getting there: From Gunnison, drive 9 miles west on US Highway 50 to Colorado Highway 149—the road to Lake City. Turn south and drive another 20 miles to Indian Creek Road (County Road 58). Turn south here and drive just over 10 miles to the trailhead, which is at road's end. This gravel road is rough in places but should be passable to most vehicles.

Although the 60,100-acre Powderhorn Wilderness Area is best known for its extensive alpine plateaus, this out-of-the-way wilderness also features some beautiful lakes and prime timbered areas. This hike accesses the heart of the wilderness in relatively short order by following the Powderhorn Lakes Trail to the wilderness area's namesake lakes. Administered by the BLM and the Gunnison National Forest, the Powderhorn Wilderness Area came into existence with the 1993 Colorado Wilderness Act. For years prior to that, the BLM's portion of the tract was included in the Powderhorn Primitive Area.

Upon entering a forest of Engelmann spruce and subalpine fir just beyond the trailhead, the

Colorado's state flower, the blue columbine

forests. In the next 1.25 miles, the route follows a mostly level grade before dropping into the West Fork of the Powderhorn Creek drainage. Although this descent is small, some short stretches of moderately steep grades must be climbed in both directions.

Upon reaching the West Fork of the Powderhorn Creek, the Powderhorn Lakes Trail intersects a trail that follows the creek downstream for a little way before crossing over to the Middle Fork of Powderhorn Creek. It eventually reaches Powderhorn Swamp and the Ten Mile Springs trailhead. The Powderhorn Lakes Trail turns right at this junction, however, and continues upstream for 0.5 mile to reach Lower Powderhorn Lake.

Situated at an elevation of 11,650 feet, Lower Powderhorn Lake sits at the base of basalt-covered Calf Creek Plateau, which rises about 500 feet to the south. While the lake itself is surrounded by trees on three sides, the top of Calf Creek Plateau, like that of nearby Cannibal Plateau, is totally treeless for several miles. These are said to be the largest alpine mesas in the lower forty-eight. From the smaller lower lake, it is another 0.5 mile and a climb of 200 feet to Upper Powderhorn Lake, which is surrounded on three sides by cliffs. This cirque resulted from glacial action during the last ice age. While the lower lake is considered to be good fishing (catch and release is encouraged), both lakes are scenic.

Some old trails head out from the Powderhorn Lakes area to access different portions of the surrounding high country. One path provides a high route for returning to the trailhead, while another leads south to Devils Lake. These routes would be fun to explore, but they are all hard to find due to lack of use. Only hikers who are skilled at orienteering should attempt to follow these routes.

Water is available along this hike, but it should be treated before drinking. Watch for lightning in higher areas along this trail. Backpackers should use existing sites and fire rings no closer than 150 feet to the lakeshores.

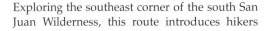

66 NO NAME LAKE

Distance: 10 miles round-trip
Difficulty: Strenuous
Hiking time: 7 hours
Elevation: 8800 to 11,450 feet
Management: Rio Grande National Forest
Wilderness status: South San Juan Wilderness Area
Map: USGS Spectacle Lake

Getting there: From Antonito, drive about 22 miles west on Colorado Highway 17 to Forest Road 250, which follows the Conejos River upstream. Turn north and drive 7.7 miles to a short side road that turns west (there is a sign for the Ruybalid Trail at the turn) at the Rocky Mountain Lodge. Continue another 0.25 mile to the trailhead located just beyond the bridge over the Conejos River. Parking is limited.

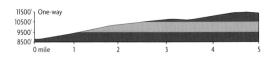

Exploring the southeast corner of the south San Juan Wilderness, this route introduces hikers to one of several lakes that dot a broad plateau above the Conejos River Valley. From the trailhead, begin by following the Ruybalid Trail southwest. The route soon enters a stand of aspen where it reaches the signed boundary of the south San Juan Wilderness. It then begins climbing along mostly easy grades as it heads southwest toward the Rough Creek drainage. A

Trail sign at No Name Lake

mix of fir, spruce, and ponderosa pine eventually replaces the aspen trees. These alternating stands of conifer and aspen characterize much of the first 3 miles of the hike as it climbs to the plateau rim above.

Within the first mile of the hike, the Ruybalid Trail intersects two side trails, both of which access Rough Creek and the spectacular Rough Creek Waterfall. An easy 1.3 miles from the trailhead, this waterfall is the destination of most hikers along the route. After keeping right at both trail intersections, the Ruybalid Trail then heads north to begin its ascent in earnest. What lies ahead is a long series of switchbacks that gain much of the hike's 2650-foot climb. Grades along this section are mostly moderate with a few steep pitches thrown in. As the trail climbs, views of the scenic Conejos River Valley periodically poke through the timber. Classically U-shaped, this valley bears the mark of past glacial activity.

Some 3 miles from the trailhead, the Ruybalid Trail reaches a small, unnamed lake on the crest of the plateau. From this point on, the route tracks across mostly level terrain with only a handful of easy ascents. It also encounters some

nice subalpine meadows ringed by stands of Engelmann spruce and subalpine fir. Because this section of the hike receives only light use, the tread may be difficult to spot in places.

After skirting to the left of the small lake, the Ruybalid Trail continues northwest before reaching a signed intersection. By keeping left at this junction you will eventually reach Alverjones Lake, which lies at the head of Rough Creek. To access No Name Lake, however, keep right and continue for another mile to a second, unsigned trail intersection. Whereas the Ruybalid Trail bears right at this point to continue to its namesake lake, the No Name Trail keeps left to reach No Name Lake. Within this last segment of the hike the trail climbs easily up and over a low ridge before ending at the lake itself. Most of this last section of the trail tracks through some nice timberlands of spruce and fir. The trail may be faint and difficult to follow in places, however. When in doubt, look for old blazes carved into trailside trees.

Rimmed by both forest and boggy meadow areas, No Name Lake is situated near the edge of the plateau and views into the South Fork

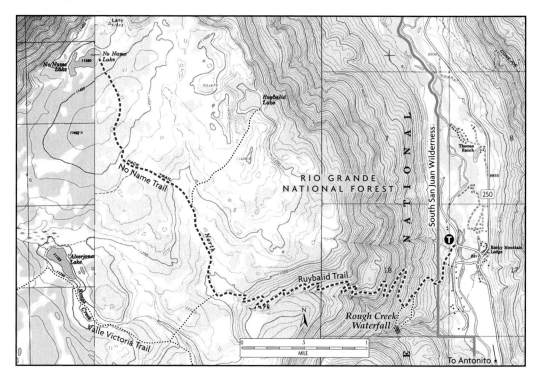

Conejos River drainage can be enjoyed from a low rise northwest of the lake. Fishing is reported to be good and a few suitable camping spots are found here. Be sure to camp at least 100 feet from the lake and trail, however.

Water is found along this hike, but it should be treated before drinking. Watch for lightning across the higher terrain. Because some sections of the trail may be faded, use caution when hiking across the plateau top.

67 FOURMILE FALLS

Distance: 7 miles round-trip
Difficulty: Moderate
Hiking time: 4 hours
Elevation: 9050 to 9800 feet
Management: San Juan National Forest
Wilderness status: Weminuche Wilderness Area
Season: June to October
Map: USGS Pagosa Peak

Getting there: From downtown Pagosa Springs, turn north onto County Road 400, which becomes Fourmile Road (Forest Road 645). A little more than 8 miles from town, be

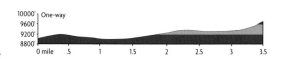

Fourmile Falls in late autumn

sure to keep right on FR 645 and drive another 4.6 miles to the trailhead, which is at road's end. Two trails begin at the Fourmile trailhead. The Fourmile Trail is the right-hand route.

Spilling hundreds of feet over a precipice of dark volcanic rock, Fourmile Falls makes an interesting destination in the Weminuche Wilderness north of Pagosa Springs. Accessed by an easy 3.5-mile trail, this spectacular feature of the rugged San Juan Mountains can be enjoyed by hikers of nearly all ages and abilities.

Within the first 0.25 mile, the Fourmile Trail drops slightly within an old-growth forest of Engelmann spruce and fir to reach a small creek. After crossing this stream, the trail climbs a short distance before crossing into the Weminuche Wilderness. The trail then enters a large meadow and continues north for about 0.25 mile. This opening provides a nice view of 12,137-foot Eagle Peak to the northeast. You might also see a few aspens growing along the meadow's edge. Entering the forest again, the Fourmile Trail continues for another 0.5 mile before climbing about 400 feet along a mostly easy grade. Upon crossing a second small creek, the trail maintains a mostly level grade until it makes one final ascent to the

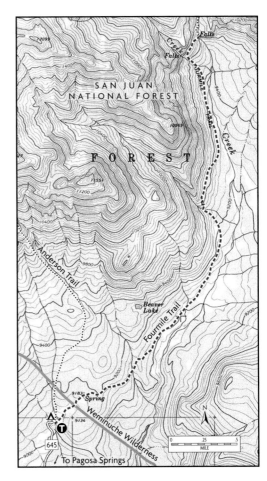

base of Fourmile Falls. The trail gains about 300 feet in this last climb, again over a mostly easy grade.

The higher of the two Fourmile Falls is created by Falls Creek as it drops some 300 feet over a sheer face of dark breccia. Breccia is a conglomerate rock that consists of debris and ash blown from volcanoes many millions of years ago. Forming an imposing wall of cliffs, this rock has obviously proven to be resistant to erosion. A short distance beyond the first waterfall is a second fall, formed where Fourmile Creek drops into the lower portion of the canyon. Although

smaller, this second cascade features a higher volume of water.

While this hike turns around at Fourmile Falls, the Fourmile Trail climbs above the falls and continues north for another 3 miles to reach Fourmile Lake. The other trail that begins at the Fourmile trailhead—the Anderson Trail—reaches Fourmile Lake in 8 miles. If you combine the Anderson Trail with the Fourmile Trail, you can enjoy a 14-mile loop hike along the eastern slopes of 12,640-foot Pagosa Peak.

Water is available along this hike, but it should be treated before drinking.

68 QUARTZ LAKE

Distance: 9 miles round-trip
Difficulty: Strenuous
Hiking time: 7 hours
Elevation: 10,040 to 11,600 feet
Management: San Juan National Forest
Wilderness status: South San Juan Wilderness Area
Season: July to September
Map: USGS Blackhead Peak

Getting there: From Pagosa Springs, drive a short distance east on US Highway 160 to US Highway 84. Turn south and drive 0.25 mile to the Mill Creek Road (Forest Road 662). Turn left and drive 6.4 miles to where the Nipple Mountain Road (Forest Road 665) branches right. Follow the Nipple Mountain Road 9.8 miles to the signed trailhead for the Little Blanco Trail. Although a good graveled road, this route is narrow in places. Drive with caution.

On a September day in 1979, an event occurred that took wildlife experts and land managers by surprise: a bow hunter killed an attacking grizzly bear with a pocketknife. The most unusual aspect about this incident was that it took place in the South San Juan Mountains of southwestern Colorado. Because grizzlies were thought to have been extinct in the state for dozens of years, this encounter rekindled the hope that they still lived in Colorado. Researchers have since

scoured the South San Juans for signs that this unfortunate sow was not a loner, but concrete evidence has yet to be discovered. Nevertheless, some experts do believe there is a good chance that a grizzly bear might eventually be spotted in some remote alpine basin or stand of timber. If hiking an area where such a legendary creature might still exist sounds intriguing, then Quartz Lake on the western slope of the South San Juan Wilderness is a good place to start.

The Little Blanco Trail begins climbing at a steady, moderate grade. The route, in fact, completes much of its 1600-foot climb in these first 2 miles. Along the lower elevations, the trail traverses small open meadows that often feature wildflowers. Glades of aspen and timbered areas of Engelmann spruce and subalpine fir are also

Quartz Lake

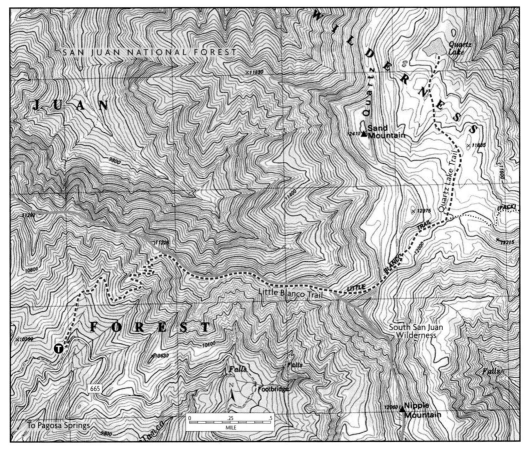

encountered. Eventually, the trail reaches a ridgeline that branches west from Quartz Ridge. Following this ridge top eastward, the trail levels off considerably and reveals scenery north toward the Wolf Creek Pass area and south to Nipple Mountain and Blackhead Peak. The volcanic origins of the South San Juans are also revealed in the interesting formations of conglomerate rock that protrude along the south face of the ridge. The Little Blanco Trail enters the South San Juan Wilderness Area along the ridge, about 2.5 miles from the trailhead, but the boundary is unsigned.

As the trail reaches the flank of Quartz Ridge, it achieves timberline and climbs a final 300 feet or so to a small notch above. The trail then turns northeast to cut across the southern face of Sand Mountain. At 12,410 feet, Sand Mountain is a high point along Quartz Ridge. Upon reaching the east side of Quartz Ridge, the Little Blanco

Trail continues east toward the Continental Divide, while the 1-mile Quartz Lake Trail heads north across rolling alpine terrain to arrive at Quartz Lake. Although Quartz Lake is not an overly popular destination, the fact that this spur trail is well worn while the Little Blanco Trail is barely visible (its location is marked by a pair of rock cairns) is telling about where most hikers in this corner of the South San Juans are headed.

Situated at timberline, Quartz Lake is ringed by trees and is quite scenic, especially when viewed from above. Except for some minor climbs back to the Little Blanco Trail and a short spur up to the notch in the Quartz Ridge, the return hike to the trailhead is downhill.

Water is available within the vicinity of the lake, but it should be treated before drinking. Watch for lightning along the higher portions of this hike.

69 REDCLOUD AND SUNSHINE PEAKS

Distance: 11.4 miles round-trip
Difficulty: Strenuous
Hiking time: 7 hours
Elevation: 10,425 to 14,034 feet
Management: Bureau of Land Management
Wilderness status: Redcloud Peak Wilderness Study Area
Season: July to September
Map: USGS Redcloud Peak

Getting there: From Lake City, drive 2.5 miles south on Colorado Highway 149 to the turnoff for the Cinnamon Pass Road, which is also signed as the Alpine Loop Scenic Byway. Follow this road for 4 miles on pavement and then another 12.5 miles on gravel to the signed trailhead on the right side of the road.

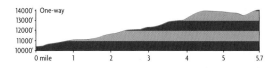

Although they barely top the 14,000-foot level, the neighboring summits of Redcloud and Sunshine make for an incredibly fun hike. Not only will you enjoy memorable views from these peaks, you can also savor the fact that you have bagged two of Colorado's elite corps of mountains. This hike following the Silver Creek Trail falls within the 37,442-acre Redcloud Peak Wilderness Study Area administered by the BLM.

Heading northeast from the trailhead, the Silver Creek Trail follows its namesake for the first 3 miles of the hike. Climbing easy-to-moderate grades, the route continues to a scenic alpine basin at the head of Silver Creek. The trail has climbed about 1500 feet when it reaches the basin. Because this basin is above timberline, it is an

Along the ridge between Sunshine and Redcloud Peaks

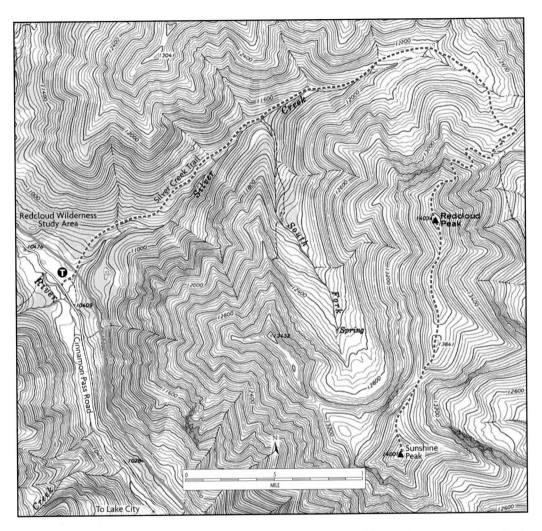

especially great place to enjoy the abundant wildflowers that grow in the San Juan Mountains.

At the head of the Silver Creek drainage, the trail turns south to begin the final 1800-foot climb up the north face of 14,034-foot Redcloud Peak. The route climbs to the top of a saddle east of the summit. It then continues on to the top by way of Redcloud Peak's northeast ridge. This final pitch ascends several switchbacks as it heads to the summit. Although the trail is fairly stable, be sure to watch your footing—especially on the return trip down. It is also important to stay on the tread; erosion and visual scars can easily result from the cutting of switchbacks.

Characterized by its deep orange hue, Redcloud Peak is heavily mineralized with iron oxides. It, along with Sunshine and other peaks in the area, is within the Lake City caldera—a huge volcano that collapsed and filled with volcanic debris. There are several such calderas in the San Juan Range.

Once you have enjoyed the panorama from Redcloud—a 360-degree view that includes Uncompahgre and Matterhorn Peaks to the north, the La Garitas to the east, the Needle Range to the south, and a jumble of peaks that stretch westward to Mount Sneffels—continue south for another 1.25 miles to 14,001-foot Sunshine Peak.

In this easy traverse, the route drops a couple of hundred feet before climbing easily to this second summit. From the top of Sunshine, you can look into the Lake Fork of the Gunnison River directly to the south and get an up-close view of 14,048-foot Handies Peak to the west. When you have completed the climb, return along the same route.

As members of the Hayden Survey discovered in 1874 when they made the first recorded ascent of Redcloud, these summits are extremely dangerous places to be during electrical storms. It is best to get an early start on the climb. Water is available along the lower half of the hike, but it should be treated before drinking. Although this route is not particularly exposed to dangerous drop-offs, the south face of Sunshine is ringed by high cliffs. The BLM suggests that overnight visitors camp below 12,500 feet to help protect endangered species habitat.

70 CONTINENTAL DIVIDE

Distance: 31.5 miles one-way
Difficulty: Strenuous
Hiking time: 4 days
Elevation: 9300 to 12,713 feet
Management: Rio Grande National Forest, San Juan National Forest
Wilderness status: Weminuche Wilderness Area
Season: July to September
Maps: USGS Howardsville, Storm King Peak, Rio Grande Pyramid,
Weminuche Pass

Getting there: This route begins near Stony Pass. To get there from Creede, drive 20.1 miles west on Colorado Highway 149 to the Upper Rio Grande River Road (Forest Road 520). Turn left and drive 33 miles west to within 0.5 mile of Stony Pass, which is on the Divide itself. The last 17 miles of this road require a 4WD vehicle. If you do not have a 4WD but you are willing to make the lengthy roundabout drive from Creede through South Fork, Pagosa Springs, Durango, and Silverton, you can access the Continental Divide Trail from the Highland Mary Lakes Trail (Hike 73). The other end of this hike is along the Upper Rio Grande River Road at the Thirty-Mile Campground and the trailhead for the Weminuche Trail. The campground and trailhead are just east of the Rio Grande Reservoir.

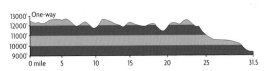

Within the more than 600 miles it covers in the state of Colorado, the Continental Divide forms the headwaters of such famous rivers as the Yampa, Platte, Colorado, Arkansas, Rio Grande, and San Juan. Along the way the Divide tracks widely east to west as it snakes from mountain range to mountain range. One of these undulations occurs where the Divide crests along the San Juan Mountains—the largest mountain range in the U.S. Rockies. Within its final 200-mile stretch to reach the New Mexico border, the Continental Divide nearly doubles back on itself as it traverses the state's largest wilderness area, the 488,544-acre Weminuche Wilderness. Encompassing more than 80 miles of the Continental Divide from end to end, the Weminuche Wilderness includes the longest undeveloped stretch of the Divide in the state. Thanks to the Continental Divide Trail, hikers can follow the Divide from Stony Pass to Wolf Creek Pass with very few intrusions. This hike covers the 26-mile segment between Stony Pass and Weminuche Pass.

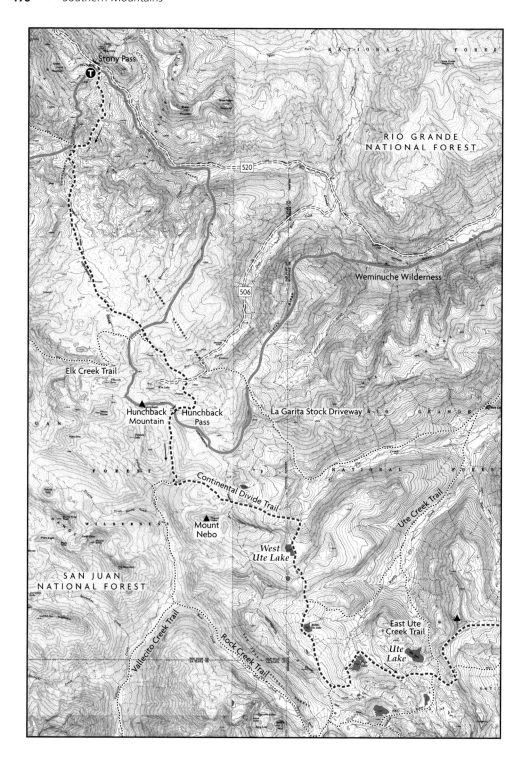

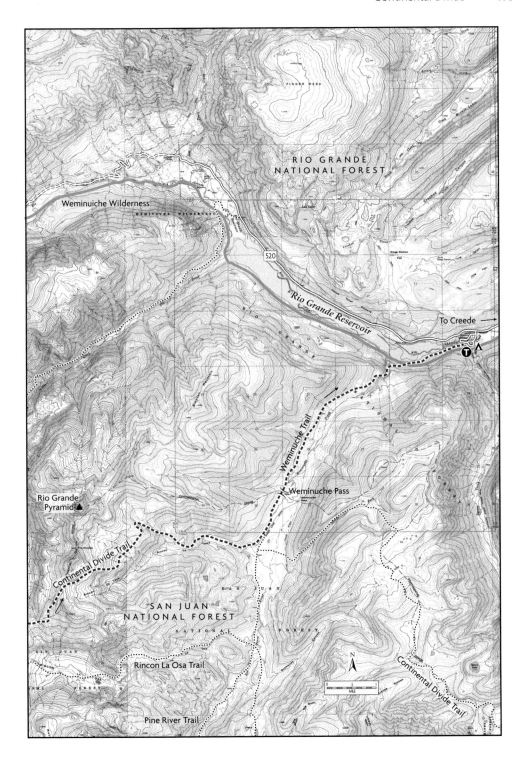

RIO GRANDE
NATIONAL FOREST

Weminuiche Wilderness

520

Rio Grande Reservoir

To Creede

Weminuche Trail

Weminuche Pass

Rio Grande
Pyramid

Continental Divide Trail

SAN JUAN
NATIONAL FOREST

Rincon La Osa Trail

N

Continental Divide Trail

Pine River Trail

Beginning about 0.5 mile east of Stony Pass, this section of the Continental Divide Trail heads due south along a mostly level grade for the first 4 miles or so. The hiking is surprisingly easy, and because this stretch is well above timberline, the scenery is incredible in all directions. Looking east you can see the forested headwaters of the Rio Grande, while to the west is Cunningham Gulch (Hike 73). About 1.5 miles from the trailhead, the route intersects with a side trail that drops into Cunningham Gulch, where it meets the Highland Mary Trail to the west.

Beyond the Highland Mary area, the Continental Divide Trail continues south—still above timberline and still along level or easy grades—to reach the head of Elk Creek, which drops west to the Animas River. The Elk Creek Trail, in fact, is now part of the Colorado Trail, which runs from Denver to Durango. Just south of Elk Creek the mountains change abruptly as the Grenadier Range spikes the skyline with a number of sharply rising 13,000-foot peaks. The

Continental Divide Trail, however, drops east to leave the Divide. In so doing it avoids the rugged slopes of 13,136-foot Hunchback Mountain and instead descends into the Kite Lake area, which lies outside the Weminuche Wilderness. In this 2-mile diversion from the actual Divide, the route drops about 1000 feet, mostly along a rough 4WD road. It then intersects the 4WD route, which accesses Kite Lake to the right. After crossing this road, the Continental Divide Trail continues south to climb 700 feet in 0.75 mile to reach 12,493-foot Hunchback Pass. Here the trail crosses the Divide and then drops steeply into the head of Vallecito Creek. In the next mile the trail descends 1000 feet to where Nebo Creek comes in from the east. The route then climbs east for a little more than a mile to cross the Divide once more. It gains nearly 1200 feet in this ascent to top a 12,500-foot saddle just north of 13,205-foot Mount Nebo.

Now east of the Continental Divide, the trail drops moderately for 2 miles to reach West Ute

The Continental Divide Trail near Ute Peak

Lake, the first of several nice lakes that dot the headwaters of the Ute Creek drainage. From West Ute Lake, the Continental Divide Trail heads south to climb up and over a 12,200-foot saddle before dropping to Middle Ute Lake. In this 2-mile stretch, the trail climbs 400 feet and then drops 200 feet to reach the second lake, which is at an elevation of just under 12,000 feet. The trail then continues south for 1 mile to meet a trail that heads south to Rock Lake. From this intersection on the Continental Divide, the route bears left before dropping moderately to Twin Lakes. Beyond Twin Lakes the trail continues east to reach Ute Lake. Ute Lake, like most in this area, offers good fishing possibilities. Hiking in the vicinity of these lakes can be slow because of thick willows and soggy ground. Additionally, some portions of the trail can be indistinct and hard to find.

From Ute Lake, the Continental Divide Trail ascends eastward to a ridge that extends south from 12,892-foot Ute Peak. At the top is an intersection with the Rincon La Osa Trail, which heads into its namesake drainage. Sometimes hikers mistakenly follow this better-defined trail. While the Rincon La Osa Trail drops east from the ridge, the Continental Divide Trail turns left to follow the ridge north toward Ute Peak. As it nears the top of this interesting little summit, the route cuts across its southern face to continue east along the Divide. It intersects the upper end of the East Ute Creek Trail in another mile, after which it reaches the head of the Rincon La Vaca drainage.

In the next 2 miles, the Continental Divide Trail drops a bit as it continues northeast into the Rincon la Vaca. Along this stretch of the trail, you get a good look at an astounding landmark known as the Window, a 140-foot-deep cut in the Divide above. Spanish sheepherders referred to the Window as the Devils Gateway.

Just north of The Window is an impressive 13,821-foot mountain known as the Rio Grande Pyramid. After reaching a point a couple of miles east of the Pyramid, the Continental Divide Trail turns due east to begin its descent into the Rincon la Vaca drainage. Within a mile it drops below timberline to reach the drainage bottom, and in another mile it reaches a wide-open park that runs north and south over low-slung Weminuche Pass. While the Continental Divide Trail continues east across this level meadow area, this hike turns north to reach 10,630-foot Weminuche Pass a mile north.

From Weminuche Pass, follow the Weminuche Trail northeast for 5.5 miles to a trailhead at Thirty-Mile Campground. Dropping easily along Weminuche Creek, this trail descends 1200 feet over its entire length. Portions of this route cross open meadows, while other parts pass through forests of Engelmann spruce and subalpine fir.

Because most of this hike is above timberline, you should take extra precautions to avoid lightning, which is common during summer afternoons. Weather conditions in general can deteriorate rapidly at this elevation. Because the Continental Divide Trail is indistinct in places, be sure you bring all necessary topographic maps. Water is found along most of this hike, but it should be treated before drinking.

71 CHICAGO BASIN

Distance: 16.8 miles round-trip
Difficulty: Strenuous
Hiking time: 2 days
Elevation: 8000 to 12,680 feet
Management: San Juan National Forest
Wilderness status: Weminuche Wilderness Area
Season: July to September
Maps: USGS Mountain View Crest, Columbine Pass, Snowdon Peak

Getting there: Most folks begin this excursion by riding the Durango and Silverton Narrow Gauge (D&SNG) Railroad north from Durango to the Needleton stopover. Not all trains make the stop to let off passengers, however, so be sure to specify that you will be hiking in from Needleton when you purchase your ticket. You will also want to find out what time to meet the train on your return trip. If you want to bypass the train ride completely, you can hike an extra 11 miles each way down Purgatory Creek from a trailhead along US Highway 550 and upstream along the Animas River to reach the Needle Creek Trail.

One of the most scenic areas in the San Juans, Chicago Basin is surrounded by the stunning 13,000- and 14,000-foot peaks of the Needle Range. Add to this the fact that the trailhead is accessible by way of a steam-powered narrow-gauge train, and you have an adventure that is steeped in both natural and historic lore. Be forewarned, however: several thousand people hike into Chicago Basin each summer, so this is no place to find solitude.

From Needleton, the Needle Creek Trail heads south along the east side of the Animas River for less than a mile to reach the Needle Creek drain-age, which continues east. After intersecting the Purgatory Trail, the Needle Creek Trail begins climbing moderate-to-occasionally-steep grades along the north side of Needle Creek. Staying on this side of the creek all the way to Chicago Basin, the trail follows what was once a stagecoach route. During the late 1800s, Needleton was a thriving little town and Chicago Basin was the site of several active mines. Today Needleton is but a few scattered cabins, and all of the mines in the basin above are nothing more than historical notations on the landscape. But, just as it was back then, access to the area is still provided by the narrow-gauge railroad.

As the Needle Creek Trail climbs, it leaves behind the scented ponderosa pine forests in exchange for a mix of Engelmann spruce and subalpine fir. Scattered aspen stands are also encountered along much of the way. About 2 miles from Needleton, the trail crosses New York Creek, which drains in from the northeast. Slide paths along this stretch of the hike testify to the fact that avalanches are a constant wintertime

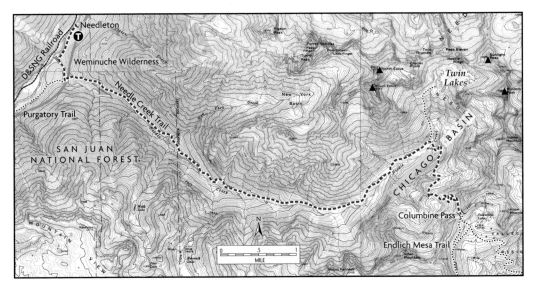

Mountain goat at Twin Lakes in the San Juan Mountains

threat in the San Juan Mountains. After another mile or so, views of the surrounding summits pop up in places where the trees thin out and in small openings. Additionally, nearby Needle Creek drops through some noisy but beautiful cascades that make for nice streamside lunch spots. The Needle Creek Trail reaches the Chicago Basin about 7 miles from the start.

Characterized by open meadows that spread across the valley floor, Chicago Basin is completely engulfed by incredibly rugged mountains. To the south, along what is known as Mountain View Crest, rise 13,125-foot Mount Kennedy and 13,310-foot Aztec Mountain. Three 14,000-foot peaks—14,083-foot Mount Eolus, 14,053-foot Sunlight Peak, and 14,082-foot Windom Peak—tower to the north. Climbers intent on bagging these three summits head north from the Needle Creek Trail along a rugged route that follows Needle Creek up the basin's north wall to Twin Lakes. From the lakes, it is a relatively easy scramble east to Sunlight and Windom, and a somewhat more difficult ascent west to Eolus. A transplanted herd of mountain goats (these animals are not native to the San Juans) roams the Twin Lakes area. They have become used to people; do not feed them.

While Chicago Basin is spectacular in its own right, it is well worth the trouble to climb beyond the basin to the top of 12,800-foot Columbine Pass—the turnaround point of this hike. In this last segment of the hike, the trail climbs 1600 feet in about 1.5 miles. From the pass, the views extend north across the Needle Mountains—indeed, they are so pointed that the name is fitting—and east into the Vallecito Creek drainage. Beyond Vallecito Creek, the San Juans continue to march eastward, stacking up against the skyline as they do. East of the pass, the Johnson Creek Trail drops to Columbine Lake before continuing on to meet the Vallecito Creek Trail below. A second route—the Endlich Mesa Trail—heads south from Columbine Pass over Trimble Pass and then on to City Reservoir. From Trimble Pass, it is also possible to access Mountain View Crest.

Within Chicago Basin are a few nice spots to camp. Because of severe overuse, however, campfires have been banned throughout the Needle Creek drainage. This has resulted in much cleaner campsites, but human impact on vegetation is still a problem. You must also camp at least 100 feet from water and have no more than 15 people per group. Additionally, the Forest Service asks that you bury human waste well away from streams and carry out toilet paper.

Water is found along this hike, but it should be treated before drinking. Lightning can pose a hazard in the higher reaches of the basin and on Columbine Pass. Because a considerable number of people hike into Chicago Basin, you might want to plan your trip for after Labor Day or, if the snows melt early, in June. Keep in mind that you will likely run into up to a hundred other hikers on any given day in Chicago Basin.

72 CRATER LAKE

Distance: 11 miles round-trip
Difficulty: Moderate
Hiking time: 7 hours
Elevation: 10,750 to 11,640 feet
Management: San Juan National Forest
Wilderness status: Weminuche Wilderness Area
Season: July to September
Map: USGS Snowdon Peak

Getting there: From Durango, drive 44 miles north on US Highway 550 to the signed right turn for Andrews Lake, which is just south of Molas Pass. Turn and continue south for about 1 mile to Andrews Lake.

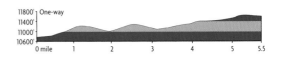

Crater Lake at twilight

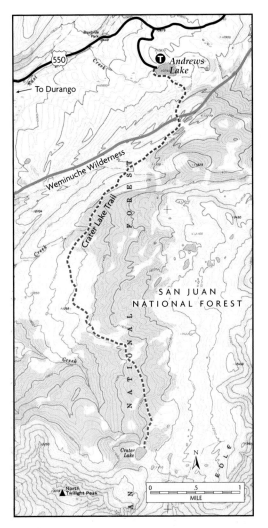

grade is easy to moderate. Because the terrain in this area is partially open, views open up in various directions. Below you can occasionally see US Highway 550 winding its way over Molas Pass. Summits that come into view include Sultan and Kendall Mountains to the north, the Twin Sisters and Jura Knob to the west, Engineer Mountain to the southwest, and Snowdon Peak directly east. The only drawback to this panorama is a powerline over Molas Pass.

The trail levels off after the first mile as it tops a ridge south of Andrews Lake. The route then begins to dip in and out of a number of shallow drainages as it heads south toward Crater Lake. Some of these grade changes may be moderate in difficulty, but they are short and never really a problem. As the trail makes its way to the lake, it crosses several open meadows where wildflowers grow in abundance. It also encounters a few small streams, some thickly timbered areas of Engelmann spruce and subalpine fir, and outcroppings of light-colored limestone.

Within the last 1.5 miles leading up to Crater Lake, the trail crosses marshy areas where the route can be a bit hard to find at first. A careful scan of the scene, though, quickly reveals the way. After 5.5 miles, the Crater Lake Trail reaches its destination, which is nestled just below timberline at the foot of 13,075-foot North Twilight Peak. A favorite among fly fishermen, Crater Lake is well stocked. Its shoreline harbors many suitable camping spots and the scenery is unsurpassed—especially at dawn and dusk, when the rugged north face of Twilight is reflected in the still lake waters. It is possible to get a good look at the Needle Mountains to the east by climbing a small saddle that sits just above the lake. And, as many climbers already know, the summit of North Twilight can be accessed from Crater Lake. The route first tops the aforementioned saddle and then follows the ridge south to the east flank of North Twilight Peak. From the summit, it is possible to reach 13,158-foot Twilight Peak. The crossover to the higher summit involves a 400-foot drop and some scrambling over steep terrain.

All water along this hike should be treated before drinking. Watch for lightning during the frequent summer thunderstorms. Camp at least 100 feet from the lake.

The hike to Crater Lake is a popular one, and for good reason. Access to the trail's start is easy and, with only one real climb, the hike is not too demanding. Along the way, the route crosses some scenic terrain to reach a real gem of a lake. Whether you are looking for a nice day hike or an overnight destination, Crater Lake is an excellent possibility.

From the Andrews Lake parking area, the Crater Lake Trail circles south around the mouth of the lake. About 0.25 mile out, the trail begins a 500-foot climb along a few long switchbacks. This section of the route is easy to follow and the

73 HIGHLAND MARY LAKES

Distance: 8 miles round-trip
Difficulty: Strenuous
Hiking time: 6 hours
Elevation: 10,450 to 12,170 feet
Management: Bureau of Land Management, San Juan National Forest
Wilderness status: Weminuche Wilderness Area
Season: July to September
Map: USGS Howardsville

Getting there: From Silverton, drive 4 miles east on Colorado Highway 110 to the old town of Howardsville. Turn right onto Forest Road 589 and drive 4 miles up Cunningham Gulch to the trailhead at road's end. Although most of this road is passable to 2WD vehicles, the last 0.75 mile might require a 4WD.

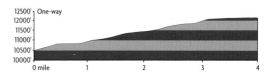

Situated in a verdant alpine basin just west of the Continental Divide, the Highland Mary Lakes are a popular destination for day hikers and backpackers alike. Some come to try their luck at fishing, while others hike the steep trail simply to enjoy the surrounding scenery. Whatever your intent, these alpine lakes are worth the effort.

From the trailhead, the Highland Mary Trail begins to climb almost immediately. Alternating between moderate and strenuous grades, this route ascends some 400 feet in the first 0.25 mile. At this point, the trail intersects a route that climbs 1400 feet to reach the Continental Divide a few miles to the east. Continuing straight at this junction, the Highland Mary Trail levels off for a short distance to reach a second turnoff for the Continental Divide (this route connects with the first a short distance east). It then begins climbing again and gains another 800 feet in the next 2 miles. Along this section the route occasionally crosses Cunningham Creek, which is not difficult to negotiate. The trail also bends and twists a bit as it climbs along moderate-to-strenuous grades. As you climb up Cunningham Gulch, be sure to notice the many old mines that dot the mountainsides. This drainage, along with most others in this part of the San Juans, was busy with mining

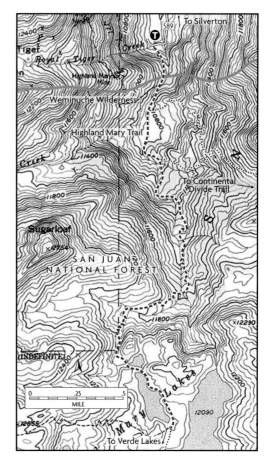

A herd of sheep near Highland Mary Lakes

activity during the last decades of the nineteenth century.

After reaching timberline at the 11,600-foot level, the trail climbs another 500 feet through open alpine tundra. Of the many wildflowers that grow here in July and August, blue columbine is the showiest. At the 12,000-foot level—about 3.5 miles from the start—the Highland Mary Trail reaches the first two lakes of the Highland Mary Lakes chain. Passing between the two, the trail continues south along the east shore of the second lake to access the third and largest of the lakes. Fishing is reported to be good to excellent in all three lakes, and vistas of the amazingly lush alpine tundra that covers the surrounding mountains are unforgettable. Domestic sheep can often be seen grazing across the slopes above the lake. While this hike turns around at the Highland Mary Lakes, it is possible to continue south for 0.5 mile to the Verde Lakes or west to the summit of 13,259-foot Whitehead Peak. In addition, the Continental Divide Trail runs along the ridges a mile east of the Highland Mary Lakes, and some people access it via this route.

Water is available along this hike, but it should be treated before drinking. Lightning is a frequent hazard in this high, open terrain during July and August, when afternoon thunderstorms are a common occurrence. Camp at least 100 feet from the lake.

74 ICE LAKE BASIN

Distance: 7 miles round-trip
Difficulty: Strenuous
Hiking time: 5 hours
Elevation: 9810 to 12,257 feet
Management: San Juan National Forest
Wilderness status: None
Season: July to September
Map: USGS Ophir

Getting there: The start of the Ice Lake Trail is adjacent to the South Mineral Campground. From Silverton, drive about 2 miles west on US Highway 550 to the

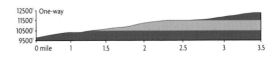

Waterfall in Ice Lake Basin

left-hand turn for Forest Road 585, which follows South Mineral Creek. Drive 6 miles on the good gravel road to the South Mineral Campground. The trailhead is located on the north side of the road.

Surrounded by some rather impressive peaks and replete with wildflowers in the summertime, Ice Lake Basin is a popular destination for hikers visiting the Silverton region of the San Juan Mountains. There are actually two Ice Lake Basins. This hike passes through the lower basin before climbing to the upper one.

From the start, the trail begins its nearly 2500-foot climb in earnest as it gains elevation at moderate-to-strenuous grades. Within the first mile, the route alternates between forested areas with aspen, Engelmann spruce, and subalpine fir, and open meadows often filled with wildflowers. Understandably, vistas along the way grow more alluring the higher you go. The trail eventually reaches a rocky area, above which is Lower Ice Lake Basin. It is here that timberline begins to take shape, trail grades ease a bit, and mostly open mountainsides become ideal showplaces for blue columbine, Indian paintbrush, mountain bluebell, and other alpine flowers. The best time of the year for enjoying this show (a show that some say rivals Yankee Boy Basin near Ouray) runs from mid-July into August.

From the lower basin, the trail then climbs a final 500 feet in less than a mile to reach Ice Lake Basin. Completely void of trees, this high basin is ringed by some beautiful 13,000-foot peaks, including Fuller Peak, Vermillion Peak, the Golden Horn, and Pilots Knob. Ice Lake itself is sizable and a popular fishing hole. If you have some spare energy you can continue on to Fuller Lake, about 400 feet higher in a basin south of Ice Lake. Fuller is actually larger than Ice Lake and includes a number of old mine structures along its shores. Fuller Lake is less than a mile beyond Ice Lake.

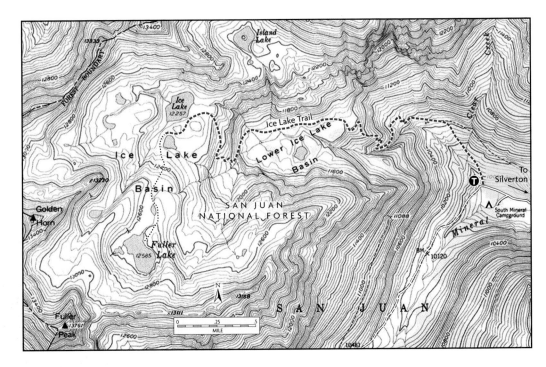

Keep in mind that all antiquities, including mining relics, are protected by law. Watch for lightning during summer thunderstorms and rapidly deteriorating weather conditions throughout the year. Water is available along the way, but it should be treated before drinking. Be prepared to encounter many other hikers along this popular trail.

75 SPUD LAKE

Distance: 2 miles round-trip
Difficulty: Easy
Hiking time: 2 hours
Elevation: 9360 to 9800 feet
Management: San Juan National Forest
Wilderness status: None
Season: June to October
Map: USGS Engineer Mountain

Getting there: From Durango, take US Highway 550 about 27 miles north and turn right onto Old Lime Creek Road (Forest Service Road 591) just past Cascade Creek. From the turnoff, it is 2.9 miles to the trailhead, which is on the left side of the

road. Old Lime Creek Road is graveled but normally passable for most vehicles.

aspens are bathed with a brilliant golden glow. Anglers might have good luck at Spud Lake, although the fishing is inconsistent. As for the geology of the area, Spud Mountain and the West Needles are actually exposed portions of the Precambrian core of the San Juan Mountains. Unlike other reaches of this extensive mountain range, traces of volcanic activity here were mostly eroded away.

Be sure to treat all water before drinking, or better yet, simply pack a quart before setting out. Although Spud Lake is not particularly exposed, you should watch for lightning during afternoon thunderstorms.

As one of the easiest hikes in this book, Spud Lake is a great excursion for family members of nearly all ages. From ages 4 to 84, all can reach this beautiful little lake for a picnic and some fine fishing. Of course, its easy access also makes this lake a popular destination, so don't count on solitude. The lake was named for nearby "Spud Mountain"—their official names are Potato Lake and Potato Hill.

The Spud Lake Trail begins by winding its way through old aspen groves. The wide route is easy to follow and grades are gentle throughout. As the route draws closer to the lake (after the 0.5-mile mark), it passes several beaver dams that offer wildlife-watching opportunities for those who can wait patiently. Mule deer and elk inhabit the forests along the way, as does a variety of smaller game. After passing a small pond on the left, the trail tops a small ridge, beyond which is the lake itself.

Shaded by 11,871-foot Potato Hill to the north and by the magnificent 13,000-foot peaks of the West Needle Range to the east, Spud Lake is a scenic destination all summer long, but September is especially beautiful, as the area's many

A young girl frolics in Spud Lake.

76 COLORADO TRAIL

Distance: 23 miles one-way
Difficulty: Strenuous
Hiking time: 3 days
Elevation: 10,880 to 12,490 feet
Management: San Juan National Forest
Wilderness status: None
Season: July to September
Maps: USGS Snowdon Peak, Engineer Mountain, Ophir, Silverton

Getting there: From Durango, drive 45 miles north on US Highway 550 to Molas Pass. The Colorado Trail crosses the highway just north of the pass. This hike begins at Little Molas Lake, however, where a trailhead provides plenty of parking. To reach the trailhead, drive about 0.5 mile beyond Molas Pass and turn left onto the graveled road to Little Molas Lake. The lake and trailhead are about 1 mile from the highway. Because this hike is one way, you will need to arrange for a shuttle at Coal Bank Pass, located farther south on US Highway 550. The trailhead is located just west of the highway at the pass.

Covering 469 miles in its journey from Denver to Durango, the Colorado Trail accesses a variety of mountain terrain throughout the state. Built mostly by volunteers under the direction of Gudy Gaskill, this trans-state trail linked many existing trails to form one continuous route. On September 4, 1987, completion ceremonies were held at three locations along the trail. One of these sites was 10,880-foot Molas Pass. This hike follows one particularly interesting stretch of the

Hikers along the Colorado Trail near Molas Pass

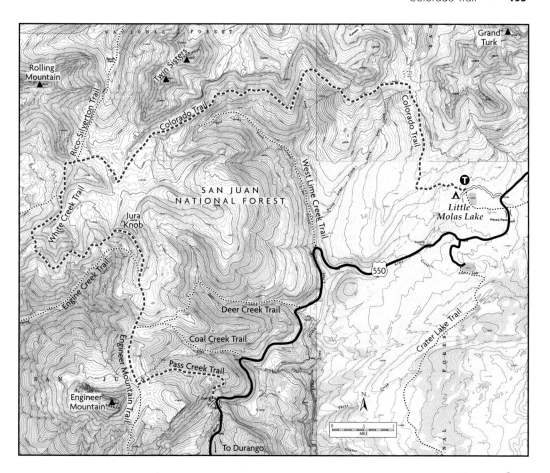

trail 12 miles west from Molas Pass to the head of Cascade Creek. It then turns south to follow three lesser routes to Coal Bank Pass. The fact that most of the route is at or above timberline makes this an especially nice excursion.

From Little Molas Lake, the Colorado Trail heads due west to switchback up a moderately sloping ridge. Widely scattered spruce and fir trees grow along this open mountainside, while a few standing dead snags serve as reminders of the Lime Creek Burn of 1879. The fact that evidence of the fire is still noticeable more than a century later demonstrates just how fragile life is in this subalpine environment. After climbing nearly 400 feet in 1 mile, the trail reaches an old road near the ridge top. Turn right and follow this road for a short distance to where the trail turns off sharply to the right. From this point,

the route continues north to begin traversing the head of the North Lime Creek drainage. Above timberline at this point, the Colorado Trail flirts with the last reaches of forest over the next 10 miles or so.

From the top of the ridge overlooking Little Molas Lake, the Colorado Trail climbs another 400 feet in 0.75 mile to reach an elevation of about 11,600 feet. In the next 2 miles, the route contours north and west at this elevation. Rising directly northeast is 13,368-foot Sultan Mountain. At mile 4 the route drops slightly to an 11,520-foot saddle that separates North Lime Creek from Bear Creek to the north. The trail then turns west again to eventually cross into the head of West Lime Creek. A number of peaks are easily visible from the trail along this segment; besides Sultan Mountain, the panorama takes in 13,432-foot

Twin Sisters, 12,614-foot Jura Knob, 12,968-foot Engineer Mountain, 13,077-foot Snowdon Peak, and the more distant Needle Mountains.

At 6 miles out, the Colorado Trail drops down a few switchbacks before heading south for a short ways. Continuing at an elevation of about 11,500 feet, the Colorado Trail travels above the head of West Lime Creek for the next 4 miles. Towering to the right is a line of dark volcanic cliffs and a pair of summits known as the Twin Sisters. At the far end of the West Lime Creek drainage, the trail encounters an open terrace that lies on the divide between the Lime Creek and South Mineral Creek drainages. From here, the Colorado Trail climbs an easy saddle to the west, where it reaches this hike's high point of 12,490 feet. From this saddle, the route drops into the head of the Cascade Creek drainage. Here, a little more than 12 miles from Molas Pass, the Colorado Trail intersects the upper end of the White Creek Trail.

At the junction between the Colorado and White Creek Trails, this hike turns east onto the latter route to begin heading south toward Engineer Mountain and Coal Bank Pass. Maintaining an elevation of around 12,000 feet, the 3.5-mile White Creek Trail circles around the west side of a 12,703-foot unnamed mountain before continuing east toward the verdant slopes of Jura Knob. Upon reaching the south slope of this interesting little summit, the route turns south again and intersects with the Engine Creek Trail and the Engineer Mountain Trail. From this junction, the hike continues south, following a 2-mile stretch of the Engineer Mountain route along a broad and mostly open ridge top. Not too far away is the unmistakable silhouette of Engineer Mountain. Along this segment of the hike, the Engineer Mountain Trail drops easily to an 11,650-foot saddle before climbing slightly to reach the foot of Engineer Mountain and the top end of the Pass Creek Trail. Climbers headed for Engineer Mountain's summit use the Pass Creek Trail to access the rugged north ridge of the mountain. The final leg of this hike turns left onto the popular Pass Creek Trail and follows it for 2.2 miles, dropping from 12,000 feet along mostly moderate grades to the trailhead at 10,600-foot Coal Bank Pass.

Water is found along much of this hike, but it should be treated before drinking. Watch for lightning all along this exposed route.

77 GOULDING CREEK

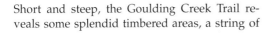

Distance: 5.4 miles round-trip
Difficulty: Strenuous
Hiking time: 4 hours
Elevation: 7880 to 10,070 feet
Management: San Juan National Forest
Wilderness status: None
Season: June to October
Map: USGS Electra Lake

Getting there: From Durango, drive about 16 miles north on US Highway 550. About a mile past the Tamarron Resort, turn left at a small sign for the trail. The trailhead itself is located less than 0.25 mile down this dirt road.

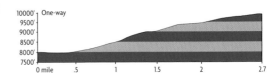

Short and steep, the Goulding Creek Trail reveals some splendid timbered areas, a string of beautiful meadows, and a dose of old-fashioned cowboy memorabilia.

Cowboy cabin along the Goulding Creek Trail

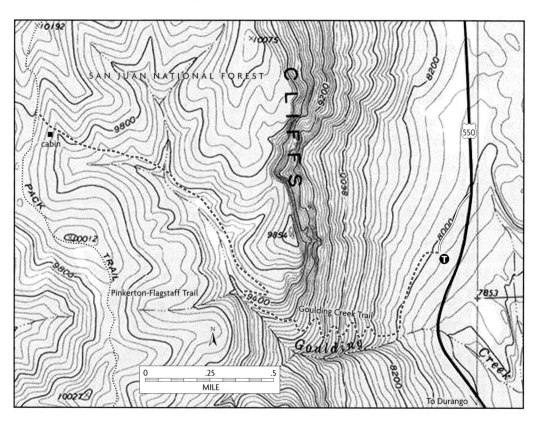

Starting out along a fairly level grade among aspen forests, the Goulding Creek Trail quickly takes up a series of often-steep switchbacks less than 0.5 mile from the start. As it climbs, the trail encounters some scattered ponderosa pines—some of them quite large—along with an occasional Douglas-fir and thick undergrowth of Gambel oak. As the route climbs, you can catch an occasional view of the highway and Tamarron Resort below, and of imposing Missionary Ridge, which rises along the eastern horizon. You might also hear the whistle of the Durango and Silverton Narrow Gauge Railroad as it winds its way through the trees below.

After climbing some 1500 feet in 2 miles, the Goulding Creek Trail levels off a bit where it passes through a cool aspen forest. In places you might spot a cliff face looming to the south. As part of the Hermosa Cliffs, which rise above US Highway 550 for several miles, this rock buttress is an example of the Hermosa Formation, which includes shales and sandstones deposited during the Pennsylvanian period in marine environments.

Upon reaching a fence and gate, the trail begins to climb along a more moderate grade before encountering the upper end of Goulding Creek. While the creek might be dry below, it is usually flowing at this elevation. The trail then enters the first of a series of beautiful tree-ringed meadows. Wildflowers are numerous in these openings, as are cows. The last meadow holds a small cabin that is still used by ranchers who run cattle in the area. Although not open to the general public, the small structure does make for an idyllic scene. About 0.25 mile above the cabin, the Goulding Creek Trail reaches the Pinkerton-Flagstaff Trail and the turnaround point for this hike. The Pinkerton-Flagstaff Trail runs for 8.5 miles along the crest of a lengthy ridge that separates the Animas River drainage from the Hermosa Creek drainage to the west. Glimpses of the heavily forested Hermosa creek drainage through the trees are impressive.

Be sure to bring plenty of water on this hike, as water might not be available during dry periods. Any water collected from Goulding Creek drainage should be treated before drinking.

78 ANIMAS CITY MOUNTAIN

Distance: 6-mile loop
Difficulty: Moderate
Hiking time: 4 hours
Elevation: 6680 to 8161 feet
Management: Bureau of Land Management and City of Durango
Wilderness status: None
Season: March to November
Map: USGS Durango East

Getting there: From downtown Durango, drive north on Main Avenue to 32nd Street. Turn left and drive uphill to West Fourth Avenue. Turn right and drive another block to the signed trailhead.

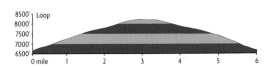

Durango residents have long enjoyed the beautiful pine forests and the spectacular scenery that a visit to the top of nearby Animas City Mountain provides. Managed by the BLM, the trail that loops across this mountain's sloping summit is currently designated as a combination hiking, biking, and equestrian route. The locally prominent mountain was named after Animas City,

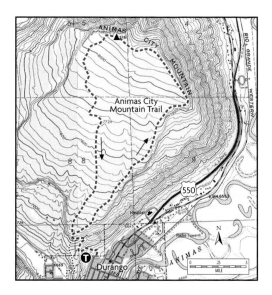

From the trailhead, the Animas City Mountain Trail begins by switchbacking up the south slope of the mountain before topping the mountain's south end. Climbing along mostly moderate grades, this section of trail is a huge improvement over a former route, which climbed strenuously along an old, rocky jeep road. Pinyon pine and juniper trees are encountered along this climb, with ponderosa pines growing here and there as the trail gains elevation. These taller evergreens are the dominant tree species on the mountain's gently sloping topside. Gambel oak also grows in patches along much of this hike.

After climbing a few hundred feet, the Animas City Mountain Trail reaches a ridgeline, at which point it intersects a side trail used by locals to access the mountain. Bear right and continue north to reach the lower, south end of the mountain. The route then begins following the east rim of the mountain, which is defined in places by high cliffs of Dakota Sandstone. Several points along this portion of the route offer some truly great scenery. Looking south you immediately get a nice view of Durango. As you continue around to the north, the vista begins to take in more of the expansive Animas River Valley. Walled in by the red cliffs of Missionary Ridge to the east, this flat-bottomed valley was carved

which preceded Durango by a few years. First settled in the 1870s, Animas City was a bit stand-offish in 1880 when General Palmer brought his Denver and Rio Grande Railroad to southwestern Colorado. Palmer instead established his own town 2 miles to the south and named it after the Mexican city of Durango. Over the years, Durango outgrew its civic rival and eventually annexed it.

View from the summit of Animas City Mountain

by the Animas River, which meanders widely as it tracks south from the San Juan Mountains. You can see how some bends in the river were eventually cut off from the river to become small oxbow lakes. You can also see that the verdant pasturelands within the valley are being swallowed up by housing developments. The trail ascends 1000 feet in the 2 miles that it follows the east rim.

Upon reaching the northeast corner of the mountaintop, the trail traverses the crest of the mountain's higher north end. Characterized by ponderosa pines, this area is frequented by mule deer and elk, especially in the winter. About 3 miles from the trailhead, the route reaches the 8161-foot summit of Animas City Mountain and a bird's-eye view of Falls Creek Valley to the north. From here, follow an old road as it descends due south down the middle of the mountain's flat top. Although closed to motor vehicles, this route is very popular among mountain bicyclists. Here, as on all stretches of the Animas City Mountain Trail, you should walk with caution as a few bicyclists career rapidly down the trail with little regard for what is around the next bend. The trail returns to the south end of the mountain in 1.75 miles. From this point, the route returns to the trailhead by way of the foot trail that it came up.

Bring plenty of water, as none is available along the trail. Lightning can pose a hazard during thunderstorms. If you are hiking with a dog, be sure to take along a leash and use the bags for waste provided at the trailhead.

79 WETTERHORN BASIN

Distance: 9 miles round-trip
Difficulty: Moderate
Hiking time: 7 hours
Elevation: 10,760 to 12,500 feet
Management: Uncompahgre National Forest
Wilderness status: Uncompahgre Wilderness Area
Season: July to September
Map: USGS Wetterhorn Peak

Getting there: From Ouray, drive 12 miles north on US Highway 550 to Owl Creek Pass Road (Forest Road 858). Turn right and drive about 14 miles to the turnoff for West Fork Road (Forest Road 860). Turn south and drive 5 miles to the trailhead, which is at road's end, north of the wilderness area. The last 1.5 miles of this road normally requires a high-clearance vehicle, and wet weather can make it impassable.

Formerly known as the Big Blue, the Uncompahgre Wilderness encompasses a pair of fourteeners, dozens of 13,000-foot summits, many miles of pristine streams, and some incredibly picturesque alpine basins. One of these scenic basins spans the head of Wetterhorn Creek in the western half of the wilderness. Accessed by a moderately easy trail, Wetterhorn Basin makes a memorable destination for hikers of varied abilities.

Following the Wetterhorn Trail, this hike sets out among scattered stands of Engelmann spruce and subalpine fir to reach timberline after the first mile. Beyond treeline, the remaining 3.5 miles traverse beautiful alpine meadows that fill with blue columbine, Indian paintbrush, and a variety of other wildflowers in the midsummer months. In places, the trail follows closely along the West Fork of the Cimarron River, a nice

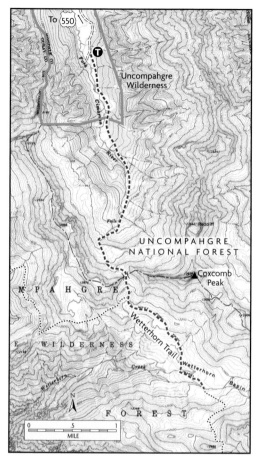

Wetterhorn Basin

stream that features many cascades and a small waterfall. The first 2 miles of the well-established and easy-to-follow Wetterhorn Trail climb along mostly easy grades. Only as it draws to within 0.5 mile of the pass that leads to Wetterhorn Basin does it take up a more moderate climb. A few switchbacks are encountered, but the grade is never overly difficult.

After 2.5 miles, the Wetterhorn Trail has climbed some 1800 feet to reach the high point of this hike—a 12,500-foot unnamed pass. Rising directly east of the pass is 13,656-foot Coxcomb Peak, and dominating the skyline to the southeast is the 14,015-foot summit of Wetterhorn Peak. Wetterhorn Peak is thought to be the conduit of an extinct volcano, later sculpted by glaciers to give it its rugged profile. From the pass, you can look south across the Wetterhorn Basin and

southwest into the Cow Creek drainage. Facing back to the north, you can look straight down the West Fork drainage toward the Owl Creek Pass area. Towering above the pass are several stunning rock pinnacles, the most visible of which is Chimney Rock.

South of the pass, the Wetterhorn Trail continues into the Wetterhorn Basin, where it reaches Wetterhorn Creek and the turnaround point of this hike. From the creek crossing at an elevation of 11,900 feet, the Wetterhorn Trail does continue on to climb another 600 feet to reach a pass that separates Wetterhorn Basin from the head of Mary Alice Creek to the south. From this point, the route drops to a trailhead south of the Uncompahgre Wilderness.

Water is available along this hike, but it should be treated before drinking. Lightning can pose a danger to hikers along most of this trail, especially on the pass and in the open basin beyond.

80 BEAR CREEK

Distance: 8.4 miles round-trip
Difficulty: Strenuous
Hiking time: 6 hours
Elevation: 8440 to 11,200 feet
Management: Uncompahgre National Forest
Wilderness status: None
Season: June to October
Maps: USGS Ouray, Ironton, Handies Peak

Getting there: From Ouray, drive 2 miles south on US Highway 550 to where the road passes through a small tunnel. The trailhead is on the right side of the road immediately beyond the tunnel. Additional parking is available on the left.

Of the four different Bear Creeks found in the western half of the San Juan Mountains, the one that drains into the Uncompahgre Gorge a couple of miles south of Ouray could well be the most spectacular. Although the creek bottom itself is far too rugged to follow, miners during the late nineteenth century were not deterred and constructed a trail into the upper reaches of

The rugged Bear Creek Trail

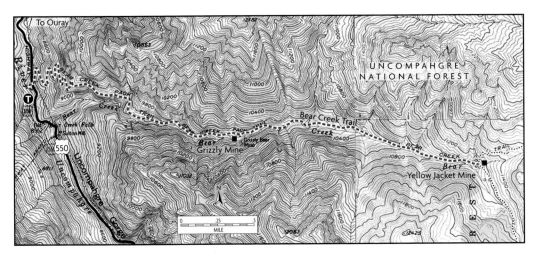

the drainage. In so doing, they built one of the most improbable mountain trails in the Colorado Rockies. This hike follows the first 4.2 miles of the route, which is designated as a National Recreation Trail.

From the trailhead, the Bear Creek Trail crosses over the road by way of the top of the tunnel. It then begins climbing up a lengthy series of moderate-to-strenuously-steep switchbacks along the east wall of the Uncompahgre Gorge. In its first mile the trail passes through scattered white firs, some of which are quite old and impressive. After about a mile of climbing, the trail encounters some picturesque limber pines as well. At an open area, you can look straight down to see the trailhead directly below. Signs on either end of the switchbacks warn against tossing rocks down the slope so as not to injure other hikers. The trail crosses a talus slope, then traverses the first of many precipitous ledges. It climbs more switchbacks before finally leveling off, having ascended some 800 feet in the first 1.5 miles.

From the top of the switchbacks, you can enjoy nice views of the Uncompahgre Gorge below and the highly scenic Mount Sneffels massif to the west. You can also begin to see the town of Ouray tucked in the canyon to the north. In addition to the terrific scenery, this vantage point provides a good perspective on the geology of the area. Exposed along the lower reaches of the rugged Uncompahgre Gorge are the quartzites and slates of the Uncompahgre Formation. This formation dates to the Precambrian era and includes some of the oldest rocks in Colorado. Exhibited in these slates are ripple marks that hint at the rock's sedimentary origins. As the Bear Creek Trail climbs up the last switchback, it crosses from this Precambrian rock to a deposit of much younger volcanic tuff above. Common across the higher reaches of the San Juan Mountains, this rock was deposited during the Tertiary period, between 40 million and 5 million years ago. Occurring in three different phases, fiery eruptions repeatedly spewed ash and lava across a broad dome of older rock to slowly build up a layer of volcanic material thousands of feet thick. The end result was the large and rugged San Juan Mountain Range.

From the top of the switchbacks, the Bear Creek Trail contours east along an elevation of about 9200 feet for the next 0.75 mile or so. It is along this stretch that you can really appreciate the hard work that went into this incredible trail. In places the miners actually blasted ledges out of the sheer canyon wall. They also built support cribbing out of logs and rocks, some of which is still visible. Soon after the trail crosses a boulder slide area, it climbs along a moderate grade for 0.25 mile to reach the old Grizzly Mine. Situated amid a stand of aspens on the left side of the creek are a few fallen-down buildings and some rusted machinery. The Grizzly Mine itself is located just across the creek and up the mountainside a bit.

Beyond the Grizzly Mine, the Bear Creek Trail continues along the north wall of the canyon until it reaches the creek bottom about 3 miles from the trailhead. The route then climbs sporadically for a little more than a mile to reach the Yellow Jacket Mine and the turnaround point of this hike. Along this last segment, the trail crosses a side creek and continues on through forests of mostly Engelmann spruce and subalpine firs, and across open meadows. Like the Grizzly Mine, the Yellow Jacket Mine features old buildings and machinery, plus open mine shafts and tunnels. For safety reasons, it is best not to enter these deteriorating mines.

Although this hike turns around here, it is possible to continue on in one of two directions. From the Yellow Jacket Mine, the Bear Creek Trail continues east to eventually reach the Horsethief Trail and American Flats in the southern tip of the Uncompahgre Wilderness. A second route turns

south at the Yellow Jacket Mine to climb to 13,218-foot Engineer Pass. While the Bear Creek Trail was built to access mines such as the Grizzly and Yellow Jacket, it also served as an alternate route to the Engineer Mountain area for miners who did not want to pay the toll levied for passage on the Million Dollar Highway, which continued up the Uncompahgre Gorge. Built by Otto Mears, the Million Dollar Highway was a real engineering feat etched out of sheer canyon walls. Today, US Highway 550 follows Mears's route.

Water is available in the second half of this hike, but it should be treated before drinking; the first 3 miles of the route are dry. Lightning can pose a hazard along the higher portions of this hike. Because of severe drop-offs, exercise extreme caution along much of this trail. Do not throw rocks over edges or cut switchbacks. Falling rocks can pose a hazard, especially after a rain.

81 BLUE LAKES

Distance: 7 miles round-trip
Difficulty: Strenuous
Hiking time: 5 hours
Elevation: 8350 to 11,730 feet
Management: Uncompahgre National Forest
Wilderness status: Mount Sneffels Wilderness Area
Season: July to September
Maps: USGS Mount Sneffels, Telluride

Getting there: From Ridgway, drive about 4 miles west on Colorado Highway 62 to Dallas Creek Road (Forest Road 851). Turn left and drive 14 miles south to the Blue Lakes trailhead, which is on a sharp bend near the road's end.

Set in a scenic glacial basin, the Blue Lakes provide a nice destination within the 16,505-acre Mount Sneffels Wilderness. In addition to the access this hike provides to higher terrain above, the fishing at all three lakes can be superb.

From the trailhead, the Blue Lakes Trail follows

the East Fork of Dallas Creek south for a short distance before beginning to climb up a ridge west of the creek. After following moderate grades for the first 1.5 miles, the trail reaches a side creek that flows east into Dallas Creek below. By this point the route has gained 2000 feet in elevation. Beyond this stream crossing, the Blue Lakes Trail climbs a bit farther to reach an

elevation of 11,700 feet, along which it contours south for the next 0.5 mile. After the trail gains another 300 feet, it reaches the north shore of the lowest and largest of the Blue Lakes. From here, the Blue Lakes Trail ascends steeply eastward to gain 600 feet in less than 0.5 mile to reach the middle lake. The climb in the last 0.25 mile to the uppermost Blue Lake is negligible.

Situated above timberline, the middle and upper Blue Lakes provide the best views of the surrounding collection of particularly rugged summits. Included in the lineup are 13,809-foot Dallas Peak and 13,694-foot Gilpin Peak to the south, an unnamed 13,242-foot-high extension of Mears Peak to the west, and—the tallest of all—14,150-foot Mount Sneffels directly east. While the dark color of these summits belies the fact that this area resulted from an extensive period of volcanic activity, Mount Sneffels itself has been identified as an igneous intrusion that pushed its way up through existing layers of volcanic rock. For all its ruggedness, Mount Sneffels is a relatively straightforward climb from the Blue Lakes Pass area above the lakes. To reach the pass, continue east from the uppermost lake for another mile or so. Climbing strenuously much of the way, this ascent gains some 1200 feet to reach the 13,000-foot pass. Beyond the pass, the route to the summit of Mount Sneffels takes off to the north to climb a couloir on the mountain's

Blue Lakes as seen from the summit of nearby Mount Sneffels

southeast face. While Mount Sneffels is accessible from the Blue Lakes, most climbers begin their ascent in Yankee Boy Basin on the east side of Blue Lakes Pass.

Water is available at the start of this hike and at the lakes, but it should be treated before drinking. Watch for lightning in the vicinity of the

lakes and above. Keep in mind that the rock in the Sneffels Range is rotten—use extreme caution when climbing around exposed areas. Because the area receives heavy use, you might want to plan your trip for a weekday. Campfires are banned within the East Dallas Creek drainage, so bring a stove.

82 SNEFFELS HIGH LINE

Distance: 14-mile loop
Difficulty: Strenuous
Hiking time: 9 hours
Elevation: 8900 to 12,250 feet
Management: Uncompahgre National Forest
Wilderness status: Mount Sneffels Wilderness Area
Season: June to September
Map: USGS Telluride

Getting there: From downtown Telluride, drive to the north end of Aspen Street and park along the last block or two. Walk the remaining way to the trailhead, which features a signboard.

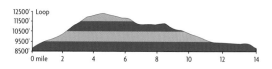

Although you would never know it by looking at the Uncompahgre National Forest map, a number of interesting trails explore the rugged mountain slopes north of Telluride. Perhaps the most intriguing route is the Sneffels High Line Trail. Completed in the summer of 1990, this loop trail connects several older routes with newer sections to climb steeply above timberline. Traversing two alpine basins, this hike reveals some memorable views along the way.

From the trailhead, walk less than 50 yards north and turn left onto the Jud Wiebe Trail. As this route climbs west along the mountainside above Telluride, it offers nice views of the town and ski area in short order. Along the way, it also encounters some big Douglas-firs. This portion of the Jud Wiebe Trail is very popular among mountain bicyclists, so watch out for them up ahead. Climbing moderate-to-steep grades, this hike gains about 600 feet in elevation in nearly a mile to reach an intersection. The Jud Wiebe Trail

turns right at the junction to reach a trailhead on the Tomboy Road just above town in a little more than 2 miles. This hike stays to the left at the junction and follows the Deep Creek Trail for about 100 yards before crossing Butcher Creek. The Deep Creek Trail intersects the Sneffels High Line Trail soon after; turn at this point to take up the less-used right-hand trail, following the loop counterclockwise.

From its intersection with the Deep Creek Trail, the Sneffels High Line Trail climbs along mostly moderate-to-strenuous grades to follow Butcher Creek uphill. Following the drainage bottom for the first mile or so, the trail passes through nice stands of aspen. The trail eventually climbs out of the drainage bottom to continue switchbacking up among grassy meadows just to the west. From these open areas, you gain views looking south across the San Miguel River Canyon to the face of the Telluride Ski Area. Some very rugged 13,000-foot peaks just to the left of the ski slopes also come into view, as do the San

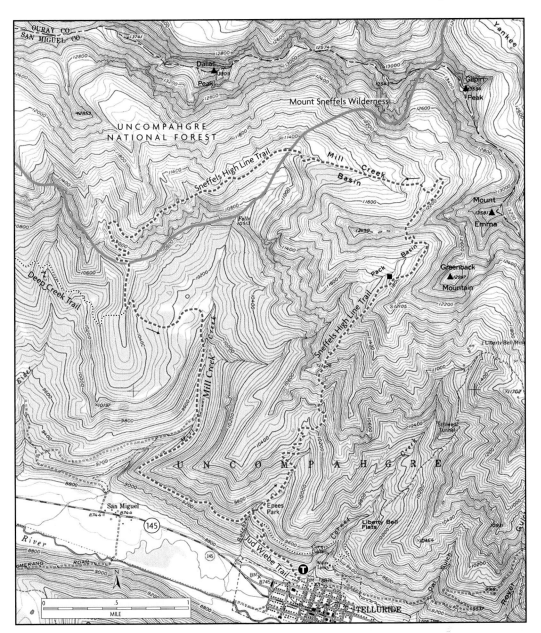

Miguel Mountains off to the southwest. Included in this distant range are three fourteeners and the lone spire of Lizard Head Peak.

Continuing to climb along the mountain slopes just west of Butcher Creek, the Sneffels High Line Trail soon passes a small notch, through which you get a stunning view of the next drainage to the west—Mill Creek. This vista reveals just how steep these mountains actually are. Beyond this point, the trail continues to climb until it reaches a stand of Engelmann spruce.

After switchbacking a bit farther, the Sneffels High Line Trail crosses into the upper end of the next drainage west, where it continues along a

A snowy scene along the Sneffels High Line Trail

short level stretch. Upon reaching the remains of an old miner's cabin at the edge of the forest, the trail climbs less than 0.5 mile amid some rather impressive old-growth spruce trees to reach timberline at the lower end of Pack Basin. Sheltered by 12,997-foot Greenback Mountain to the south, 13,581-foot Mount Emma to the east, and an unnamed 12,490-foot ridge to the north, Pack Basin is a scenic little hideaway on the head of a side fork of the Mill Creek drainage. While the only distant view from this basin takes in the San Miguel Mountain Range to the southwest, the immediate peaks are incredibly rugged and scenic.

From Pack Basin, the Sneffels High Line Trail climbs north to a small saddle from which it drops into Mill Basin at the head of Mill Creek

itself. Marking the 12,250-foot high point of this hike, the saddle offers views of 13,809-foot Dallas Peak, among other rugged summits to the north. Composed of a dark volcanic rock, these jagged summits owe their existence to an intensive period of volcanic activity that occurred some 40 million years ago. The highest of these is 14,150-foot Mount Sneffels, which rises northeast from here.

After dropping into Mill Basin, the Sneffels High Line Trail briefly crosses a southern extension of the 16,505-acre Mount Sneffels Wilderness. Skirting its way around the head of Mill Creek, the route contours below Dallas Peak at about the 11,200-foot level before dropping southward along a ridge that separates Mill Creek from Eider Creek to the west. Switchbacking down this steep descent, the trail loses some 800 feet in less than a mile before intersecting the Deep Creek Trail west of Mill Creek. Turn left at this point, and continue to drop to reach Mill Creek. From this point, the hike covers a little more than a mile along the Deep Creek Trail to reach the start of the Sneffels High Line Trail, and then about a mile more along the Jud Wiebe Trail before returning to the Aspen Street trailhead.

Water is found along portions of this hike, but it should be treated before drinking. Watch for lightning in the higher terrain and mountain bicyclists along the lower Deep Creek Trail portion of the loop.

83 SHARKSTOOTH PASS

Distance: 4 miles round-trip
Difficulty: Moderate
Hiking time: 3 hours
Elevation: 10,900 to 11,936 feet
Management: San Juan National Forest
Wilderness status: None
Season: July to September
Map: USGS La Plata

Getting there: From Mancos, drive less than 0.5 mile north on Colorado Highway 184 to County Road 42. Turn right and follow

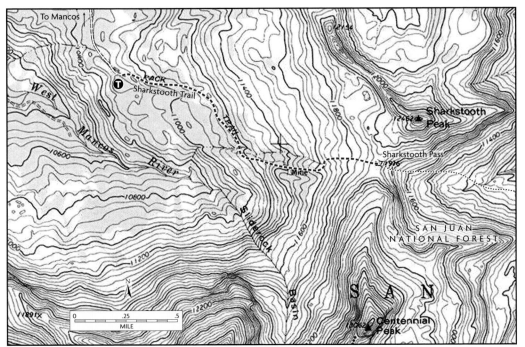

Hikers dwarfed by the Sharkstooth

sharply triangular summit is unmistakable, especially when viewed from the west. A short hike accesses Sharkstooth Pass, which, in turn, offers an up-close view of the rugged mountain.

Heading east from the trailhead, the Sharkstooth Trail begins by climbing moderately through a forest of Engelmann spruce and subalpine fir. After the first 0.75 mile, the route begins a more moderately difficult ascent. Near the 1-mile mark it encounters the old Windy Williams Mine. Besides tailings, little of the operation is left today. Beyond the mine the trail soon reaches timberline, then continues to climb among alpine meadows. Following a few switchbacks (be sure not to cut), the route finally reaches 11,936-foot Sharkstooth Pass, which separates Sharkstooth Peak from Centennial Peak to the south. Along this last portion of the hike, nice views looking west across the forested foothills of the range and south to banded 13,232-foot Hesperus Mountain (the La Plata Range's highest summit) are afforded. From the pass itself, you can look east into the upper reaches of the Bear Creek drainage.

Although Sharkstooth Pass marks the turn-around point for this hike, it is possible to add to your excursion. The first option is to continue east along the Sharkstooth Trail, and drop into the Bear Creek drainage. After descending 1400 feet from the pass in about 1.5 miles, the Sharkstooth Trail reaches Bear Creek and the Highline Loop Trail. A National Recreation Trail, the Highline Loop Trail follows Indian Ridge and upper Bear Creek to complete a 16-mile loop hike. The second option is to scramble up 13,062-foot Centennial Peak, which rises just south of Sharkstooth Pass. The moderately difficult climb reaches the top in less than a mile, and the summit offers some interesting views. Looking across at Hesperus Mountain to the southwest and other peaks to the south, you gain an appreciation for the true ruggedness of the La Plata Mountains. And looking north back at Sharkstooth Peak, you realize that, while the 12,462-foot summit is somewhat small in comparison to its neighbors, its profile is memorable.

Because water is not available along most of this hike, be sure to pack a quart or two. Watch for lightning in the exposed higher terrain.

this road (it becomes Forest Road 561 after it enters the national forest) for 12 miles to Spruce Mill Road (Forest Road 350). Turn right and continue east for another 6.5 miles to Forest Road 346. Turn right and drive 1.5 miles to the Sharkstooth trailhead. The last few miles of this drive are rough but passable to most carefully driven vehicles.

Although Sharkstooth Peak is one of the smaller summits in the La Plata Mountains, it is one of the most spectacular. Protruding in splendid isolation a short distance north of the rest of the range, this

84 GEYSER SPRING

Distance: 2.5 miles round-trip
Difficulty: Easy
Hiking time: 2 hours
Elevation: 8600 to 9120 feet
Management: San Juan National Forest
Wilderness status: None
Season: June to October
Maps: USGS Dolores Peak, Groundhog Mountain

Getting there: This hike begins at an obscure trailhead on the West Fork Road. To find it, drive 13 miles northeast from Dolores on Colorado Highway 145 to the West Fork Road (Forest Road 535). Turn left and follow this road for 20.3 miles to the trail's start on the right side of the road. Although the Forest Service has installed a sign at the trailhead, it is hard to see. The trail begins at a point along the road just to the right of a private

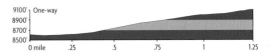

drive. It then follows a fenced access corridor for a short way to the West Dolores River.

Short and easy, the hike to Geyser Springs reveals one of Colorado's most surprising geological features: the state's only true geyser.

Diminutive Geyser Spring

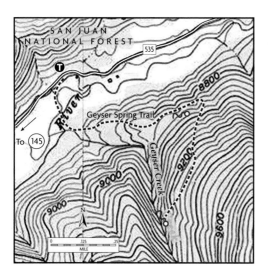

From the trailhead, the Geyser Spring Trail follows the West Dolores River upstream for a short distance before crossing to the east bank. As there is no bridge (plans in the offing might see construction of a footbridge in the near future) here, you might get your feet wet, and you might not be able to cross at all during periods of high water. Beyond the crossing, the trail winds easily among stands of aspen. After crossing a small creek, the route continues to climb up an easy grade on an old road. Barren patches of brine-encrusted ground along the way are evidence of old thermal springs that have dried up. Depending on the direction of the wind, you might get a whiff of sulfur—an aroma similar to that experienced in the geyser basins of Yellowstone National Park. You might even see a wisp of steam floating up from small springs that are hidden in the woods.

After climbing for a bit, the trail drops for a short distance farther into the Geyser Creek drainage, where it reaches this hike's destination. Situated alongside the streambed, Geyser Spring is enclosed in a stone-lined pool. Although the spring does not produce the fury and spectacle that Old Faithful and other Yellowstone geysers do, it does gurgle and bubble for about twelve to fifteen minutes at thirty- to forty-minute intervals. Unlike the thermal springs of Yellowstone, this one is not particularly hot. Rather, it is a constant 82.4 degrees Fahrenheit—a bit cool for soaking in. Upon erupting, Geyser Spring does emit sulfurous gases.

Water is available in the West Dolores River and Geyser Creek, but it should be treated before drinking. Use caution when crossing the West Dolores River in late spring, early summer, and after rainy periods.

85 NAVAJO LAKE

Distance: 9.6 miles round-trip
Difficulty: Strenuous
Hiking time: 7 hours
Elevation: 9393 to 11,154 feet
Management: San Juan National Forest
Wilderness status: Lizard Head Wilderness Area
Season: July to September
Map: USGS Dolores Peak

Getting there: From Dolores, drive 13 miles northeast on Colorado Highway 145 to the turnoff for the West Fork Road (Forest Service Road 535). Drive 26 miles north, past the end of the pavement and the Burro Bridge Campground, to a signed left turn for the trailhead.

It is easy to understand why Navajo Lake is perhaps the most popular destination in the Lizard

Head Wilderness. Not only is the lake situated in a beautiful alpine basin, but it also offers a handy base camp for climbers intent on climbing the nearby fourteeners of El Diente, Mount Wilson, and Wilson Peak. Heavy use has forced a fire ban to be put into effect in the Navajo Lake Basin.

Shortly beyond the trailhead, the Navajo Lake Trail intersects the Groundhog Trail, which climbs west. This route stays right at this junction and begins an easy climb along the east bank of the West Dolores River. Within 0.75 mile the route crosses the river via a footbridge to climb up the west bank. Beyond the crossing, the trail climbs along easy-to-moderate grades through beautiful meadows and sporadic forests of Engelmann spruce and subalpine fir. A great variety of wildflowers grow in these meadows in July and early August. At the 1.5-mile mark, the Kilpacker Trail comes in from the Meadows area to the southeast. Views along this portion of the hike include Dolores Peak to the northwest and El Diente to the east.

After 2.5 miles, the trail begins to climb a much more strenuous grade along a series of steep switchbacks. This ascent climbs about 1000

Along the trail to Navajo Lake

feet in less than a mile. At the top of the switch-backs the Navajo Lake Trail intersects the Woods Lake Trail. A left turn at this point leads 4.5 miles to Woods Lake, which lies north of the wilderness. This hike takes the right fork, however, and continues on for another 0.5 mile to Navajo Lake. The route drops about 250 feet in this last stretch.

Situated at 11,154 feet in elevation, scenic Navajo Lake lies just below timberline. Fishing in Navajo Lake is reported to be poor, although the West Dolores River is considerably better. Artificial flies and lures are required in both the lake and the river. Beyond its namesake, the Navajo Lake Trail continues to climb eastward through Navajo Basin before topping out on a 13,000-foot saddle just below 14,017-foot Wilson Peak. Climbers often use this route to access the peak. Camping within 100 feet of the lakeshore is prohibited due to overuse.

Water is available along much of the hike, but it should be treated before drinking. Also, watch out for lightning in the higher terrain. There is a permanent fire ban throughout the Navajo Basin, so backpackers will need to bring a stove. Because Navajo Lake receives heavy use in midsummer, you might want to plan your visit for a weekday or after Labor Day.

86 LIZARD HEAD

Distance: 12-mile loop
Difficulty: Strenuous
Hiking time: 9 hours
Elevation: 10,040 to 12,147 feet
Management: Uncompahgre National Forest, San Juan National Forest
Wilderness status: Lizard Head Wilderness Area
Season: July to September
Map: USGS Mount Wilson

Getting there: From Telluride, drive 14.5 miles south on Colorado Highway 145 to Lizard Head Pass. The well-marked trailhead is located just west of the highway.

For at least the last hundred years, the sight of Lizard Head Peak has enthralled those traveling across Lizard Head Pass between the towns of Rico and Telluride. Protruding abruptly above the eastern end of the San Miguel Mountains, this 13,113-foot pinnacle of rock was featured in the logo of Otto Mears's Rio Grande Northwestern Railroad. In 1912 an erroneous newspaper story claimed that the landmark had collapsed, much to the shock of its readers. Today, the stunning spire still captures the imaginations of motorists heading north on Colorado Highway 145. Those who want a much closer look at Lizard Head can follow a roundabout route to its base for a worm's-eye view.

From the trailhead, the Lizard Head Trail contours north along the east slope of Blackface Mountain for about 2 miles before turning west to climb up a number of switchbacks. This first section of the route passes through patches of aspen and open meadows as it roughly parallels Colorado Highway 145 above Trout Lake and the Lake Fork Valley. After crossing a talus slope, the trail begins ascending the switchbacks along moderate-to-strenuous grades. The surrounding forest includes stands of Engelmann spruce and subalpine fir. The route encounters a junction at a small meadow. A right turn here leads 2 miles to Wilson Meadows, a beautiful open park located north of Blackface Mountain. The Lizard Head

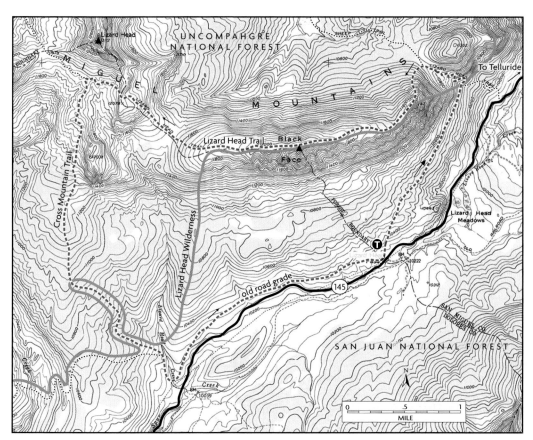

Trail heads left to continue climbing up Blackface Mountain.

Beyond the turnoff for Wilson Meadows, the Lizard Head Trail ascends more steeply among tall stands of spruce and fir. Around the 11,600-foot level the trail reaches timberline, where it levels off somewhat to follow the crest of Blackface Mountain west. While this open mountaintop is no place to be during inclement weather, it does provide exceptional views. To the south, it is possible to pick out Highway 145 as it winds north toward Lizard Head Pass. To the east are the rugged summits of Pilot Knob, Golden Horn, and Vermilion Peak, among others. To the north, you can look down upon Wilson Meadows, where you might spy mule deer or elk. Westward stand the spectacular San Miguel Mountains. Among these impressive wonders are three fourteeners, a number of slightly lower mountains, and Lizard Head itself.

After topping the 12,147-foot summit of Blackface Mountain, the trail begins to drop down the relatively gently sloping west flank of the mountain. The route eventually reaches a saddle situated between the headwaters of Lizard Head and Wilson Creeks. From here, it climbs up a moderately steep ridge that extends south from Lizard Head. Views of the monolith are unobstructed and spectacular all along this section of the trail. About 6 miles from the trailhead, the route passes just beneath Lizard Head itself to reach a junction with the Cross Mountain Trail. Composed of old volcanic ash and cinder, Lizard Head is nearly unclimbable due to the crumbling condition of the rock. Climbers do, however, scale nearby 14,246-foot Mount Wilson, 14,017-foot Wilson Peak, and 14,159-foot El Diente with considerable frequency. Of these three fourteeners, El Diente and Mount Wilson are considered difficult, and several climbers have died trying to scale them.

Trailside geology on Blackface Mountain

Although this hike turns left at the Lizard Head–Cross Mountain Trail intersection, it is possible to continue following the Lizard Head Trail north into Bilk Basin. Heading south on the Cross Mountain Trail, however, this hike drops some 1800 feet in 3 miles to reach Colorado Highway 145 a couple of miles south of Lizard Head Pass. The Cross Mountain Trail segment of the hike descends easily among open meadows that afford wonderful views in various directions. Upon reaching the highway, you can return to your car via a trail that parallels the highway to the north. Although not signed, this last 2-mile stretch of the hike actually follows an old roadbed. You will be within plain view of the road, but there is still plenty of fine mountain scenery.

Water is available along portions of this hike, but it should be treated before drinking. Watch for lightning during summer thunderstorms, especially along the exposed summit of Blackface Mountain. Although there are no exposed drop-offs along the Lizard Head Trail, those who attempt ascents of nearby peaks should be very careful.

Opposite: Wild Horse in Main Canyon

PLATEAULANDS

Whereas Colorado is best known for its alpine terrain, the western portion of the state serves up another personality that is strikingly different yet alluring in its own right. Typified by isolated mesas, slickrock gulches, and verdant river bottoms, the state's plateauland provides a look at some pristine and truly lonesome stretches of canyon country. A number of memorable treasures reward hikers who visit this rugged upland desert, including natural arches, ancient cliff dwellings, indecipherable petroglyphs, and, of course, stunning panoramas.

87 DILLON PINNACLES

Distance: 4 miles round-trip
Difficulty: Easy
Hiking time: 3 hours
Elevation: 7450 to 7847 feet
Management: Curecanti National Recreation Area
Wilderness status: None
Season: Year-round
Map: USGS Sapinero

Getting there: From Gunnison, drive 21 miles west on US Highway 50 to where the road crosses to the south shore of Blue Mesa Reservoir. The Dillon Pinnacles trailhead is at the picnic area just before the bridge.

Dillon Pinnacles

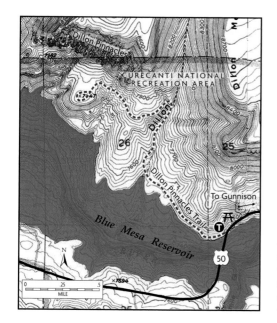

mostly easy grade. Upon reaching the 7800-foot level, the trail turns left to contour west to a knoll that sits directly in front of the Dillon Pinnacles. Throughout this hike, the plant community is predominantly sagebrush and grasses. Views of the reservoir to the south are nice throughout.

While the Dillon Pinnacles are visible from most of this hike, the best view is at the trail's end, which is marked by a small loop. Composed of West Elk Breccia, the pinnacles consist of ash and rock that was spewed from fiery volcanoes some 30 million years ago. Deposited in a layer thousands of feet thick, this volcanic material was eventually cemented together to make a conglomerate rock that has subsequently eroded into the cliff of spires before you. While palisades of West Elk Breccia tower over portions of the Blue Mesa Reservoir, the lower reaches of the Curecanti National Recreation Area feature the much older Precambrian rock that typifies the Black Canyon of the Gunnison.

Eagles—golden eagles year-round and bald eagles during the winter—may be spotted soaring in the vicinity of Blue Mesa Reservoir, and a variety of migratory birds frequent the shores of the reservoir below. Mule deer and elk are common to the Curecanti area, while coyotes, mountain lions, and black bears reside here as well. Given the fact that a lot of activity occurs on and about the lake, however, you will likely not see these shyer creatures along the Dillon Pinnacles Trail.

Bring water on this hike, especially on warm summer afternoons. Watch for lightning, as thunderstorms can move quickly through the area.

This short and easy hike along the north shore of Blue Mesa Reservoir culminates with an up-close vista of the impressive Dillon Pinnacles. Rising at the south end of the West Elk Mountains, these unusual formations offer picturesque evidence that the topography of this region resulted from an extended period of volcanic activity.

Tracing the shore of the Blue Mesa Reservoir, the Dillon Pinnacles Trail follows a mostly level grade for about 0.75 mile until it reaches Dillon Gulch. The route then turns north to follow the gulch's bottom for another 0.25 mile. Along this stretch, the trail climbs about 300 feet on a

88 OAK FLAT LOOP

Distance: 2-mile loop
Difficulty: Moderate
Hiking time: 2 hours
Elevation: 8160 to 7800 feet
Management: Black Canyon of the Gunnison National Park
Wilderness status: Black Canyon of the Gunnison Wilderness Area
Season: Year-round
Map: USGS Grizzly Ridge

Getting there: The Oak Flat Loop begins at the South Rim Visitor Center of the Black Canyon of the Gunnison National Park. To reach the visitor center, drive 8 miles west from Montrose on US Highway 50 to Colorado Highway 347 and the turnoff for the park. The visitor center is 7 miles north.

Reaching a depth of 1800 feet and spanning as little as 1100 feet from rim to rim in one spot, the Black Canyon of the Gunnison is unmatched for its combination of narrowness and depth. Although most visitors view the Black Canyon from the south or north rim, a handful of hardy souls descend into the canyon's depths by way of a few rough routes that access the bottom. While such an endeavor is beyond the realm of this guidebook, one established trail—the 2-mile-long Oak Flat Loop—does drop beneath the south rim for a short distance to offer a more in-depth look at the canyon and its ecosystems.

Heading west from the visitor center, the signed Oak Flat Loop descends easily through a thicket of Gambel oak for about 0.25 mile to reach the first trail junction. After turning right here the route descends steeply through a few switchbacks to reach Oak Flat itself. Along this descent the trail passes among Douglas-firs and a small stand of aspens. Both of these tree species find suitable moisture and protection from direct sun in this below-the-rim location. After dropping nearly 400 feet from its start, the Oak Flat Loop reaches the signed turnoff for a river-access route. Quite rugged and unmarked, this route to the bottom drops some 1500 feet in less than a mile. A permit is required from the Park Service to continue down this route; it can be obtained from the visitor center.

The Black Canyon of the Gunnison

Beyond the river-access turnoff, the Oak Flat Loop begins heading west along a ledge of sorts. Shortly, the trail passes a rock outcrop with an incredible view of a mile-long stretch of the canyon below. Of particular note is a narrow section a short distance downstream. Consisting of Precambrian schist and gneiss that date back 1.7 billion years, the dark walls of the canyon feature several lighter streaks that were formed when molten rock was injected into fissures and cracks. Thought to have been formed within the last 2 million years, the Black Canyon was cut into the dome-shaped Gunnison Uplift by the Gunnison River. Geologists theorize that the river first established its present course in a layer of softer volcanic rock before it reached the underlying Gunnison Uplift.

From the overlook, the Oak Flat Loop heads west for a short distance before beginning the climb back up to the canyon's rim. The trail passes another stand of aspens nestled at the base of a cliff, as well as more Douglas-firs. The climb out of the canyon on this end of the loop is not as steep as where the trail drops in below the visitor center. After reaching the rim, the Oak Flat Loop heads east to return to the trailhead.

Bring water on this hike, as none is found along the way. Watch for lightning during thunderstorms and use caution when hiking near dangerous drop-offs.

89 EXCLAMATION POINT

Distance: 3 miles round-trip
Difficulty: Easy
Hiking time: 2 hours
Elevation: 7710 to 7650 feet
Management: Black Canyon of the Gunnison National Park
Wilderness status: Black Canyon of the Gunnison Wilderness Area
Season: May to October
Map: USGS Grizzly Ridge

Getting there: This hike begins at the North Rim Ranger Station. From Crawford, drive 3 miles south on Colorado Highway 92 to the signed turnoff for Black Canyon of the Gunnison National Park. Turn right and drive 11.9 miles to a fork in the road (inside the park). Turn right and drive 0.4 mile to the ranger station. The last half of this drive is on good gravel road.

Somewhat isolated, the North Rim of the Black Canyon of the Gunnison offers all of the scenic rewards that the majority of visitors to the national park find along the South Rim—without the crowds. Interestingly, most of the park's hiking trails are also found here. One of these leads to the appropriately named Exclamation Point.

This hike follows the North Vista Trail west from the ranger station. First traversing open sagebrush parks and clumps of Gambel oak, and then passing among mature stands of pinyon pine and Utah juniper, the North Vista Trail reveals plant communities typical for this elevation. The route to Exclamation Point is mostly level, with only a few minor grade changes. It is also fairly easy to follow. Along the way, two small side trails marked by signs that read "overlook" branch left to access overlooks of a side canyon known as SOB Draw.

About 1.25 miles from the trailhead, you will reach a fork in the trail. The right-hand route continues west to access the top of Green Mountain 2 miles farther, while Exclamation Point is accessed by bearing left. Located a short distance

Old juniper trunk at Exclamation Point

farther, Exclamation Point is an undeveloped overlook that offers some of the finest views into the inner canyon to be found in the park. Especially noteworthy is the view upstream (to the east) of the chasm. You can see the Gunnison River 1800 feet below, and you will be amazed by the sheer walls of Precambrian igneous rock that drop to it. You might also notice how close the South Rim is from here.

Bring water, as none is found along the hike. Use extreme caution when you are close to the canyon rim. Watch for lightning during thunderstorms.

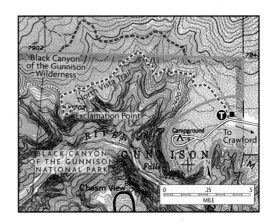

90 GUNNISON GORGE

Distance: 9 miles round-trip
Difficulty: Moderate
Hiking time: 6 hours
Elevation: 6500 to 5300 feet
Management: Bureau of Land Management
Wilderness status: Gunnison Gorge Wilderness Area
Season: Year-round
Map: USGS Black Ridge

Getting there: From Montrose, drive about 9.5 miles north on US Highway 550 to Falcon Road. Turn right and continue 3.6 miles to the end of the pavement. Here the route becomes the Peach Valley Road. About 7.5 miles beyond the pavement's end, turn right onto Ute Road and follow it 2.6 miles to the trailhead. The last half of this road requires a 4WD vehicle. A trailhead use fee is charged.

Designated as wilderness in 1999, the BLM-administered Gunnison Gorge Wilderness Area encompasses some truly beautiful canyon country that extends north from the Black Canyon of the Gunnison National Park. Included in this area is one of Colorado's more alluring river corridors. So coveted is the run through this gorge that rafters go to the trouble of packing their gear into the canyon (down the 1-mile-long Chukar Trail upstream) just so they can then float down the next several miles of river. Four hiking trails drop into this scenic canyon from the west rim. The longest of these routes, the 4.5-mile Ute Trail, offers as fine an introduction to the Gunnison Gorge as any. Currently, the Gunnison Gorge Wilderness encompasses 17,700 acres of prime canyon country.

From the trailhead, the Ute Trail drops easily down arid hillsides studded with pinyon pine, juniper trees, sagebrush, and Mormon tea. After descending through a broad basin, the Ute Trail reaches a bench that follows the top of the inner gorge's harder Precambrian rock. Following this bench north for less than a mile, the route then turns east to drop down a series of steeper switchbacks. Up to this point, the Ute Trail has descended along mostly easy grades. At the

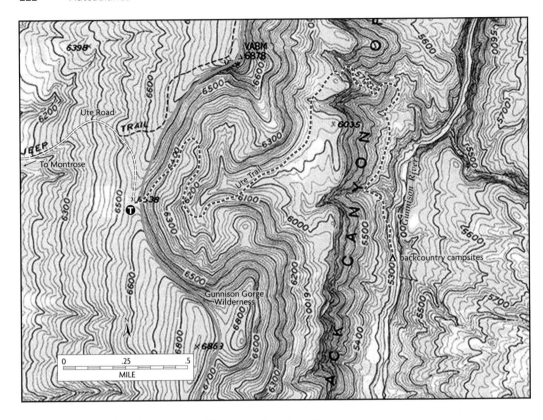

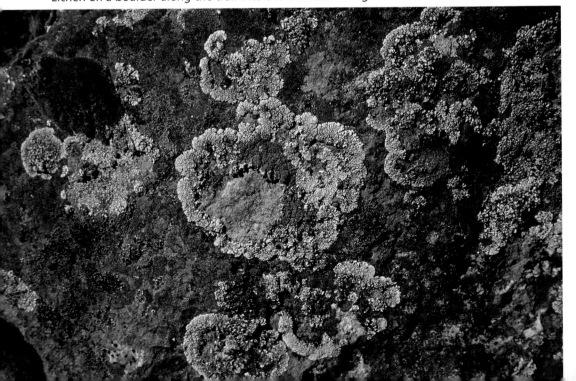

Lichen on a boulder along the trail into the Gunnison Gorge

bottom of these switchbacks, it then heads due south across a bench area known as Ute Park before it reaches the river. Stretching along a straight, comparatively open stretch of the Gunnison River, Ute Park historically served as a crossing point for the Ute Indians who once inhabited much of Colorado.

Once at the river, you can travel some distance both upstream and downstream before being turned back by impassable terrain. The scenery includes canyon walls that tower hundreds of feet above. Exposed within the inner portion of the Gunnison Gorge are the same dark Precambrian schists and gneisses that are found upstream within the Black Canyon of the Gunnison National Park. Because this stretch of the Gunnison River is considered Gold Medal

water for trout fishing, you might want to bring a rod and reel. You might also encounter a rafting party camped at one of four backcountry campsites (hikers must sign up at the trailhead to use one of these sites, for which a fee is charged). Anyone who is interested in floating through the Gunnison Gorge should keep in mind that some class III and IV rapids are found downstream. In an effort to minimize impact on the fragile canyon environment, the BLM has regulations for hikers and boaters. Parties cannot exceed twelve persons, open fires are prohibited, and portable potties are required.

Bring water on this hike, as none is available until the river. This hike can be a hot one, especially in the summer. Watch for rattlesnakes in rocky areas.

91 MOUNT GARFIELD

Distance: 4 miles round-trip
Difficulty: Strenuous
Hiking time: 4 hours
Elevation: 4800 to 6765 feet
Management: Bureau of Land Management
Wilderness status: None
Season: Year-round
Maps: USGS Clifton, Round Mountain

Getting there: From Grand Junction, drive east on Interstate 70 to the Palisade exit—a distance of about 10 miles. From the exit, drive south a short way to the first paved road that runs west. Follow this road (signed as the G7 Road) for 1.5 miles through a residential area. Turn right onto a gravel road and drive 0.2 mile under the interstate to the trailhead just north of the highway.

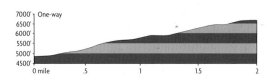

One of the main geographical features of the Grand Valley, the Book Cliffs rise sharply to form a strikingly scenic wall that stretches deep into Utah. In the Grand Junction area, the Book Cliffs top out at a height of 6765 feet in Mount Garfield. The short but challenging Mount Garfield Trail climbs to the top of Mount

Garfield from a trailhead just west of the town of Palisade.

From the trailhead, the Mount Garfield Trail heads north across a level area to reach a steep-sided ridge of Mancos Shale. Following the spine of this ridge, the route climbs a very strenuous grade for the next 0.5 mile. Deposited in a shallow sea over 75 million years ago during the Cretaceous period, Mancos Shale is a soft clay-like material that swells greatly when wet and shrinks upon drying. Because of this, few plants

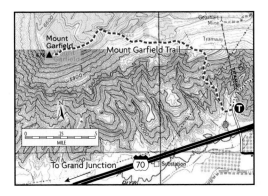

can grow in the soil, thereby allowing rapid erosion. Along the Book Cliffs and in many other places, Mancos Shale features exaggerated patterning. Mancos Shale is very slick and gooey when wet, so this hike is dangerous after a rain or snowfall.

After gaining approximately 600 feet along this ridge of Mancos Shale, the route continues to climb up a slope strewn with boulders of the Mesa Verde Group sandstones. The Mesa Verde Group is composed of sands deposited in a shoreline environment along Cretaceous seas. Sandwiched in among these buff-colored layers are seams of coal, which resulted from plant-rich lagoons. While this section of the trail winds

its way through rocky areas, it is not difficult to follow. Eventually, the trail reaches a shelf of relatively level ground that is not visible from below. After crossing this grassy area the route climbs again to a hidden valley that was burned over relatively recently. The result is thick grasses studded by a few charred skeletons of juniper trees. From here, the Mount Garfield Trail climbs to a saddle just below the rim above. Beyond this climb, it is a short distance farther to the crest of the Book Cliffs. From the crest, the trail continues less than 0.5 mile west to the summit of Mount Garfield. Although the scenery up to this point is spectacular, it is especially so from the very top.

Marked by a memorial to two brothers who died some years back, the Mount Garfield summit provides a 360-degree vista that is indeed tremendous. Spreading out directly below and to the west are highly eroded Mancos Shale slopes, which contrast sharply with the irrigated orchards and farm fields of the Grand Valley. Coursing across the valley and through the city of Grand Junction is the Colorado River. The Uncompahgre Plateau is draped across the horizon beyond. Grand Mesa rises to the east, as does Battlement Mesa. To the north in the distance are the light-colored Roan Cliffs, and opening up between the Roan Cliffs and Mount Garfield is Coal

Formation along the Mount Garfield Trail

Canyon. Whereas Mount Garfield is included in the 36,113-acre Little Book Cliffs Wild Horse Range, Coal Canyon lies even deeper in the range and it, along with adjacent areas, is home to a herd of wild horses. These impressive animals are occasionally spotted from Mount Garfield.

Bring plenty of water on this hike, as none is available along the way. During the summer you might want to head out early so that you can avoid the heat of the day. Lightning can pose a threat, especially on the summit. Avoid this hike in wet or icy weather. In addition, proceed cautiously along portions of this hike, as a fall could prove disastrous.

92   MAIN CANYON

Distance: 8 miles round-trip
Difficulty: Easy
Hiking time: 5 hours
Elevation: 4900 to 5200 feet
Management: Bureau of Land Management
Wilderness status: Little Book Cliffs Wilderness Study Area
Season: Year-round
Maps: USGS Cameo, Round Mountain

Getting there: From Grand Junction, drive about 20 miles east on Interstate 70 to the Cameo exit. After leaving the highway, continue across the Colorado River to a power plant. Pass through the plant area and drive about 1.5 miles north on a good gravel road to the signed Coal Canyon trailhead.

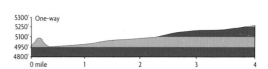

The collection of canyons that dissect the Little Book Cliffs northeast of Grand Junction is also a

Wild horses graze in Main Canyon.

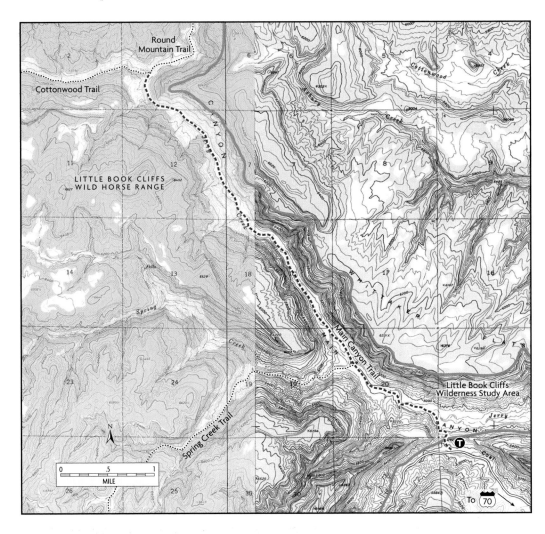

well-known wild horse range by the same name. An estimated 80 to 100 wild horses call this area home and, thanks to such natural impediments as canyon walls, the chances of spotting some of these magnificent mustangs are good. Among the many hiking routes that the BLM has identified and established in the Little Book Cliffs Wilderness Study Area, the Main Canyon Trail is most easily accessed and easiest to follow.

The Main Canyon Trail begins by climbing a short but steep and rocky road to the right from the trailhead. On top of a saddle (about 0.1 mile from the trailhead), a gate blocks most vehicular traffic while a trail gate to the left allows passage of hikers and horseback riders. The old road then drops quickly to the bottom of Main Canyon and continues up canyon for a number of miles. Closed to motor traffic (ATV riders do occasionally sneak into the canyon), this old road now serves as a suitable hiking trail. It follows the canyon floor, crossing the wash bottom on several occasions. About 1 mile from the trailhead, the Main Canyon Trail intersects the lower end of the Spring Creek Trail, which follows its namesake west for 5 miles. This route is single track and was first created by the horses themselves. About 4 miles from the trailhead, the Main Canyon Trail reaches its end where the Round Mountain

Trail begins climbing 1.5 miles north to the top of Round Mountain and the 3-mile Cottonwood Trail begins to head west up Cottonwood Canyon. While this intersection of three routes serves as the turnaround point for this hike, additional explorations could be rewarding.

Typified by sagebrush flats occasionally studded with widely scattered Utah junipers, the bottom of Main Canyon is an ideal place to spot the wild horses. Typically, they are sighted in small groups often consisting of a stallion, his brood of three or four mares, and perhaps a colt. Marking the territories of these stallions are "stud piles," or piles of manure. Whereas the lineage of these horses can be traced back to Indian ponies, a majority of the bloodline stems from horses that escaped from or were turned loose by ranchers. The horses are usually relatively easy to approach and observe, although caution should be used just the same. While the higher reaches of the horse range are best for spotting horses in the hot summer months, horses are often found throughout the canyon.

Bring plenty of water on this hike, as no potable water is available along the way. Watch for flash flooding in wash bottoms after heavy downpours. Keep in mind that these canyons can be hot on summer afternoons.

93 MONUMENT CANYON

Distance: 8 miles round-trip
Difficulty: Moderate
Hiking time: 4 hours
Elevation: 6200 to 5300 feet
Management: Colorado National Monument
Wilderness status: None
Season: Year-round
Map: USGS Colorado National Monument

Getting there: From Grand Junction, drive west on Interstate 70 to the Fruita exit and follow the signs for Colorado National Monument. Continue south on Colorado Highway 340 for 2.4 miles to the entrance to the Colorado National Monument. Follow the monument's only road, Rim Rock Drive, south for 8.2 miles to the signed trailhead. There is limited parking for hikers on the left side of the road.

Embracing a ruggedly beautiful cross-section of canyons, cliffs, and mesa tops, Colorado National Monument offers some wonderful hiking opportunities within a short drive from Grand Junction. The hike described here follows the Monument Canyon Trail to the base of Independence Monument, the monument's flagship landform.

From the trailhead, the Monument Canyon Trail begins dropping immediately into the head of a side drainage that eventually feeds into Monument Canyon. Within 200 yards is the turnoff for the 0.5-mile trail to the Coke Ovens—a cluster of beehive-shaped formations of Wingate Sandstone. Created by the erosion of the softer sandstone beneath caps of more resistant Kayenta Sandstone, these monoliths are clearly visible from the Monument Canyon Trail, which turns left at the trail junction.

Beyond the turnoff for the Coke Ovens, the Monument Canyon Trail begins to really drop in elevation as it negotiates steep switchbacks, areas of loose rock, and exposed drop-offs. The route descends some 600 feet in about 0.5 mile to

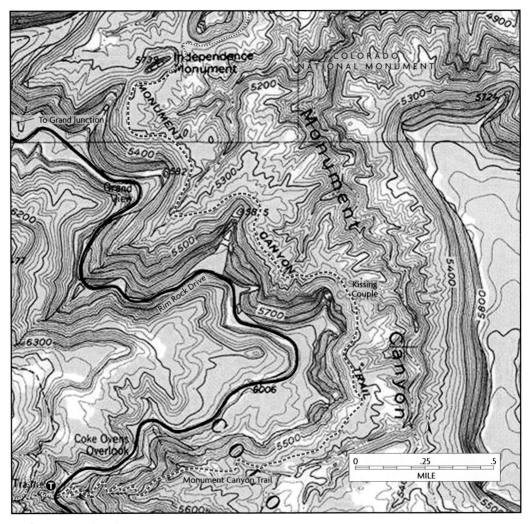

reach the relatively level canyon bottom. Along this descent you might want to stop and take in the geology of the canyon. Like the Coke Ovens, the canyon walls consist of Wingate Sandstone, a rock that tends to form sheer cliffs several hundred feet high. Wingate Sandstone was deposited as sand dunes during the Jurassic period more than 200 million years ago. Atop the Wingate Formation is a layer of Kayenta Sandstone, and above that a layer of salmon-colored rock known as Entrada Sandstone. Like the Wingate Formation, Entrada Sandstone was formed from windblown sands.

At the canyon bottom, the Monument Canyon Trail heads east through forests of pinyon pine and Utah juniper. Such an ecosystem is standard for this elevation, since semidesert conditions predominate here. Other plants include mountain mahogany, Mormon tea, yucca, and a renegade cottonwood tree or two stashed away along the dry streambeds. Among the resident fauna of the monument are mule deer, desert bighorn sheep, antelope, ground squirrels, coyotes, and mountain lions.

After continuing 0.5 mile east from the bottom of its descent into the canyon, the Monument Canyon Trail begins to bend north as it follows the canyon wall. A little more than 2 miles from

Formations in Monument Canyon

the trailhead, the trail passes almost directly beneath an interesting formation called the Kissing Couple. From this up-close vantage, the landmark is impressive. By this point you might have also noticed some dark metamorphic rock along the lower reaches of the canyon. Dating back 1.5 billion years, these Precambrian schists and gneisses form the core of the Uncompahgre Plateau, which reaches its northeastern terminus at Colorado National Monument.

After passing beneath an additional tower of Wingate Sandstone, the Monument Canyon Trail reaches the base of Independence Monument. While a spectacular view of this 450-foot-high monolith can be enjoyed from Rim Rock Drive above, the rock's base provides an equally impressive but very different vantage point. Once part of a large dividing wall, Independence Monument was worn away by erosion on both sides, leaving the freestanding monolith behind. This whole scenario can best be envisioned from

a low saddle just west of the formation. From this point, you can see how Independence Monument separates Monument Canyon from Wedding Canyon to the north. From here, you can also see the Pipe Organ, Window Rock, and Sentinel Spire on the far side of Wedding Canyon. And framed in the mouth of Wedding Canyon just as it is framed in the mouth of Monument Canyon is the verdant patchwork of farmlands that spread across the Grand Valley beyond.

Although the 6-mile Monument Canyon Trail continues for another 2 miles from the base of Independence Monument to reach a trailhead just east of the national monument boundary, this hike turns around here to return to the upper trailhead. Don't forget that you have a 600-foot climb back to your car before finishing this hike.

Water is not available along this hike, so bring plenty, especially in the hot summer months. Although rattlesnakes tend to shy away from people, watch out for them anyway.

94 RATTLESNAKE ARCHES

Distance: 11.4 miles round-trip
Difficulty: Strenuous
Hiking time: 9 hours
Elevation: 4500 to 5700 feet
Management: Bureau of Land Management
Wilderness status: Black Ridge Canyons Wilderness Area
Season: Year-round
Map: USGS Mack

Getting there: The hike begins at the Pollock Canyon trailhead in the northeast corner of the Black Ridge Canyons Wilderness. From Grand Junction, drive about 10 miles west on Interstate 70 to Fruita. Exit here and drive 1.2 miles south on Colorado Highway 340. Turn right onto Kings View Road and drive 3.3 miles to the well-developed trailhead facility.

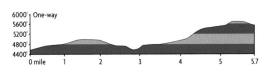

Containing a significant collection of natural arches, Rattlesnake Canyon is as nice a slickrock wonderland as any to be found in Colorado. These arches make for a worthy destination, but the route also traverses some tremendous scenery and offers a real adventure as it follows the challenging Rattlesnake Arches Trail. Given the route's rugged nature, novice hikers should avoid this hike.

The hike begins innocently enough on the Pollock Bench Trail, which utilizes an old road as it crosses gently rolling terrain typified by

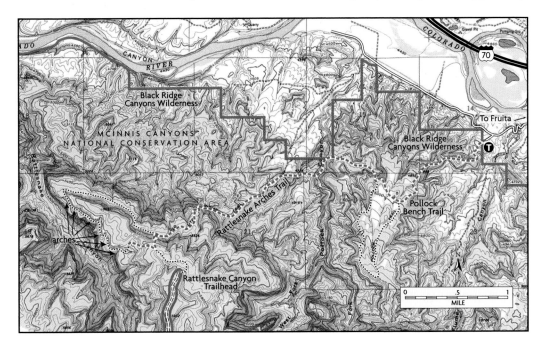

A natural arch in Rattlesnake Canyon

pinyon pines, junipers, Mormon tea, sagebrush, saltbush, and a variety of grasses. The route enters the Black Ridge Canyons Wilderness in this initial section. It then ascends a benchland between Flume Creek and Pollock Canyons. About 1 mile from the trailhead, the Pollock Bench Trail forks to form a loop route. Keep right here and continue about 0.5 mile farther to where the Pollock Bench Trail intersects the Rattlesnake Arches Trail. This second trail junction is located just below where the trail begins dropping into a side canyon of Pollock Canyon. Continuing along the Rattlesnake Arches Trail from this point, the route takes on a radically changed character as it makes the first of several scrambles over a slickrock drop-off. To find the Rattlesnake Arches Trail, look for steps carved into the slickrock just below the Pollock Bench Trail junction.

Once below the canyon wall, the Rattlesnake Arches Trail continues west toward its namesake in a deep and narrow drainage ringed by sheer sandstone walls. A little more than 2 miles in, the route is a steep scramble that leads into the main drainage of the canyon. In the canyon bottom, a signed trail intersection indicates private land 0.3 mile to the right. Turn left here and follow the canyon bottom among scattered cottonwoods and tamarisk. After walking up canyon for a little

less than 0.25 mile, turn right to begin the short but rugged ascent out of Pollock Canyon. Here again, the going consists of scrambling uphill over steep rocks and along severe drop-offs.

Once beyond the inner canyon, the Rattlesnake Arches Trail continues west across benchland that drops and climbs with each drainage. Eventually, a signed intersection points the way to more private land. Keep left here and continue west toward the final climb. Steep and rocky, this ascent is the largest along the entire route: about 800 feet in 2 miles. Near the top of this climb—at mile 5—hikers have a choice of either continuing directly to the top to reach the first of the arches or bearing right to follow a bench around the base of the point along which most of the arches are located. While this hike takes the most direct route to the first of the arches, a right turn would allow visitors to take in a number of the arches from below. This route reaches the base of the first arch in 2 miles, thereby completing a loop.

From the intersection at mile 5, the Rattlesnake Arches Trail climbs a final steep pitch to reach the top of the elongated point of land where it intersects a short trail leading 0.5 mile to the remote Rattlesnake Canyon trailhead. (While this trailhead would make for easy access to the arches, getting to it requires a lengthy drive along the rugged 4WD Black Ridge Road.) Turn right at this intersection and continue 0.5 mile to the first arch. To reach the other arches, descend through this arch to the benchland below, then continue northwest along the base of the cliffs to the right. The arches are tucked away in these folds of rock. Formed partly by water and wind erosion, these arches also owe their existence to the cleaving action of ice in the wintertime. Water that has seeped into cracks freezes and expands, flaking off chunks of rock. The rock, Entrada Sandstone, is the same stuff of which most of the arches in Arches National Park are made.

Bring plenty of water, as none is available along this hike and it can get very hot in the summer. Watch for rattlesnakes when hiking in rocky areas, and exercise caution when climbing around the arches and near all precipices. Take care not to trample across cryptogamic soil, which forms a stabilizing crust over loose soil that might otherwise blow away. This combination of lichens and mosses is very fragile and takes many years to heal after it is stepped on. The arches area is closed to camping and campfires. It is best to avoid this hike when conditions are muddy or snowy.

95 RABBITS EAR MESA

Distance: 5 miles round-trip
Difficulty: Easy
Hiking time: 3 hours
Elevation: 4950 to 5723 feet
Management: Bureau of Land Management
Wilderness status: None
Season: Year-round
Map: USGS Ruby Canyon

Getting there: From Grand Junction, drive 30 miles west on Interstate 70 to exit 2, which is less than 2 miles from the Utah border. From this exit, continue south and drive 0.4 mile to where the road splits. Turn left (east) and drive another 4.4 miles on a good gravel road. The signed trailhead is on the right.

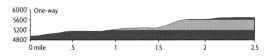

If you show up at Rabbit Valley on a busy weekend, you might think this is the last place in Colorado to find an interesting and peaceful hike. As a BLM-administered recreation area, Rabbit Valley is often rife with noisy ATVs, motorcycles, and 4WD vehicles. While many trails and dirt roads in Rabbit Valley do accommodate the off-road vehicle enthusiasts who frequent the area, the 2.5-mile Rabbits Ear Trail leaves the mechanized hum behind for a lonesome, wind-swept mesa top with one of the best vista points in the entire Grand Valley area.

Named for the shape of the mesa's edge that it follows, the Rabbits Ear Trail climbs a few hundred feet along an easy grade for the first 0.5 mile to reach a ridgeline, which it follows a short distance. From this section of the hike, it is possible to look out toward the Book Cliffs to the north. The dominant plant species along this trail is Utah juniper, but scattered rabbitbrush, saltbush, and Mormon tea are found here as well. Around the 1-mile mark is a nice view of a large meander in the Colorado River to the east. The trail then passes through an interesting cut in the sandstone before contouring up to the northern point of an unnamed mesa. At this point, the Rabbits Ear Trail forks to form a loop. Keep left at this intersection. Within the next 0.25 mile the

The Colorado River as seen from Ruby Canyon Overlook

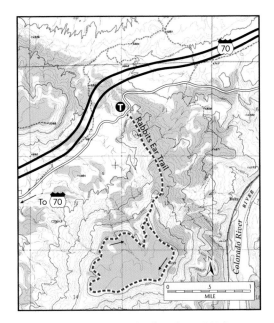

the mesa for slightly less than a mile to reach the Ruby Canyon Overlook on the southern edge of the mesa.

The views from the overlook are indeed wonderful. Front and center is Ruby Canyon, through which flows the Colorado River. This stretch of the river is popular among rafters and kayakers, in large part due to the colorful sandstone walls that follow the river as it snakes its way toward Utah. Rising farther south is the 75,168-acre Black Ridge Canyons Wilderness Area. A real highlight among BLM wildlands, the Black Ridge Canyons Wilderness includes tangled slickrock canyons, isolated mesas, and a large collection of natural arches (Hike 94). Beyond the Black Ridge Canyons area is the Uncompahgre Plateau, and in the distance to the southwest rise the La Sal Mountains near Moab, Utah. The Grand Valley and the city of Grand Junction are visible to the east, as are Grand Mesa and the Roan Cliffs beyond. The aforementioned Book Cliffs line the skyline to the north as they stretch far into Utah's Green River Desert.

Beyond the overlook, the Rabbits Ear Trail

trail makes its steepest climb—about 300 feet—to reach the mesa top directly to the south. Upon reaching the top, the trail follows the east rim of continues westward, roughly following the rim of its namesake mesa. This section of the hike continues to offer up scenic vistas, as well as an up close look at the beauties of rimrock formations. The route connects back up with the return trail after about 2 miles.

Bring plenty of drinking water on this hike, as none is available along the way. Hiking in the summer can be especially hot in this arid desert terrain. Watch for rattlesnakes in rocky areas. Biting gnats can be a problem from mid-May to mid-July.

96 DOLORES RIVER CANYON

Distance: 6 miles round-trip
Difficulty: Easy
Hiking time: 4 hours
Elevation: 5000 to 5100 feet
Management: Bureau of Land Management
Wilderness status: Dolores River Canyon Wilderness Study Area
Season: Year-round
Map: USGS Paradox

Getting there: From Naturita, drive 2 miles west on Colorado Highway 141 to where Colorado Highway 90 turns off. Turn left and drive about 22 miles to Bedrock. Just beyond where the highway crosses the Dolores River (and just before the Bedrock Store), turn left and drive 2 miles south to where the road is closed. Because parking is limited, you might consider parking just upstream from the Bedrock Store—which would add 4 extra miles of walking to the hike.

After gathering strength in the San Juan Mountains, the Dolores River flows west and north before emptying into the Colorado River just inside Utah. While still in Colorado, the Dolores River twists and turns through a series of deep wilderness canyons that thrill rafters, canoeists, and kayakers each spring. One of these canyons, the 30-mile-long Dolores River Canyon, is the centerpiece of a 28,668-acre BLM wilderness study area of the same name. Hikers interested in exploring this corridor can follow an old jeep road, now closed to vehicles, that accesses the first few miles of the canyon's mouth. Along the way, you can enjoy spectacular red-rock scenery, and some prehistoric and paleontological treats as well.

From the road closure, follow this old Jeep route south along the river's west bank for about 1 mile to where it turns west to continue upstream. Rounding a prominent point in the canyon wall, this turn in the route is almost directly above the river itself. It offers a good view of the Dolores River as it meanders downstream toward Bedrock and a stretch straight upstream to the west. Already towering nearly 1000 feet high at this point, the walls of the Dolores River Canyon include several layers of rock that represent different episodes of geologic history. Most impressive are the sheer faces of Wingate Sandstone that provide the canyon walls with much of their vertical rise. Wingate Sandstone was formed as giant sand dunes during the Triassic period. Below these cliffs is the Chinle Formation, which includes sandstones and shales that were deposited in large floodplains and shallow lakes. Above the Wingate cliffs is Kayenta Sandstone, which originated in floodplains in the Triassic period. And above it is the Entrada formation, which also began as large sand dunes. Younger deposits of the less-distinct Summerville,

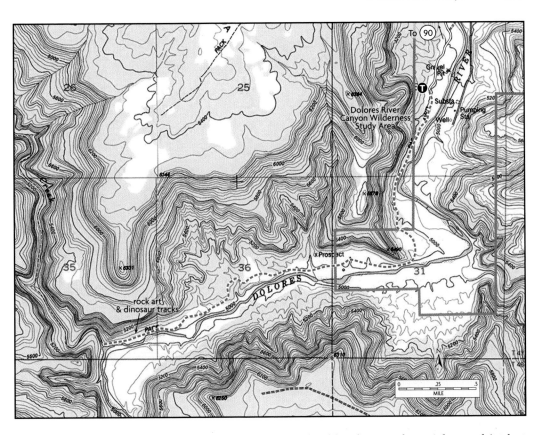

Morrison, and Dakota Formations constitute the highest reaches of the canyon corridor.

After turning west, the route continues upstream for another 2 miles to reach the mouth of La Sal Creek, which drains from Utah to the west. Maintaining a level grade as it follows a bench above the river bottom, the route encounters pinyon pine and juniper forests along with open areas of sagebrush. Two additional interesting features that are a short distance north of the road lie about 2 miles from the trailhead. If you turn right onto a small trail that river runners have worn down, you will soon reach several large boulders. Some of these boulders have petroglyphs etched into protected faces. These images, thought to have been created by the Archaic, Fremont, and Ute Indians several centuries ago, still mystify archaeologists and laypersons alike. Be sure not to touch, trace, or chalk in the petroglyphs, as direct contact can hasten erosion of the images. Then, across the flat side of a particularly large boulder that stands upright, are faint but unmistakable bird-like dinosaur tracks.

After visiting these two relics of the past, continue on the road for a short distance to reach the mouth of La Sal Creek and the turnaround point for this hike. It is possible to continue exploring both the Dolores River Canyon and La Sal Creek upstream, but you should expect to get your feet wet before too long. Once a wild and free-flowing waterway, the Dolores River has been tamed by the McPhee Dam upstream. This means that the river usually flows at a fraction of its full strength. While this drop in volume might allow hikers to wade across in the low-water season, it also means that rafters can enjoy the river for only a few weeks each year.

Bring water on this hike, as any found along the way is not potable. Watch for flash floods, especially in the narrow side canyons. Rattlesnakes are found in the area, although they typically shy away from people.

97 PETROGLYPH POINT

Distance: 2.8-mile loop
Difficulty: Moderate
Hiking time: 2 hours
Elevation: 6970 to 6640 feet
Management: Mesa Verde National Park
Wilderness status: None
Season: April to November
Map: USGS Moccasin Mesa

Getting there: From Mancos, drive 8 miles west—or 10 miles east from Cortez—on US Highway 160. Turn into the park and drive 20 miles south to the park headquarters. From the museum at the headquarters, follow the paved trail that leads down to the Spruce Tree House. After the trail makes a sharp bend, turn right at the signed start of the Petroglyph Point Trail. Before setting out, however, be sure to register at the trailhead. You can pick up a trail guide here as well.

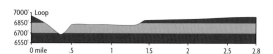

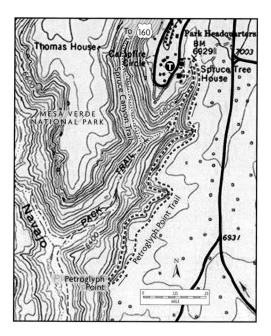

The chief attractions at Mesa Verde National Park are its impressive cliff dwellings, which were constructed during the thirteenth century. Counted among the largest such ancient structures in the Southwest, these classic sites are enjoyed by hundreds and even thousands of visitors each summer day. Meanwhile, the hike to Petroglyph Point offers a considerably less crowded look at some of the park's other archaeological resources, including a panel of exquisite rock art that dates back several hundred years.

Following the canyon wall just below the rim all the way to Petroglyph Point, this trail encounters several rocky areas and small stone stairways. It also cuts through some narrow passageways that might prevent heavier people from completing the hike. A few places could pose unsure footing for some, and a steep climb at the far end of the loop might be a bit precipitous for others. Such trail conditions might deter some people from hiking this route, but it is an otherwise easy trail to follow. Along the way the route also intersects the Spruce Canyon Trail, which branches to the right.

This route accesses a number of archaeological and ecological points of interest. A short distance after turning off the paved way to Spruce Tree House, the Petroglyph Point Trail passes a 300-year-old Douglas-fir. Early ranchers incorrectly identified a Douglas-fir growing next to nearby Spruce Tree House as a spruce, but the name has managed to stick to this day. Additional stands of this evergreen species are encountered later

Ancestral Puebloan rock art at Petroglyph Point

on, as well as Utah serviceberry bushes, Utah junipers, pinyon pines, and a patch of shrub live oak that is growing well north of the plant's normal range.

About 1 mile out, the Petroglyph Point Trail reaches a shaded grotto with a small cliff dwelling. Nearby boulders have characteristic scrape marks from the sharpening of stone axes. This site dates back to about AD 1200, when the ancestral Puebloan Indians (formerly called the Anasazi) began building their homes among the canyon walls of the Four Corners region. Shortly after, however, they left the canyons of Mesa Verde and moved south to the Rio Grande and Little Colorado River drainages. While a lengthy drought occurred at this time, other factors such as the depletion of topsoil also might have served to force their migration. Of course, all sites and artifacts within the park (and on all federal lands, for that matter) are strictly protected. Do not climb on any of the masonry walls or harm them in any way.

From this cliff dwelling, the Petroglyph Point Trail continues south for another 0.4 mile to reach the rock art for which Petroglyph Point is named. A number of animals, human figures, designs, and handprints are etched into the smooth sandstone across a few square feet of the cliff face. While archaeologists remain somewhat perplexed by the meaning of this prehistoric rock art, some Hopi elders did provide a translation during a visit in 1942. As the direct descendants of the ancestral Puebloans, these elders identified a number of clan symbols that indicate each clan's presence in Mesa Verde during previous times. They pointed out spiral designs that represent the Sipapu, or the place of emergence for the Pueblo and Hopi Indians, and they indicated some kachina figures as well. It is important not to touch these images; the oils on your hand can deteriorate the rock.

Just beyond the petroglyph panel, the trail climbs steeply to gain the canyon rim above. Offering a somewhat different view of the scenery and ecology of Mesa Verde National Park, the remaining half of this hike follows the canyon rim back to park headquarters. Various points along the mesa's edge offer nice views of Spruce and Navajo Canyons. Because the mesa tops are considerably drier than the areas just below the rim, the only trees that grow in appreciable numbers here are pinyon pines and junipers. After rounding the head of Spruce Canyon, the trail returns to the park headquarters.

Water is not available along this hike, so pack a quart or two before heading out. Lightning can pose a threat during periodic thunderstorms. Although the trail is open year-round, some icy spots might be present after heavy snowfall. Use extreme caution when hiking near drop-offs. Be aware that federal law strictly prohibits removing or disturbing artifacts in any way.

98 SAND CANYON

Distance: 6 miles round-trip
Difficulty: Easy
Hiking time: 4 hours
Elevation: 5470 to 5900 feet
Management: Canyon of the Ancients National Monument
Wilderness status: None
Season: Year-round
Maps: USGS Battle Rock, Woods Canyon

Getting there: From Cortez , drive 3 miles south on US Highway 491 to McElmo Canyon Road (County Road G). Turn right and follow this paved road west for 12.5 miles to the trailhead, which is on the right, just past where the road crosses McElmo Creek.

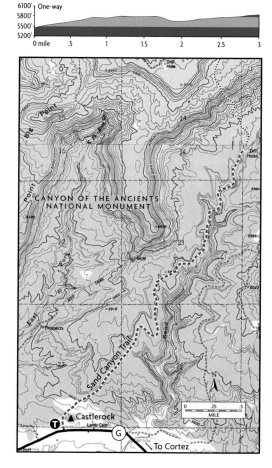

Characterized by sandstone canyons and broad mesas, the southwestern corner of Colorado features a variety of prehistoric cliff dwellings and ruins. The best known of these archaeological sites are found in Mesa Verde National Park and Hovenweep National Monument, but countless other ruins exist as well. So rich in archaeological treasures is this remote region that 164,000 acres of it were declared the Canyons of the Ancients National Monument by President Clinton in June 2000. A great hike within the monument that highlights archaeological wonders and splendid slickrock scenery follows picturesque Sand Canyon.

From the trailhead, the Sand Canyon Trail heads north for 100 yards or so across mostly bare sandstone to continue to the left of the nearby rock formation known as Castlerock. A large Ancestral Puebloan pueblo dating back to AD 1250 once stood at the foot of Castlerock. From Castlerock, the Sand Canyon Trail continues north, mostly across bare sandstone. The route along this section is marked by rock cairns and small signs.

About 0.25 mile beyond Castlerock, the Sand Canyon Trail bears right at a sign to continue in a more northeasterly direction, heading up the Sand Canyon drainage along a broad shelf above the canyon bottom. The trail beyond this point is well worn and easy to follow as it traverses an open forest of pinyon pines and junipers. For the next 1.5 miles the route is mostly level as it continues north along benches within the canyon. This section of the hike passes some nice cliffs and formations of Entrada Sandstone.

About 1 mile from the trailhead, the Sand Canyon Trail reaches the first of several prehistoric cliff dwellings along this hike. Tucked into a small but protective alcove, this well-preserved structure dates to around AD 1200. Built by the Ancestral Pueblo Indians, cliff dwellings such as these represent the culmination of ancient civilization in the Four Corners area. Prior to AD 1200, the Ancestral Puebloans lived in scattered settlements along valley bottoms and on mesa tops. It was not until the thirteenth century that they began constructing these cliff dwellings. Shortly after—just prior to AD 1300—an extensive drought, along with other factors, forced these cliff dwellers to abandon the region in favor of the Rio Grande and Little Colorado River drainages to the south. While these cliff dwellings have survived many hundreds of years, they are still fragile. Do not climb on the walls or camp within the ruins. Keep in mind that all artifacts—pottery shards, arrowheads, corncobs, and so on—are protected by law and must be left alone. Some hikers have created small collections of artifacts on flat rocks (perhaps some sort of museum mindset); this practice is frowned upon by the BLM.

Beyond this first cliff dwelling, the Sand Canyon Trail rounds the next bend in the canyon wall to continue north. About 0.25 mile beyond, the trail encounters the head of a small but deep side drainage of Sand Canyon's inner gorge. Soon the trail drops about 100 feet into the next side canyon north to reach the next lower bench. You might notice some additional cliff dwellings along the north wall of this side canyon. After visiting the first two cliff dwelling sites, it is easy to recognize a pattern in these ancient structures. Nearly all were built along south-facing canyon

Ancestral Puebloan cliff dwelling in Sand Canyon

walls. This was undoubtedly to take advantage of the warm rays of the low winter sun. Still more dwellings are found around the next turn in the canyon to the north. Piles of rocks lying at the base of these ruins indicate that there were once many more rooms. You might also notice the remains of a round underground room on the west side of the ruin. This was probably a kiva, which served as a center of religious activities.

Within the next mile, the Sand Canyon Trail encounters still more cliff dwellings before finally reaching the bottom of the canyon. From this point the route follows the normally dry wash bottom for another 0.5 mile before turning left to climb out of the canyon bottom to the west. This final section of the hike is also quite interesting as it passes through a narrow corridor of sandstone rock. A few cottonwood trees and tamarisks grow within this riparian community.

Although this hike turns around where the Sand Canyon Trail begins climbing from the canyon bottom, it is possible to continue for another 3 miles up the canyon to reach its head to the north. The trail becomes steep and less distinct beyond this point, but it does reach the expansive Sand Canyon Pueblo at its far end.

Bring plenty of water on this hike, especially in the hot summer months. Watch for flash flooding when in drainage bottoms. Keep in mind that ancient cliff dwellings are very fragile and should be treated with utmost care. Federal law protects all artifacts found on public lands; you can enjoy these relics, but leave them as they were. And be sure to stay on the trail so as not to damage fragile cryptogamic soil.

99 HARPERS CORNER

Distance: 2 miles round-trip
Difficulty: Easy
Hiking time: 2 hours
Elevation: 7600 to 7400 feet
Management: Dinosaur National Monument
Wilderness status: Dinosaur National Monument Wilderness Area
Season: Year-round
Map: USGS Jones Hole

Getting there: The Harpers Corner Trail begins at the end of the Harpers Corner Scenic Drive in the central portion of the Dinosaur National Monument. To reach the trailhead, drive 90 miles west from Craig on US Highway 40 to the monument headquarters. Turn right onto the Harpers Corner Scenic Drive and continue 31 miles north to the trailhead, which is at road's end.

Dinosaur National Monument is best known for its paleontological resources, but the Dinosaur Quarry in the far west end is the only place in the entire 210,844-acre monument where you can see dinosaur bones. What this unit of the National Park system does have in prodigious supply, however, are slickrock canyons, lonesome mesas, and miles of pristine river corridor. The short but highly scenic Harpers Corner Trail offers a memorable look at these treasures.

From the trailhead, the 1-mile-long Harpers Corner Trail heads northeast along a narrow and precipitous ridge to reach Harpers Point at the end. This trail dips and climbs a bit throughout, yet it is an easy route to follow. Several numbered features correspond to a printed trail guide available at the visitor center. This pamphlet also mentions various species of flora that grow along the way, including pinyon pines and junipers, Douglas-firs, such desert bloomers as phlox and Indian paintbrush, sagebrush, and even some grasses. The pamphlet points out some brachiopods and crinoids, or sea lilies, that are embedded in a limestone shelf near the end of the trail. It further describes in some detail the folding and faulting action that led to the peculiar geology of this area. This geologic history is made evident by the fact that the walls of Whirlpool Canyon to the west consist of dark limestones and shales, while the Yampa River Canyon to the east has been cut into lighter-colored sandstone. Although the two canyons are at the same level, the rocks they are cut into were greatly displaced by the bending and fracturing that took place as the area was being uplifted.

Geological discourse aside, these two canyons offer what may be the most dramatic view in Colorado's plateau region. Some 2500 feet deep,

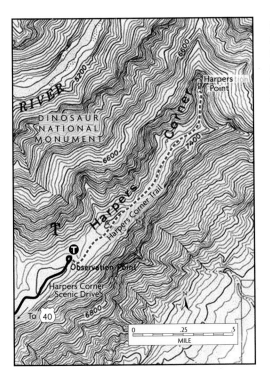

corridor of rock. To the right, Echo Park is reminiscent of southern Utah's canyon country with its entrenched meanders set in sheer walls of sandstone. Flowing in from the east, the Yampa River joins forces with the Green River in Echo Park. Their combined waters then flow around the north end of Harpers Corner, where they enter Whirlpool Canyon. In addition to naming Whirlpool Canyon during his epic 1869 float down the Green and Colorado rivers, John Wesley Powell also assigned titles to a number of other features in Dinosaur National Monument, among them the Gates of Lodore, Disaster Falls, and Hells Half Mile. In more recent times—the 1950s, to be exact—these canyons were threatened by a proposed dam. Fortunately, conservationists won out.

While the views are spectacular all along the Harpers Corner Trail, the panorama is best from the observation point at trail's end. With a little luck you might even be the only visitors at the point during your visit. If so, be sure to take the time to really soak in the ambience of this special place. Return to your car along the same route.

Bring water, as none is available along the way. Watch for lightning along this exposed route, and use extreme caution around the many precipices.

Whirlpool Canyon—on the left side of Harpers Point as you are hiking out to the overlook—engulfs the Green River within a spectacular

The Green River in Dinosaur National Monument

100 CHOKECHERRY DRAW

Distance: 7 miles round-trip
Difficulty: Easy
Hiking time: 4 hours
Elevation: 5650 to 6300 feet
Management: Bureau of Land Management
Wilderness status: Diamond Breaks Wilderness Study Area
Season: Year-round
Maps: USGS Lodore School, Swallow Canyon

Getting there: From Craig, drive 31 miles west on US Highway 40 to the turnoff for Colorado Highway 318. Drive 60 miles northwest on this route to graveled County Road 83 in Browns Park. Turn south and drive 2 miles to the narrow bridge that spans the Green River. Immediately after crossing the bridge, turn left and drive east on a Browns Park National Wildlife Refuge road. Continue for 1.7 miles to a 4WD road that branches right. Follow this road for less than a mile to where it is closed.

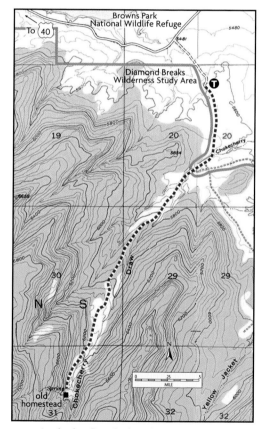

Situated in the remote northwest corner of the state, the 35,380-acre Diamond Breaks Wilderness Study Area encompasses a rugged extension of Utah's Uinta Range known as Diamond Mountain. Although few maintained trails enter this proposed wilderness, one well-established route follows an old road, now closed to vehicles, up Chokecherry Draw. In addition to views of this little-known corner of Colorado, the hike up this drainage reveals the remains of an old homestead.

Following an old road the entire way, this route is easy to follow. The road climbs a mere 650 feet over 3.5 miles. About 0.75 mile beyond the trail's start, the road reaches a fork in the drainage. After crossing the normally dry wash, the road begins climbing along a gentle ridge that separates the two forks. A variety of plants are common to this upland desert area. The two primary tree species that grow across these dry hillsides are pinyon pine and Utah juniper. These stunted forests are occasionally interspersed with sagebrush flats. Deciduous trees include Gambel oaks and, of course, chokecherry trees.

Beyond the 2.5-mile mark, the trail reaches a

grassy meadow that stretches for nearly a mile to the homestead site and the turnaround point of this hike. A good place to spot mule deer at dawn and dusk, this meadow also allows unobstructed views north into Browns Park below. A sparsely populated valley that is well off the beaten path—even by Colorado's standards—Browns Park constitutes quite a find for anyone searching for the back of beyond. The Browns Park National Wildlife Refuge encompasses much of the valley's floor and a lazy stretch of the Green River. The refuge harbors some important waterfowl habitat, while the Diamond Breaks area is home to a variety of wildlife, including mule deer, elk, coyotes, mountain lions, and black bears.

At the upper end of the meadow are the remains of an old homestead that dates to the early 1900s. All that is left today are some scattered fence posts, a house foundation, and a few gnarled fruit trees. As early as 1826, Browns Park served as a rendezvous site for the famed mountain men of the era. Later, because of its isolation, the Browns Park area served as a hideout for such notorious outlaws as Annie Bassett, Butch Cassidy and the Sundance Kid, and Tom Horn. A short distance beyond the homestead is a small spring, and beyond that is a nice outcrop of rock, the top of which makes an ideal place to take in the views.

Water is scarce in Chokecherry Draw, and any that is found should be treated before drinking; it is best to bring your own.

One of many flowering jewels in the San Juan Mountains

APPENDIX

NATIONAL FORESTS

Arapaho and Roosevelt National Forests
www.fs.fed.us/r2/arnf

Boulder Ranger District
2140 Yarmouth Avenue
Boulder, CO 80301
303-541-2500

Canyon Lakes Ranger District
2150 Centre Avenue, Building E
Fort Collins, CO 80526
970-295-6700

Clear Creek Ranger District
101 Chicago Creek Road
P.O. Box 3307
Idaho Springs, CO 80452
303-567-3000

Sulfur Ranger District
9 Ten Mile Drive
P.O. Box 10
Granby, CO 80446
970-887-4100

Grand Mesa, Uncompahgre, and Gunnison National Forests
www.fs.fed.us/r2/gmug

Grand Valley Ranger District
2777 Crossroads Blvd., Suite 1
Grand Junction, CO 81506
970-242-8211

Gunnison Ranger District
216 North Colorado
Gunnison, CO 81230
970-641-0471

Norwood Ranger District
1150 Forest
P.O. Box 388
Norwood, CO 81423
970-327-4261

Ouray Ranger District
2505 South Townsend
Montrose, CO 81401
970-240-5300

Paonia Ranger District
North Rio Grande Avenue
P.O. Box 1030
Paonia, CO 81428
970-527-4131

Pike and San Isabel National Forests
www.fs.fed.us/r2/psicc

Leadville District
810 Front Street
Leadville, CO 80461
719-486-0928

Pikes Peak Ranger District
601 South Weber
Colorado Springs, CO 80903
719-636-1602

Salida District
325 West Rainbow Blvd.
Salida, CO 81201
719-539-3591

San Carlos District
3170 East Main Street
Canon City, CO 81212
719-269-8500

South Park Ranger District
320 Highway 285
P.O. Box 219
Fairplay, CO 80440
719-836-2031

South Platte District
19316 Goddard Ranch Court
Morrison, CO 80465
303-275-5610

Routt National Forest
www.fs.fed.us/r2/mbr

Hahns Peak/Bears Ears Ranger District
925 Weiss Drive
Steamboat Springs, CO 80487-9315
970-879-1870

Yampa Ranger District
300 Roselawn Avenue
P.O. Box 7
Yampa, CO 80483
970-638-4516

Rio Grande National Forest
www.fs.fed.us/r2/riogrande

Divide Ranger District
13308 West Highway 160
Del Norte, CO 81132
719-657-3321

Saguache Ranger District
46525 Highway 114
Saguache, CO 81149
719-655-2547

San Juan National Forest
www.fs.fed.us/r2/sanjuan

Columbine Ranger District
110 West 11th Street
Durango, CO 81301
970-884-2512

Dolores Ranger District
29211 Highway 184
P.O. Box 210
Dolores, CO 81323
970-882-7296

Pagosa Ranger District
180 Second Street
P.O. Box 310
Pagosa Springs, CO 81147
970-264-2268

White River National Forest
www.fs.fed.us/r2/whiteriver

Aspen District
806 West Hallam
Aspen, CO 81611
970-925-3445

Blanco Ranger District
317 East Market Street
Meeker, CO 81641
970-878-4039

Dillon Ranger District
680 Blue River Parkway
Silverthorne, CO 80498
970-468-5400

Eagle Ranger District
125 West 5th Street
Eagle, CO 81631
970-328-6388

Holy Cross District
24747 US Highway 24
Minturn, CO 81645
970-827-5715

NATIONAL GRASSLANDS

Comanche National Grassland
27204 Highway 287
Box 127
Springfield, CO 81073
719-523-6591
www.fs.fed.us/r2/psicc/coma

Pawnee National Grassland
660 "O" Street
Greeley, CO 80631
970-346-5000
www.fs.fed.us/r2/arnf/png

NATIONAL PARKS, MONUMENTS, AND RECREATION AREAS

Black Canyon of the Gunnison National Park
102 Elk Creek
Gunnison, CO 81230
970-641-2337
www.nps.gov/blca

Colorado National Monument
Fruita, CO 81521-0001
970-858-3617
www.nps.gov/colm

Curecanti National Recreation Area
102 Elk Creek
Gunnison, CO 81230
970-641-2337
www.nps.gov/cure

Dinosaur National Monument
4545 East Highway 40
Dinosaur, CO 81610-9724
970-374-3000
www.nps.gov/dino

Florissant Fossil Beds National Monument
15807 Teller County 1
P.O. Box 185
Florissant, CO 80816-0185
719-748-3253
www.nps.gov/flfo

Great Sand Dunes National Park & Preserve
11500 Highway 150
Mosca, CO 81146-9798
719-378-6300
www.nps.gov/grsa

Mesa Verde National Park
P.O. Box 8
Mesa Verde, CO 81330-0008
970-529-4465
www.nps.gov/meve

Rocky Mountain National Park
1000 Highway 36
Estes Park, CO 80517-8397
970-586-1206
www.nps.gov/romo

BUREAU OF LAND MANAGEMENT
www.co.blm.gov

Grand Junction Field Office
2815 H Road
Grand Junction, CO 81506
970-244-3000

Gunnison Field Office
216 North Colorado
Gunnison, CO 81203
970-641-0471

Little Snake Field Office
455 Emerson Street
Craig, CO 81625
970-826-5000

San Juan Public Lands Center
15 Burnett Court
Durango, CO 81301
970-247-4874

San Luis Public Lands Center
1803 West Highway 160
Monte Vista, CO 81144

Uncompahgre Field Office
2465 South Townsend Avenue
Montrose, CO 81401
970-240-5300

STATE PARKS

www.parks.state.co.us

Barr Lake State Park
13401 Picadilly Road
Brighton, CO 80603
303-659-6005

Castlewood Canyon State Park
2989 South Highway 83
Franktown, CO 80116
303-688-5242

Golden Gate Canyon State Park
92 Crawford Gulch Road
Golden, CO 80403
303-582-3707

Roxborough State Park
4751 Roxborough Drive
Littleton, CO 80125
303-973-3959

CITY AND COUNTY PARKS

Boulder Open Space & Mountain Parks
P.O. Box 791
Boulder, CO 80306
303-441-3440
www.bouldercolorado.gov/index.php

**Colorado Springs Parks, Recreation
     and Cultural Services**
1401 Recreation Way
Colorado Springs, CO 80905-1975
719-385-5940
www.springsgov.com

Jefferson County Open Space
700 Jefferson County Parkway
Golden, CO 80401
303-271-5925
www.co.jefferson.co.us/openspace/index.htm

INDEX

ABOUT THE AUTHOR

Scott S. Warren has lived in Colorado for over twenty-five years and in that time he has hiked in virtually every corner of the state. "Colorado's variety and breadth are truly amazing," Warren says. "Yes, Colorado's collection of high summits is unmatched, but the state's hidden treasures are just as memorable."

In addition to writing about the outdoors, Warren is also a photographer. He holds a bachelor of fine arts degree in photography from Utah State University, and his images have appeared in *Smithsonian, Audubon, Nature Conservancy, Sierra, Outside, Time, Newsweek,* and various *National Geographic* publications.

THE MOUNTAINEERS, founded in 1906, is a nonprofit outdoor activity and conservation club, whose mission is "to explore, study, preserve, and enjoy the natural beauty of the outdoors...." Based in Seattle, Washington, the club is now the third-largest such organization in the United States, with seven branches throughout Washington State.

The Mountaineers sponsors both classes and year-round outdoor activities in the Pacific Northwest, which include hiking, mountain climbing, ski-touring, snowshoeing, bicycling, camping, kayaking, nature study, sailing, and adventure travel. The club's conservation division supports environmental causes through educational activities, sponsoring legislation, and presenting informational programs.

All club activities are led by skilled, experienced instructors, who are dedicated to promoting safe and responsible enjoyment and preservation of the outdoors.

If you would like to participate in these organized outdoor activities or the club's programs, consider a membership in The Mountaineers. For information and an application, write or call The Mountaineers, Club Headquarters, 300 Third Avenue West, Seattle, WA 98119; 206-284-6310. You can also visit the club's website at *www.mountaineers.org* or contact The Mountaineers via email at *clubmail@mountaineers.org*.

The Mountaineers Books, an active, nonprofit publishing program of the club, produces guidebooks, instructional texts, historical works, natural history guides, and works on environmental conservation. All books produced by The Mountaineers Books fulfill the club's mission.

Send or call for our catalog of more than 500 outdoor titles:

The Mountaineers Books
1001 SW Klickitat Way, Suite 201
Seattle, WA 98134
800-553-4453
mbooks@mountaineersbooks.org
www.mountaineersbooks.org

The Mountaineers Books is proud to be a corporate sponsor of The Leave No Trace Center for Outdoor Ethics, whose mission is to promote and inspire responsible outdoor recreation through education, research, and partnerships. The Leave No Trace program is focused specifically on human-powered (nonmotorized) recreation.

Leave No Trace strives to educate visitors about the nature of their recreational impacts, as well as offer techniques to prevent and minimize such impacts. Leave No Trace is best understood as an educational and ethical program, not as a set of rules and regulations.

For more information, visit *www.LNT.org,* or call 800-332-4100.

OTHER TITLES YOU MIGHT ENJOY FROM THE MOUNTAINEERS BOOKS

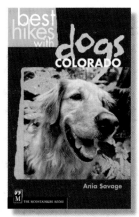

Best Hikes with Dogs: Colorado
Ania Savage
A handy guide to
paw-friendly terrain

Colorado Snow Climbs
Dave Cooper
A year-round guide to
Colorado's best snow climbing

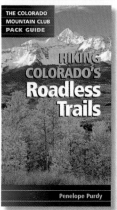

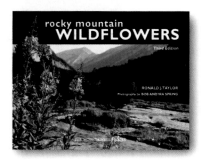

Hiking Colorado's Roadless Trails
Penelope Purdy
Colorado's most precious,
pristine wilderness areas!

Don't Forget the Duct Tape
Kristin Hostetter
Secrets to saving your
trip from disaster

**Rocky Mountain
Wildflowers, 3rd Ed.**
Taylor & Spring
Easy, fun, and portable
wildflower identification!

**Digital Photography
Outdoors, 2nd Ed.**
James Martin
"A great all-in-one reference"
—*Digital Photography* magazine

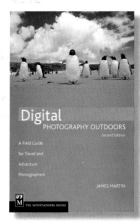

Find The Mountaineers Books' entire catalog of outdoor titles online at *www.mountaineersbooks.org.*